P9-DDX-148

GIVE & TAKE

Other books by Willard F. Harley, Jr.

His Needs, Her Needs
Love Busters
5 Steps to Romantic Love

Give & Take

The Secret to Marital Compatibility

Willard F. Harley, Jr.

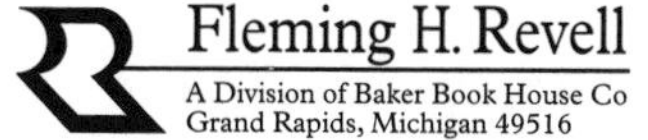

Fleming H. Revell
A Division of Baker Book House Co
Grand Rapids, Michigan 49516

Published by Fleming H. Revell
a division of Baker Book House Company
P.O. Box 6287, Grand Rapids, MI 49516-6287

Third printing, February 2000

Printed in the United States of America

Library of Congress Cataloging-in-Publication Data

Harley, Willard F.
Give and take : the secret to marital compatibility / Willard F. Harley, Jr.
p. cm.
ISBN 0-8007-1726-0 (cloth)
1. Marriage. 2. Marital conflict. 3. Married people—Psychology. 4. Emotions. 5. Negotiation. I. Title.
HQ734.H2844 1996
306.81—dc20 96-28511

To Joyce
My best friend

Contents

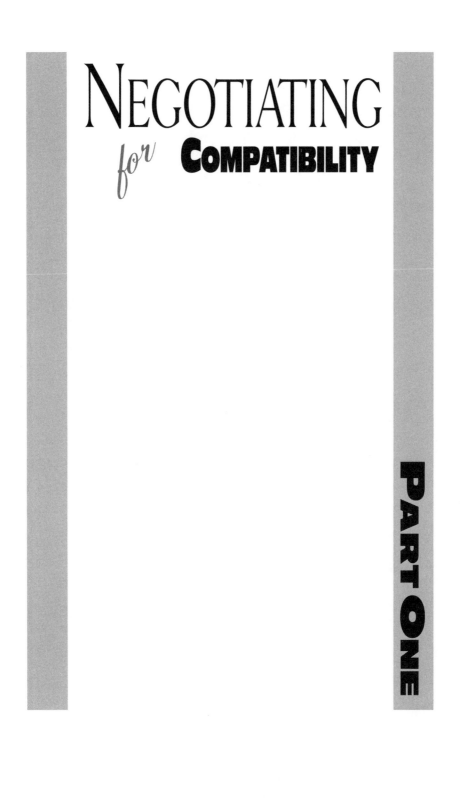

NEGOTIATING *for* COMPATIBILITY

PART ONE

Chapter One

Why Can't We Just Get Along?

The Struggle for Compatibility in Marriage

Marrying Mike was the worst mistake she'd ever made. That's how it looked to Joan as, day after day, she tried to survive a husband who ignored, belittled, or yelled at her. She often wished she were dead.

Mike also painted a desperate situation. He left the house each day while his wife was asleep and his children were running wild. He returned from work to a house in shambles, his kids still on a rampage. Dinner was every man for himself. He spent most evenings trying to settle his children down while Joan escaped to watch TV in their bedroom. On weekends, to avoid fights, they went their separate ways. They had not made love for over a year.

Joan and Mike came to my office in a last-ditch effort at marriage counseling. The counselor who referred them to me described them as "incredibly incompatible." As I met with them and heard their stories, I could see what he meant.

> **Compatibility:** The ability to live together in harmony.

Mike was a day person, Joan a night person. He would get up early for exercise and reflection, while she liked to roll out of bed around eleven. By ten at night, he was ready for bed, and she was ready to rock and roll.

Joan was abstract in her thinking, a free spirit, creative and whimsical. Mike was concrete, down-to-earth, no-nonsense. She loved to dance, but he wouldn't be caught dead on a dance floor. He loved sporting events; she hated them. In my office, they went on and on, describing all the ways they had nothing in common.

They *did* have one thing in common, however: They hated each other.

I had to concur that *incompatible* was a good way to describe them—they seemed incapable of living together in harmony. Again and again they had proven that they simply could not get along. It was hard to imagine how these two had ever been deeply in love.

How Do Loving Couples Become Hating Couples?

What happens to the care and affection that mark the beginning of a romantic relationship? Where do they go?

Or more to the point, how do two people fall in love to begin with? And then how do they fall out of love?

It's a matter of emotional needs.

Simply stated, people fall in love when their emotional needs are met. They fall out of love when those needs are no longer met.

During courtship, we consider how well a prospective spouse can meet our emotional needs. Some prospects do a poor job, some do a good job, and one of them does a great job. That's the one we fall in love with and usually marry.

But what goes wrong? Why do so many marriages fail?

Marriages fall apart when spouses stop loving each other, and they stop loving each other when they stop meeting each other's emotional needs. This can happen for a host of reasons. Sometimes one partner's needs change—what used to work doesn't anymore. Some spouses get lazy. Some give up when they feel the relationship has been unfair—and they go on strike.

Indeed the business of meeting needs in marriage is very delicately balanced. The balance can be tipped in many ways and, once broken, a marriage is very hard to restore. Both spouses must meet each other's needs if the balance is to be preserved, because when one fails, the other usually quits.

Good marriages are not all "give" or all "take." They're "give *and* take." They're well-balanced. When spouses communicate their emotional needs to each other and meet them simultaneously, they've discovered the formula for lasting love and a fulfilling marriage.

So there you have it, Mike and Joan. Just return to the days when you were meeting each other's emotional needs, and your marriage will be fine!

Not so fast.

Mike and Joan had not been getting along for years. In that time, they had developed a lifestyle of habits and activities that made each other miserable. Their marriage was not just a graveyard of unmet needs, lacking any spark of love; it was a war zone, where land mines went off every day. The pain they suffered had caused them to become bitter enemies.

Need meeting was out of the question. First they needed to declare a truce—put down their weapons. After the bullets stopped flying, when it was safe to step out into the open, they could begin thinking about meeting each other's needs. But that seemed a long way off.

I invite you to join me in the counseling sessions with Mike and Joan. If your marriage is anything like theirs, you may have given up hope. But let me assure you, there is a way back to the days when you found each other irresistible. It worked for Joan and Mike, and it can work for you.

But you have to take it one step at a time. Halfway through this book, we'll be looking at what drew you and your spouse together in the first place—those important emotional needs that must be fulfilled in your marriage. But first you must be emotionally ready to meet your spouse's needs and to have your needs met by someone who may, at this moment, be your enemy. We must tackle those hurtful habits that threaten the safety of a marriage—I call them Love Busters.

But before we tackle those, let's consider some basic principles of how relationships work. What goes into the making of that delicate balance we call marriage?

Chapter Two

The Love Bank

How Couples Fall In and Out of Love

It started in science class. Joan's good looks and great figure got Mike's attention. Since science was not her strong suit, Mike proved very helpful in explaining new concepts. When she finally asked him to study with her, he was blown away.

Soon they were getting together to "study" almost every day. Once in a while they even opened their science books. Most of their time, of course, was spent getting to know each other. It seemed so easy to talk in those days; their conversations would last for hours. During this time they discovered what made each other happy.

Sports made Mike happy. Joan liked to shop. Mike was into politics. Joan enjoyed talking about her friends and family. Mike wanted to be told how smart he was. Joan wanted to know she was loved. Mike liked passionate women. Joan liked to be pampered.

Their differences were new and exciting, and each tried to accommodate the other. Joan studied up on politics and sports, especially football. Mike went shopping with her and made a special effort to get to know her friends and family. Joan praised his achievements. Mike showered her with affection, and Joan responded passionately. They were trying to become compatible.

There was a bittersweet taste in the way they told me of those early days in their relationship. The memories seemed like a dream, but both had to admit that those were the best years of their lives. Still, the dream sure didn't last very long, especially after marriage. Where had they gone wrong?

Starting an Account

Years ago, I created a concept that helped me explain how married couples, once in love, can come to hate each other, how they change from compatibility to incompatibility. I call it the Love Bank.

> **Love Bank:** The way your emotions keep track of compatibility. Good experiences deposit "love units," leading you to like or even love a person. Bad experiences withdraw units, leading you to dislike or even hate a person.

You have a Love Bank within you; so do I. Your Love Bank has an account in the name of each person you encounter, and it keeps track of each encounter you have, from the simplest, "Hello, how are you?" to the deep and intimate experience of a lover.

With every interaction you have, a deposit or withdrawal is made. When you feel good being with someone, love units are deposited into his or her own personal account in your Love Bank. The better you feel, the more love units are deposited.

Meet a pleasant person at work and you put, say, one "love unit" in that person's account. A friend compliments you in passing and—ka-ching!—you deposit two units in that account. There are three units for someone who makes you feel particularly good. And when you have such a good experience that you remember it years later, four units are deposited.

People also make withdrawals from the Love Bank. Suppose your encounter with someone isn't much fun. In fact, suppose it's downright unpleasant most of the time. As you have daily encounters with this person, one love unit would be withdrawn from his or her account in your Love Bank when you feel uncomfortable; two units would be withdrawn when you feel bad; three when you feel very bad; and four when you feel terrible.

Of course, we don't actually sit and think about how many love units are being deposited or withdrawn in each of our encounters. But be assured your Love Bank is keeping score.

As you go through life, all the people you know have different balances in your Love Bank. Some may be "in the red," with more withdrawals than deposits, leaving negative balances, because you've had more bad experiences than good ones. Others stay "about even" as you sometimes have a comfortable encounter and other times find yourself uncomfortable or feeling bad. Still others have positive balances, because they make you feel good more often than they offend or hurt you.

The Love Bank is the way our emotions keep track of compatibility. When people treat us with kindness and consideration, building positive balances in their accounts, our emotions encourage us to be with them, by giving us the feeling of attraction. It's our emotions' way of telling us that we're compatible.

But when people treat us with contempt or insensitivity, depleting their accounts, our emotions encourage us to avoid them by giving us the feeling of repulsion or hatred. In other words, they're telling us we're incompatible.

Obviously no one knows the precise balance in any account, but you probably have distinct feelings about people who have piled up large amounts of deposits or withdrawals. When someone accumulates a great number of deposits in your Love Bank, that someone has become a very good friend. If that person happens to be of the opposite sex and if the number of love units crosses a threshold—say, 1,000 love units—you experience the feeling of incredible attraction that is known as romantic love. It's your emotions' way of encouraging you to be with that person as much as possible—for life, if you can.

Similarly, when someone rampantly disregards your feelings, crossing the threshold of *minus* 1,000 love units, you experience the feeling of incredible repulsion we call hate. Your emotions are telling you to run for the hills. Avoid that person at all costs!

Mike and Joan's Banking History

Apparently Mike and Joan had gone from one extreme to the other. As they told me how they met in science class and got to know each other, I could imagine them building balances in their Love Bank accounts with each other. Joan's beauty was scoring points with Mike from day one, and his attentive interest was attracting her to him. As they dated, they showed each other more and more kindness, making new deposits nearly every day.

It wasn't always easy. For instance, what exactly is "a date"? Joan wanted a formal invitation from Mike to go out to dinner and dance afterward. But Mike preferred to just "drop by." He would formally invite her to football games, but that wasn't exactly her idea of a romantic evening.

Yet they both learned to adapt. Eventually Mike invited her to dinner and dancing more often and sometimes he would even dress up for it. Meanwhile, Joan encouraged him to come over more often, even to watch football on TV! The more they learned how to make each other happy, the more love units were deposited.

Mike also had an obsession about being on time, and Joan tended to be late. Once in a while his frustration would get out of hand, and he would begin lecturing her on the values of promptness. Her feelings would be hurt whenever he criticized her, and sometimes she would start to cry. His show of disrespect always withdrew love units from his account. Although her tears would prompt a quick apology from Mike, it would take at least a day for her to warm up to him again. This emotional distance on her part would make Mike feel bad, withdrawing love units from her account in his Love Bank.

Still, these were temporary debits in rapidly growing accounts. Both Mike and Joan were making adjustments to each other. Mike, who tended to be somewhat judgmental, made a special effort to curb his criticism of Joan. Joan tried hard to be on time.

As they learned to accommodate each other, more love units were being deposited all the time. They were learning how to make each other happy.

They were also learning how to avoid making each other unhappy, and this kept them from making withdrawals from their Love Bank accounts.

As soon as their Love Bank accounts both reached 1,000 love units, they became irresistible to each other. They had fallen in love.

Because of their high Love Bank balances, their emotions were encouraging them to spend more time with each other, so marriage was an easy choice. Convinced that they would love each other forever, they both said "I do" with no reservations at all.

Joan was eager to spend her life with a man she loved and respected, who respected her, who treated her with kindness, and who made every effort to meet her needs and avoid making her unhappy. Mike was equally enthusiastic about spending his life with a woman who was committed to meeting his needs.

With such a hopeful beginning, how could Joan and Mike have come to hate each other? How could they have lost that compatibility?

How Did Joan and Mike Fall Out of Love?

It all started on their honeymoon, in Cancun. Mike was looking forward to touring the nearby Mayan ruins, and Joan was expecting to relax on the beach between shopping excursions. Before they got married, Joan would have insisted on seeing the ruins, just to make Mike happy, and Mike would have expressed enthusiasm about sunning and shopping. But on this day, a change took place that would alter the course of their marriage.

Mike felt that it was time for him to exert his leadership by directing Joan toward activities that would be educational and edifying instead of frivolous.

"Honey," he said, "today we'll be going to Tulum!"

If he had asked, she would have been willing to join him, but he made it sound as if she had no choice in the matter. On the defensive, she replied, "If that's how you want to spend your day, go right ahead, but you'll be going alone."

In the past, Mike would have apologized immediately, sensing her hurt feelings. But this time he thought she was being stubborn and foolish. "Open your eyes and take in the world around you," he pontificated. "You'll miss the best life has to offer."

Joan shot right back, "My eyes are open, wide open—and I don't like what I'm seeing."

"Honey," Mike responded, pushing even harder, "if you don't broaden your horizons, you'll become an ignorant housewife, just like your mother."

Oops. In a flash, there were more ruins in Mexico, the ruins of what could have been a happy honeymoon.

In a moment, everything changed. Mike wanted to go to the ruins so badly that he sacrificed Joan's happiness. When he tried to justify his own itinerary by mocking her plans for the day (and her mother), she was doubly offended.

The patterns they had followed before marriage—apology, recovery, and accommodation—were smashed to bits. There were no apologies. Thus, there was no accommodation. What should have been a time of major love unit deposits was bringing massive withdrawals instead.

Eventually Mike apologized, but he didn't mean it. If Joan had really cared about him, he felt, she would have joined him cheerfully on the trip to the Mayan site. He also felt she was trying to punish him by withholding sex throughout the rest of their honeymoon. By the time they got back home, two days early, he was steaming.

The honeymoon disaster was a sign of things to come. Back home, they had trouble agreeing on anything—how to divide household chores, what friends to be with, how to spend their money, when to visit relatives, and what to watch on TV. Few conflicts were resolved, and new ones arose steadily. Love units were being withdrawn at an alarming rate.

Mike and Joan were becoming incompatible.

Oh, every so often they would try to patch things up, desperately grasping for the feelings that had brought them together. But there wasn't much left in their accounts, and every disagreement tore them apart again.

The birth of little Kathy made matters worse. At first, Mike felt he needed to work long hours to help pay for the added expense of a child, leaving Joan alone most of the time. When he did arrive home, Joan would welcome him with a litany of criticisms and a list of things to do. Soon, he found his most relaxing moments were at work, especially at the end of the day when the others had gone home. So he often stayed late, whether or not there was work to do.

Meanwhile, Joan was feeling trapped, especially after two more children were born. With three kids and half a husband, she grew depressed. It became hard to do anything, and she had trouble getting up in the morning to face another day.

Mike had always been judgmental, though he had managed to protect Joan from it during their courtship. After the wedding, though, the safety catch was removed, and he aimed his criticism at her, point-blank. Of course, Joan was dishing out plenty of criticism herself, but Mike's barbs were taking their toll on her. The more he criticized her, the more depressed she became. And the more depressed she became, the less she did around the house, which gave him more to criticize. When she finally saw a counselor, he told her family that she had "flipped out."

Love Bank balances: negative and falling fast. By the time Joan and Mike saw me, they were easily 1,000 units down, hating each other with a deep revulsion. They were truly and completely incompatible.

The Difference between Romantic Love and Caring Love

There are two kinds of love at work in marriage. We have already discussed romantic love in the case of Mike and Joan. Their level of emotional attraction—the account balance in their Love Banks—became high enough to become romantic love. Romantic love is what we experience when someone meets our needs. But that isn't enough.

We also need caring love, which is a decision to try to contribute to someone's happiness or help someone avoid unhappiness.

People often have caring love in many different relationships, not just marriage. In fact, we often care for people we don't even know as we decide to invest time and resources with charitable organizations that help people. As a psychologist, I spend much of my time caring for people I did not know before I made the decision to care for them.

Caring love is our effort to meet someone else's needs. The caring kind of love *does not* depend on one person having a certain balance in the other person's Love Bank. It has nothing to do with compatibility. You can care for people whether or not they have been effective in caring for you.

So what happened to Joan and Mike?

During their courtship, both made the decision to care for the other, based on their first impressions. That decision was a decisive moment because, once it was made, romantic love was almost inevitable. The effectiveness of their mutual care drove Love Bank balances through the threshold of romantic love, and then they had both kinds of love—the decision to care and the feeling of irresistible attraction.

The concepts of caring love and romantic love usually come together in marriage. We care for our spouses when we try to make them happy and avoid making them unhappy. That, in turn, causes our spouses to feel romantic love for us. Our spouse's care for us causes us to feel romantic love in return.

You see, romantic love is a litmus test of our ability to care. If we are effective in our care, romantic love is the outcome, because we are depositing love units and avoiding their withdrawal. When our spouses no longer feel "in love" with us, we are failing to care for them effectively.

Romantic love is simply the result of effective mutual care. When a husband and wife both care for each other in a way that results in romantic love, they are unquestionably effective in their care. And without a doubt, they are truly compatible.

But remember what I said earlier: Care is a decision. It's possible to care for someone who doesn't care effectively for you; it's just harder.

Romantic love and hate are feelings, not decisions. Yet these feelings often influence our decisions to care. The feeling of romantic love encourages us to provide care and protection to the one we love. It can make a great marriage seem almost effortless. On the other hand, the feeling of hatred can make it seem impossible to protect and care for your spouse the way you should.

When you lose motivation, you reduce your effort. Even if you really want to do the right thing and show your spouse the proper care, hateful feelings will make it tough. Your reduction of effort, in turn, will deplete your Love Bank balances even further, which will make it tough for your spouse to care for you. Scientists call this a "negative feedback loop." This downward spiral is at the heart of marital incompatibility.

What started that negative feedback? Mike and Joan were madly in love—or were they suddenly just plain mad? Why did they stop making deposits in their Love Banks and start making withdrawals?

Why Did Joan and Mike Stop Caring for Each Other?

Care is a decision, as I've said. While it's relatively easy to care for those you love, it's also possible to make the decision not to care. And if that decision is made, it has the effect of encouraging the other person to make a decision not to care. That's where the spiral starts.

Before marriage, Joan and Mike had followed a basic rule: *Do whatever you can to make the other person happy and avoid anything that makes the other person unhappy.*

Any couple who follows this rule will have an excellent chance of creating the feeling of romantic love in each other. Their Love Bank accounts will be full, and their emotions will encourage them to be together for life. They will have been successful at creating compatibility.

But after marriage, Mike followed a new rule: *Do whatever you can to make yourself happy and avoid anything that makes you unhappy.*

It wasn't long before Joan was following the same rule. Couples who follow this rule during courtship destroy their chances of creating romantic love. Their Love Banks soon go bankrupt, and their emotions warn them to avoid each other.

What's wrong with doing whatever you can do to make yourself happy? Shouldn't we care for ourselves as well as others?

Yes, but look at that rule again. *Do whatever you can to make yourself happy and avoid anything that makes you unhappy.* Those words, *whatever* and *anything* mean you can make yourself happy at any cost, even if it is at the expense of others. Once Mike chose to please himself at Joan's expense, love-unit withdrawals were inevitable—the negative feedback loop had begun.

When the rule changes after marriage, as it did for Joan and Mike, a tragedy occurs. The love that encouraged them to marry is replaced with a hatred that drives them apart. They are faced with two ugly choices: living together in a loveless marriage or destroying the family through divorce.

What caused the rule change? Why would a loving Mike suddenly become a selfish Mike? More important, what can Mike and Joan do to turn their marriage around?

The answers to these questions are at the core of understanding compatibility. To answer them properly, we need to get to know two important "characters" who reside within our hearts and minds. Sometimes these characters help us but often they wreak havoc on our relationships. The better you know them, the better prepared you are to avoid Joan and Mike's nosedive into incompatibility.

Chapter Three

Meet Your Giver and Taker

Why Marital Negotiation Is So Tough

Joan had fallen in love with the charming Dr. Jekyll but found herself married to the gruesome Mr. Hyde.

"It was our marriage that did it," Joan told me. "Before we were married, he was kind and thoughtful. Now he's cruel and selfish. I had no idea that marriage could change a man so much."

Mike also resented the changes in Joan. "She was nice to me long enough to get married, but then she let me see her true colors. I thought she really cared about me, but now I know that, all along, she only cared about herself."

Each of them had a different take on what had happened to their marriage, but they agreed on one point: A change had taken place in their relationship when they got married—a change that was a devastating surprise to both of them.

Before the wedding, both Mike and Joan focused their attention on how to please each other. They gathered data about each other's likes and dislikes and used this information to make each other happy and avoid offending each other. The balances in both their Love Banks went up in a hurry, and they basked in the bliss of romantic love that led them straight to the altar.

If they had conflicts, they resolved them quickly through self-sacrifice: one of them giving in and agreeing with the other. While their strategy worked well enough to catapult them into romantic love, they never learned to negotiate a compromise that would take into account the feelings of both of them at the same time. They were so eager to agree that they didn't care whether their own needs were met.

The strategy of self-sacrifice broke down, of all places, on their honeymoon. If this disagreement had happened before the wedding, they would probably have sailed through it smoothly. *What should we do, visit ruins or sun on the beach? Well, what do you want to do?* Joan would have agreed to a trip to the ruins, even though she had no interest in them, and Mike would have suggested that they sun on the beach instead.

But with the sound of wedding bells still ringing in their ears, they tried a whole new strategy, one of self-centeredness. Mike insisted on visiting the ruins, and Joan was going to the beach, with or without him. Almost overnight, the bliss of what had been a loving, caring, intimate relationship slipped into the unfathomable pain of criticism and judgment.

As they explained the situation to me, starting with the disagreement over where to go that day on the honeymoon, they were describing a familiar problem. I had seen it many times before.

Prior to marriage, each had witnessed the other person's other-centered personality, incredibly thoughtful to the point of self-sacrifice. Each assumed that the other would always be like this. But they were seeing only half the person. Lurking in the background, each of them had another "personality," a self-centered side, that could (and nearly did) wreck their marriage.

Everyone Has a "Dual Personality"

No, you're not Jekyll and Hyde or the multifragmented Sibyl. But you have two very real characters within you that I have named the Giver and the Taker.

Most of the time the Giver and the Taker are kept in balance so that others see only one integrated personality. But when you get to know a person well, particularly in the most intimate of relationships—marriage—you get a much clearer picture of these two distinct sides.

The Giver and Taker are very powerful forces in determining what you do in life, affecting every decision you make. If you want to understand yourself or someone else, you must know how these characters operate.

They represent two necessary but conflicting roles that you play. Although they are in conflict, they can be satisfied if the interests of both are taken into account. But when one or both of them are not satisfied, they fight each other for control of your life. It's very important for you to know your Giver and Taker well, because the more successful you are at satisfying them, the less likely that either one will try to take control. As it turns out, when either the Giver or the Taker takes total control at the other's expense, it can leave your life in shambles.

Getting to Know Your Giver

Your Giver tries to make you follow its rule, one I introduced to you earlier: *Do whatever you can to make the other person happy and avoid anything that makes the other person unhappy.* This is the rule Joan and Mike used during courtship.

> **Your Giver:** The part of you that wants what is in the best interest of others.

If your Giver had its way, your house would be dominated by large plaques hanging on the wall, proclaiming messages like, "Love Unconditionally," "Live for the Joy of Making Someone Happy," and "Don't Think of Yourself." You see, it's the Giver's mission in life to help as many people as possible without consideration for self. The Giver is not concerned about being repaid. In fact, the Giver often feels that it's more important to help those who cannot repay than to help those who might be able to reciprocate.

The Giver's self-sacrificing spirit would be reflected in books lining the library shelves with titles such as *Ask Not What Others Can Do for You but What You Can Do for Others, Learning to Give Until It Hurts,* and *The Virtue of Self-Sacrifice.* The Giver wants you to make a constructive difference in the lives of others during your lifetime and wants you to do it without thought for yourself. In short, the Giver's goal in life is to make other people happy. Your Giver wants you to meet the needs of others but is not concerned about your own needs.

The Giver grows out of a basic instinct that we all share. If we search deep within ourselves, we find a reservoir of love and concern for those around us. We feel compassion for people we don't even know and are willing to give up our own resources to help those halfway around the world.

Everyone has a Giver. The cruelest terrorist is fighting for a cause he thinks will ease the suffering of those he cares for. Some of the most evil, sociopathic people I've ever known have a compassionate, loving side. That's why some murderers, rapists, and child molesters can appear to be rehabilitated. They sincerely want to avoid ever hurting anyone again—at least some of the time.

Although we all have this caring, other-centered side to us, each person's Giver is somewhat different. The way we express our care for others is a reflection of our cultural background and genetic predispositions. Masculinity and femininity play a major role as well.

I've been fascinated by those who choose marriage partners with serious social and physical limitations—alcoholics, addicts, criminals, the chronically unemployed. They seem to be attracted to the obvious needs of these individuals. Why? It's the Giver within them.

Remember that the Giver is looking for someone to care for. So being needed is a powerful reason to marry, because the Giver in each of us wants to provide care for one special person. I know that's how I felt when I married Joyce, and she felt the same way toward me. In fact, that's also how Joan and Mike felt when they were first married.

But giving is only half of the story. There's another powerful force that affects all the decisions we make, especially the decision to marry. It's the Taker.

Getting to Know Your Taker

Just as your Giver tries to make others happy or tries to prevent the suffering of others, your Taker tries to make *you* happy and tries to prevent *your* suffering. This is the Taker's rule: *Do whatever you can to make yourself happy and avoid anything that makes you unhappy.*

The Taker grows out of our basic instinct for self-preservation and survival. Even those who appear to be the most self-sacrificing have a Taker that lurks in the background. If you've ever worked with those who have dedicated their lives to the welfare of others—social workers, disaster-relief volunteers, missionaries, and, yes, even psychologists—you know that they're not totally selfless. They have Takers too.

Your Taker: The part of you that wants what is in your own best interest.

If the Taker had its way, your house would be dominated by plaques reading, "Self-Esteem Is the Greatest Virtue," "What's in It for Me?" and "Don't Let Those Turkeys Get You Down." The Taker is not concerned for the happiness of others and is quite willing to gain happiness at their expense. Your Taker wants you to have friends but it wants friends who can contribute the most to your happiness and protect you from pain.

The Taker would want your library shelves lined with books titled, *Learning to Love Yourself Unconditionally, Getting the Most Out of Life with the Least Amount of Effort,* and *Happiness Is a Choice: It's Either Yours or Theirs.*

The Taker wants you to spend your life understanding your needs and seeing that they're met—at any cost!

How does your Taker express itself? That depends on your cultural and genetic predispositions, your gender, and of course, your unique personality. How do you generally go about making yourself happy? How do you try to prevent your own suffering?

Marriage is viewed by your Taker as an opportunity to have some of your most important needs met. In selecting a spouse, your Taker considers all the pluses and minuses. What will you get, and what will you be expected to give? It wants you to strike a good bargain—get as much as you can for as little as possible.

Love Bank balances are very important to your Taker because they reflect how much happiness you receive from people. Your Taker wants you to marry the one with the largest Love Bank account, because that's the person who makes you the happiest.

Your Taker thinks that the idea of unconditional love is great, as long as it's the other person who's loving *you* unconditionally. It likes the security of getting your needs met with no strings attached. But it will strongly advise you not to care for someone else unconditionally.

When you go to the altar, you promise to take your partner as husband or wife, to have and to hold from this day forward, for better or for worse, in sickness and in health, to love and to cherish, until you are parted by death—as God is your witness you give your promise. Yet more than half of all marriages end in divorce, and two-thirds of those who remain married for life report an absence of love and cherishing. That vow doesn't seem to mean much to people. But do you know why? It's because their Takers never agreed to it in the first place! It's a Giver's vow, not a Taker's vow.

Your Shortsighted Giver and Taker

It's tempting to consider the Giver as our loving and caring nature and the Taker as our hating and thoughtless nature. But that's not what they are. Actually, both of them are caring: Your Giver cares for others, and your Taker cares for you.

Both Giver and Taker also have their thoughtless sides. Your Giver does not care how you feel, and your Taker does not care how others feel. In fact your Giver is willing to see you suffer, even to a point of deep depression, as long as you continue to care about others. Your Taker, on the other hand, is willing to see others suffer if it means that you are prevented from suffering.

The truth is, your Giver and Taker are both good and bad. They're good because they both care, the Giver for others and the Taker for you. But they're bad because they don't care, the Giver caring nothing for your feelings and the Taker caring nothing for the feelings of others. Because each of them ignores someone's feelings, they are both shortsighted. The Giver and Taker fail to see that you and others should be cared for simultaneously.

What happens when the interests of the Giver and Taker are in conflict? Your Giver wants you to run errands for your spouse, and your Taker wants you to spend the day playing golf. Should you try to decide which of the two is right? No. Instead, you should see that each has a valid point to make. Your spouse needs help with errands, and you need to take some time to relax. The interests of both Giver and Taker are important, and your decision should satisfy them both.

Here's a secret that neither your Giver nor your Taker understands: We are more effective in meeting the needs of others (satisfying the Giver) when our own needs are being met (satisfying the Taker). Conversely, we are more effective in meeting our own needs when we meet the needs of others.

It's very much like feeding the horse that plows the field. If we push the horse to plow, but never feed it, it will eventually stop plowing (and may die). Work with no reward ultimately results in no work. On the other hand, if we feed the horse and never hitch it up to the plow, sooner or later we run out of feed, because no one plowed the field.

Reciprocity is essential for the survival of a relationship. It needs both give and take.

Who Calls the Shots?

So what happened to Mike and Joan? As with many couples, their Givers were in charge during courtship, but their Takers surfaced after the vows were made.

During most successful and extended dating experiences, the partners are reaching out to meet each other's needs. Selfish desires are regularly overruled in an effort to be thoughtful. Both people are on their best behavior, because they want the relationship to succeed. They're willing to sacrifice their own interests in order to be more appealing to the other.

It's as if there's a meeting in your mind:

TAKER: Hey, there's someone who could meet my needs. I think I'll introduce myself. Wait a minute! This is too good to botch. I think I need some help on this one. Giver, why don't you introduce yourself?

GIVER: Why should I? That person doesn't need anything from me. I'd rather help someone in need.

TAKER: Who knows, maybe that person needs something you have to offer. Wouldn't hurt to ask, would it?

GIVER: Okay, I'll see if I can help that person.

From that moment on, we tend to put our Givers in charge of developing the relationship, recognizing that our Takers' self-centeredness is likely to ruin things. And our Givers are usually effective in making the other person happy.

And this is the part that makes it all work: If the one you're dating does the same thing, putting the Giver in charge of each encounter, you end up being happy, too. Your Taker is satisfied with the arrangement, because your Giver's care is being reciprocated. There's no need for your Taker to meddle. You're as happy as you've ever been.

As a result, at the time of marriage, a man and woman are under the impression that they are committed unconditionally to each other's happiness. When they stand at the altar, they are quite willing to say they will care for each other in joy and in sorrow, in sickness and in health, in plenty and want, as long as they both shall live.

These familiar wedding vows seem reasonable as long as both spouses are successful in meeting each other's needs. If this is the case, the Taker within each of them is willing to stay in the background. But when one partner has an important unmet need, the Taker can come back with a vengeance.

Marriage partners often fail to realize that their success depends not only on their willingness to make each other happy, but their long-range ability to do so. When either a husband or wife engages in thoughtless behavior, even briefly and unintentionally, the Taker becomes alarmed and tries to push the Giver aside. The Giver's love and care take a holiday, and withdrawals are made from Love Banks in a hurry.

How the Taker Ruined a Honeymoon

That's what happened on Mike and Joan's honeymoon. Oh, they were doing beautifully on the first day of their new marriage. Their Givers were pulling out all the stops to provide mutual happiness.

But day two dawned with a disagreement over how to spend the day. Mike had decided that it was time for him to assert his leadership. He put his foot down—and squashed their marital bliss. It was his Taker's unfortunate intrusion into their relationship.

Why did Mike's Taker suddenly emerge? It was essentially due to the fact that he wanted to see the ruins very badly—so badly that he was willing to sacrifice Joan's happiness to get what he wanted. Now that he was married, he thought his Taker could get away with a demand now and then.

"The Mayan ruins are educational, and the beach is a waste of time," he announced to his bride. "It's time we began spending our time constructively."

This was a smoke screen, to be sure. Mike loved prowling archaeological sites, and Joan hated it. Joan loved lying on the beach, while Mike was bored and worried about getting sunburned. Mike just wanted to see the ruins—his appeal to "educational" value was a rationalization. Remember that Mike had more of a logical, get-down-to-business personality, while Joan was a free spirit. Mike was implying that everything Joan wanted was frivolous and that only his plans were constructive. He would lead her out of her meaningless existence and into a truly meaningful life. Maybe he didn't say that, but that's what Joan heard. They were fighting words.

So Joan's Taker came out of hibernation. "If you want to see the ruins so badly, you can go alone. I'm going to the beach." It was her Taker talking, seeing to it that her interests were protected.

Her Taker's solution to the problem was to part ways—she would do what she wanted and let Mike do what he wanted. *Why waste your time trying to make Mike happy, when he has no interest in making you happy?* her Taker whispered in her ear.

Mike was a bit surprised, but he stuck to his guns. *Let her lie on the beach,* whispered his Taker. *Show her that she can't control you.*

From that moment on, Mike and Joan's honeymoon was controlled by their Takers. Naturally, things went downhill in a hurry.

Do you remember when you met your spouse's Taker for the first time? Probably. It was that Jekyll-and-Hyde moment that left you wondering, *What's come over him? What's happened to her? Where did that come from?* The moment usually causes disillusionment, fear, and eventually, anger. Your spouse, the very one you have been depending on for emotional strength and support, seems to have turned against you. Your own Taker is summoned to the surface, and you respond in kind. Bliss turns to battle.

How Your Giver and Taker Resolve Marital Conflict

Your Giver and Taker have very different ways of resolving conflicts, as you might expect. But neither strategy is very effective.

When the Giver is in charge, the solutions you propose reflect your desire to make your spouse happy and help him or her avoid suffering. You tell your spouse how much you care and that you're willing to do anything to make peace. You avoid subjects that upset your spouse and you try to build your spouse's self-esteem. You listen, attending sincerely to your spouse's concerns. All in all, you approach the conflict in a way that makes your spouse feel good.

But if your Taker is in charge of conflict resolution, you focus attention on your needs and your interests. You interrupt, criticize, and pick on your spouse. You use biting words as weapons. You listen only to gain new ammunition. If you can catch your spouse in an error, you think you've won.

If you ever fight with your spouse, it's your Taker that has chosen your words. You may apologize later (and your Giver's doing the apologizing), but don't ever say you didn't mean something your Taker led you to say. Your Taker means it, even if your Giver doesn't.

On first glance, you might say, *Keep the Giver in charge of a relationship and prevent the Taker from interfering.* After all, the Giver helps create the feeling of romantic love, and the Taker destroys it.

Not so fast. On the surface, this is true: The Giver tends to defuse conflict in the short term. But the Giver ignores your own needs. It is quick to apologize and give in, but the issue is not necessarily resolved in your interest, just submerged until the day when you cannot control your Taker's frustration.

The fact is, both the Giver and the Taker represent important forces that influence your decisions, but it's shortsighted to let either of them speak for you. If your Giver is in charge, your personal happiness will be seriously neglected. If your Taker is dominant, you become Attila the Hun, and the happiness of others is at risk.

You must resolve marital conflict by balancing the interests of your Giver and Taker. This is the only way you will ever succeed in building marital compatibility. Unless you negotiate for both your Giver and Taker, working out compromises whenever a marital conflict arises, you are destined for a slide into marital incompatibility.

For Mike and Joan, the problems didn't start on the honeymoon, but during their courtship. Their Givers created illusions that could not stand the test of time. By letting their Givers dominate their interactions while they were dating, they presented a distorted view of themselves. Mike and Joan rarely allowed their Takers to express the inevitable reactions of resentment, anger, jealousy, envy, greed, and all the other human, but self-centered, emotions. So they were stunned when their Takers burst onto the scene and took over negotiations. They had never learned to balance their own needs with the other's needs.

Thrown out of balance like this, Joan and Mike started a roller-coaster ride that rocketed them through different states of marriage, with their Givers and Takers fighting for control.

Chapter Four

The Three States of Marriage

How the Giver and Taker Can Mess Up Your Mind

Some of the brightest people I know become idiots when faced with marital conflict.

I've seen this happen in case after case. An intelligent man listens to his wife talking about her needs, her desires, her interests—and it's as if she's speaking a foreign language. A brilliant woman hears her husband describe his perspective of their marriage, and she doesn't get it. They seem to be on entirely different wavelengths. Reason is replaced by rage; intelligence becomes ignorance.

Why is this? What is it about conflict in marriage that saps our brainpower?

Emotion.

Even though you might try to analyze your marital problem rationally, your feelings will come crashing through, distorting your perception and twisting your logic. Marital disputes strike us at the core of our beings, shaking our dreams, our expectations, and our sense of fairness. As a result, we react to these disputes emotionally.

It's as if you're on a roller coaster, high one second, low the next. Just when you begin to level off, you go crashing down again. And it's hard to hold an intelligent conversation on a roller coaster. Go to an amusement park and listen: What do you hear? Unintelligible screams.

That's basically what I hear in a lot of the marital counseling I do—screams of uncertainty and fear. *Where are we going? What are we doing? I don't know what to expect from you anymore!*

Before they can make sound decisions and reasonable progress, couples desperately need to get off the roller coaster and plant their feet on solid ground. Only then can they use their intelligence to solve their problems.

I help couples like Joan and Mike get off the roller coaster by helping them understand what it is. I introduce them to the emotions that rattle their reason by describing the three states of marriage: Intimacy, Conflict, and Withdrawal.

In the past, I've referred to them as "stages" of marriage, but that term has led to some confusion. The word *stages* indicates that couples routinely spend a certain number of years in one stage, then several more in another, and so on. But that's not what I mean. I am referring to something that can change as easily as we change our minds.

In fact, the three states of marriage are *states of mind*—three different ways we tend to view our relationship. The states can, and often do, change daily, even hourly. Like most truckers, you can be in one state for breakfast, another for lunch, and the third for dinner.

For many, it's a roller-coaster ride—high, low, fast, slow—through the three states of marriage. Couples *can* remain in a particular state for months or years, but even then there are probably flashes of Intimacy amid the Conflict or sparks of Conflict amid the Withdrawal.

This can be very confusing, if you don't recognize which state you're in or which state your spouse is in. Each state of marriage is dominated by either your Giver or Taker. So, as we move through the different states, we become incredibly inconsistent. Agreements made one day can be completely forgotten the next. This makes it difficult to resolve conflicts.

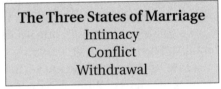

The Three States of Marriage
Intimacy
Conflict
Withdrawal

Joan and Mike had clearly passed from one state of marriage to another on that second day of their honeymoon and they had experienced a few other ups and downs since then. Before they could chart a course for the restoration of their marriage, they needed to understand how their emotions had been jerking them around and what they could do to stop it.

The First State of Marriage: Intimacy

I'm not sure what it was about Joan that first got Mike's attention, but I suspect it was her good looks. She deposited love units in his Love Bank just sitting there in science class, taking notes. It triggered a phenomenon that we're all familiar with, infatuation. For a moment in time, Mike was in love, and his Taker was so satisfied with the pleasure that the Giver had free reign over Mike's thinking.

Remember, your Taker doesn't have anything to do when your needs are being met, because it's there to see to it that you're happy. When you're already happy, it can relax and take the day off. That leaves it up to your Giver to determine what you do that day. As a result, when you're happy, you're much more likely to be generous.

Joan was everything Mike needed. His Love Bank was overflowing, so Mike's Giver had free reign over his relationship with her—Mike was willing and able to meet Joan's needs. He helped her understand the science lectures, keep up with the reading, and pass the tests. His helpfulness built enough units in her Love Bank to satisfy her Taker, and she fell in love with him. When her Giver took charge, Mike and Joan were both in the state of Intimacy.

In this most enjoyable state of a relationship, both spouses are building their Love Bank accounts at a rapid pace. They're following the Giver's rule, *Do whatever you can to make the other person happy and avoid anything that makes the other person unhappy.* When both partners follow this rule, both are getting their emotional needs met, and their Takers are satisfied. All is well with the world.

In this state, the Giver's rule seems almost instinctive. Both partners have a great desire to make each other happy in any way they can and want to avoid hurting each other at all costs.

As they protect each other, trust builds. They can share their deepest feelings, becoming emotionally vulnerable, because they know that they both have each other's best interests at heart. They feel so close to each other that to hurt the other person would be the same as hurting themselves.

Conversation in the state of Intimacy is respectful and nonjudgmental. The partners also express their deepest love for each other and gratitude for the care they are receiving. By lowering their defenses and forming a close emotional bond, they feel even greater pleasure when they meet each other's needs. This is the way marriage was meant to be.

Of course, Mike and Joan entered this state before marriage. (In fact, what I'm calling states of marriage are actually states of a relationship.) Mike and Joan actually began their marriage in the state of Intimacy because they were still meeting each other's needs right up to the second day of their honeymoon.

The Second State of Marriage: Conflict

Something happened on Joan and Mike's honeymoon to awaken their Takers. In their case, it seemed deliberate on Mike's part. Seeing the ruins was so important to him that he gave his Taker momentary control and took an intentionally self-centered stand.

Yet in many cases it is completely unintentional. Suppose, while a couple is in the state of Intimacy, the husband is unintentionally inconsiderate. He promised to pick up orange juice on the way home from work and forgot. Or perhaps, through no fault of her own, the wife is ineffective in meeting one of her husband's most important emotional needs, causing him frustration. Because of their vulnerability and close emotional bonding, every negative experience feels like a stab in the back.

"Why are you treating me this way?" is the normal reaction to such pain. "I haven't done anything to hurt you."

If this was just a temporary lapse, if the errant partner is still following the Giver's rule, apologies abound and efforts are made to compensate for the pain. The husband promises that he will be more thoughtful in the future, and the wife makes an effort to meet her husband's unmet need. Such a reaction keeps the couple in the state of Intimacy.

But what happens if there are no apologies, as was the case with Joan and Mike? What if the damage is not repaired quickly? What if a partner continues to be thoughtless?

Pain? I do believe I'm experiencing pain! says the Taker within us, rousing from its slumber. *That will never do. I'll get right on the problem!*

Why has the Taker been slumbering? Because it has been feeling great in the state of Intimacy. The Taker is satisfied: There's nothing for it to do. But once it sees us suffer, it jumps to our rescue.

As soon as you can say, "Bull in a china closet," you are in the second state of marriage, Conflict, and the Taker is making a number of suggestions to help you avoid future pain.

You recall the Taker's rule, *Do whatever you can to make yourself happy and avoid anything that makes you unhappy.* When one spouse follows the advice of his or her Taker in response to a conflict, it isn't long before the other spouse's Taker is ready for battle. In this state, partners are no longer willing to meet each other's needs but demand that their own needs be met first. They no longer guarantee protection, but instead, threaten each other with pain unless their demands are met.

In the state of Conflict, conversation tends to be disrespectful, resentful, and even hateful. Mutual care and concern have been replaced by mutual self-centeredness. Your Taker no longer trusts your spouse to look after your interests, but pulls out all the stops to see to it that you are treated fairly. The problem, of course, is that your Taker does not know how to treat your spouse with that same fairness. Fairness is viewed by each Taker as getting its way.

In the state of Conflict, couples are still emotionally bonded—and that makes the pain of thoughtlessness even worse. Love units are withdrawn at a very fast rate. The partners may still hope that the hurting will stop and there will be a return to the state of Intimacy, but they don't trust each other to stop the madness. Occasionally, one spouse may revert to the Giver's rule, but if peace is to return, they must both do it simultaneously. The only way the Takers calm down is for both of them to be satisfied at the same time.

Couples can return to the state of Intimacy from Conflict if, and only if, they satisfy each other's Takers. How do they do that? By putting an end to their hurtful behavior and meeting each other's emotional needs again.

This is difficult because, in the state of Conflict, your Taker urges you to return pain whenever you receive it. For most couples, the state of Conflict inspires them to think with the shortsightedness of their Taker. Instead of wanting to meet each other's needs, they want their own needs met before they'll do anything. That makes resolving the conflict seem almost impossible, because Takers would rather fight than try to make the other spouse happy.

The Third State of Marriage: Withdrawal

If intelligence does not prevail, and Takers keep fighting, couples eventually enter the third state of marriage, Withdrawal. Like the state of Conflict, this is dominated by the Taker. But it represents a radical change in the Taker's strategy.

In the state of Conflict, your Taker tries to force your spouse to meet your needs, making demands and threatening your spouse with pain to get its way. But if that doesn't work—if your spouse does not meet your needs—your Taker suggests a new approach to the problem: Withdrawal. It tries to convince you that your spouse is not worth the effort, and you should engage in emotional divorce.

In the state of Withdrawal, spouses no longer feel emotionally bonded or in love, and emotional defenses are raised. Neither one wants to try to meet the other's needs, and both have given up on attempts to get their own needs met by the other. One becomes two. They are completely independent, united only in living arrangements, finances, and child rearing, although they often have to keep up appearances for neighbors and friends.

When one spouse enters the state of Withdrawal, the other usually follows. After all, what is the point? If she is meeting none of his needs and rebuffing every effort he makes to meet hers, he might as well give up, too. The thoughtless behavior by each spouse toward the other becomes too great to bear, so they stop caring. Trust is a faint memory.

Emotional needs can be met only when we are emotionally vulnerable to someone who meets those needs. When we become emotionally defensive, our emotional needs cannot be met. Couples in Withdrawal are really in a state of emotional divorce. When they've been in Withdrawal for any length of time, they will sleep in separate rooms, take separate vacations, and eat meals at different times. They will not communicate unless they must. If that doesn't work, they either separate or obtain a legal divorce.

Mates in Different States

Marriage partners do not necessarily experience the same state of marriage at the same time. One spouse may mar the peace and tranquility of Intimacy and cause the other spouse to go into the state of Conflict. That's when complaints, nagging, and arguments start. As these disagreements escalate, the other spouse is dragged into the Conflict state as well, and then both spouses behave selfishly.

Typically, if they fail in their efforts to resolve the conflict and if the unpleasant effects escalate, one spouse will go into Withdrawal first and raise his or her emotional barriers. The spouse who remains in the state of Conflict continues to argue, while the withdrawn spouse tries to escape. If the arguing spouse persists, the withdrawn spouse may be goaded to reenter the Conflict state and fight back. Or the arguing spouse may give up and enter Withdrawal, too.

One spouse may also lead the other on the road back from Withdrawal to Conflict and eventually to Intimacy. In Withdrawal, a husband may decide to make a new effort to restore Intimacy and toss out an olive branch. That effort places him back into the Conflict state, leaving his wife in Withdrawal.

Suppose his effort is an encouragement to her, and she joins him in the state of Conflict. Now they are both willing to have their needs met by the other, but their Takers encourage them to fight about it, rather than negotiate peacefully.

This step from Withdrawal to Conflict is a positive one, a step in the right direction. Withdrawal may seem more peaceful, but it is actually a shutting down of the marriage. A return to the Conflict state is a sign that the partners have restored hope—the marriage is worth fighting over. They are lowering their emotional defenses and taking the risk of getting close to each other again.

While fighting and arguing are instinctive in the Conflict state, one spouse can lead the other back to Intimacy by resisting the temptation to fight. It takes two to fight, and if one spouse makes an effort to avoid making hurtful and judgmental statements and tries to meet the other's needs, the other usually calms down and does the same thing.

Once their Takers are satisfied by each other's caring efforts, they reenter the state of Intimacy. But here's an irony that trips up some couples. Which spouse do you think is the first to move back into the state of Intimacy: the one who makes the first effort to meet the other's needs or the recipient of that effort?

You guessed it! The recipient, not the one who made the greatest effort to save the relationship.

If you set a good example by meeting your spouse's needs first, alas, that usually means that your own needs are met last. Your Taker is not pleased with this arrangement and will try to sabotage it. It generally requires a deliberate and patient effort to override the Taker's instinct to retreat back to fighting and name-calling. When both spouses' needs are finally met, the struggle is over. They have restored Intimacy.

As any roller-coaster ride will prove, it's easier to go downhill. The passage from Intimacy, through Conflict, to Withdrawal can be almost effortless. It takes more work to climb back up that hill. One of you *can* pull both of you back up the hill, but you *should* work together. In the next chapter I will introduce you to principles that will help you both climb the hill, making the job much easier and making the outcome successful.

Chapter Five

The Policy of Joint Agreement

How to Be Thoughtful and Caring When You're Not

Saving marriages is a difficult business. The Taker can ruin a relationship more easily than the Giver can restore it. Couples find it much easier to move away from the state of Intimacy toward the state of Withdrawal than from Withdrawal back to Intimacy.

In the state of Intimacy, a couple is motivated to be thoughtful and considerate because the relationship is paying such rich emotional dividends. Takers are getting a free ride on the mutual giving, so they don't want to do anything to spoil it. The Givers have their way in each conversation, and the Taker is satisfied.

But satisfaction is a temporary delight. Sooner or later someone makes a mistake. For example, if your spouse promised to pick you up at 5:00 and didn't show up until 6:00, what should you say? You may expect an apology and a promise that it won't happen again. But even if you get that apology, it may not be enough to keep your Taker quiet. After all, how can your Taker avoid telling your spouse that it's the fifth time this month that you've been left stranded and that apologies don't mean much to you anymore?

Or suppose your spouse doesn't even try to apologize. Now your Taker is definitely in high gear. After all, isn't it reasonable to impress on your spouse the importance of being on time, particularly when you are left cooling your heels, wondering what's going on?

Possibly worst of all, your spouse may think it's funny that you had to wait. Hell hath no fury like the Taker scorned. Your spouse is sure to get a verbal blast that will send him or her reeling!

You see, your Taker is just trying to protect you. Your Giver has been shoved aside because it was letting your spouse get away with murder. Someone has to stick up for your rights, and the Taker is more than willing to do the job. You justify your Taker's blowtorch approach by admitting that the conversation may not be pretty, but at least you're being *honest.*

Suppose, however, your spouse has moved into the state of Withdrawal while you're still in Conflict. Now you may wish for the days when you could at least argue with your spouse's Taker, because your spouse isn't talking much, if at all. Your spouse's Taker advises him or her to keep quiet and avoid conflict, because it's just too painful to do otherwise, and there's no point to it anyway. Your spouse's emotional barriers are up because the marriage just isn't worth getting hurt over. *Stop the fight. I give up!* is the message. Conversation practically grinds to a halt because your spouse's Taker, in protective mode, has put an end to it.

Meanwhile, you're still back in the Conflict state, and your emotional barriers are still down. You are still trying to get your spouse to change, to meet your needs, but you are doomed to disappointment. Your spouse's Taker has lost all hope of gaining pleasure (getting emotional needs met) in the relationship, and it is advising your spouse to avoid all but the most essential conversation with you (such as, "Please pass the salt").

Now, consider what an uphill battle it is to get back to the state of Intimacy once you're in the state of Withdrawal. Your Taker and your spouse's Taker are both overpowering. The Givers in you are being suffocated by the relentlessly convincing arguments of your Takers. You are both facing each other's worst sides, and the scene is truly ugly!

Somehow you must encourage your Givers to give again. But they seem imprisoned by your Takers' rule of self-protection: *Avoid anything that makes you unhappy.* Any effort to call a truce and seek his or her best interest might result in rebuff or ridicule. You can't trust your spouse to say a civil word to you, much less reach out to meet your needs. Even waving a white flag can get your arm blown off!

You desperately need peace talks but how do you get to the table? If you knew that your spouse's Giver was attending the meeting, maybe you could take a chance. But the last time you tried, the room was filled with attorneys—the hard-bargaining representatives of your spouse's Taker.

It's harder to mend than to rend. The Taker's reign of terror keeps most couples in Conflict or Withdrawal most of their married lives. But there is a way to beat it.

How to Restore the State of Intimacy

If you followed my excursion through the three states of marriage in the last chapter, you probably recognize that you've gone through them yourself. In fact, you may go through all three in a single day!

It's not unusual for married couples to wander through these states of marriage from time to time. But isn't it important to know how to get out of Withdrawal and Conflict and back into Intimacy as quickly as possible?

You could try putting your Giver in charge. After all, your Giver creates the environment for Intimacy, and it's your Taker that ruins it all.

But it's not that simple. Your Taker is not a potted plant, passively waiting for you to call it in when you need it. It is an aggressive force for your survival and takes over whenever it thinks you're in trouble. You cannot simply ignore it. You must reason with it and convince it that your interests are being served.

The rule of the Giver does not take the Taker's interests into account—that is the Giver's fatal flaw. We need a rule for marriage that takes the interests of both Giver and Taker into account at the same time. Teaching Joan and Mike to negotiate the interests of their Givers and Takers simultaneously was my biggest challenge.

Let's reiterate the rules of the Giver and Taker.

The Giver's Rule: Do whatever you can to make the other person happy and avoid anything that makes the other person unhappy.

The Taker's Rule: Do whatever you can to make yourself happy and avoid anything that makes you unhappy.

Your Giver always wants you to sacrifice your happiness so that others can be happy. Your Taker wants others to give up their happiness so that you can be happy. No matter which rule you follow, someone gets hurt.

Relationships can flourish only when our interests and the interests of others are met simultaneously. Then no one is hurt, everyone is happy, and compatibility is created.

So what we need to restore a shattered relationship is a new rule that takes the good from the rules of the Giver and Taker and eliminates the bad. We need to give and take, simultaneously, considering our own feelings and those of others.

Let's take a stab at revising the rules of the Giver and Taker.

The Revised Giver's Rule: Do whatever you can to make the other person happy, *unless it makes you unhappy,* and avoid anything that makes others unhappy, *unless avoiding it makes you unhappy.*

The Revised Taker's Rule: Do whatever you can to make yourself happy, *unless it makes the other person unhappy,* and avoid anything that makes you unhappy, *unless avoiding it makes the other person unhappy.*

It's beginning to look like a tax form, isn't it? Much too complicated. So I've come up with a simpler version of these revised rules. I call it the Policy of Joint Agreement: Never do anything without an enthusiastic agreement between you and your spouse.

The word *enthusiastic* should get your attention. It's a Taker's word, believe it or not. Your Taker will be enthusiastic about an agreement that's in your own best interest, and your spouse's Taker will be psyched about things in his or her best interest.

Policy of Joint Agreement
Never do anything without an enthusiastic agreement between you and your spouse.

Givers never show much enthusiasm, although they're willing to help sacrificially when they're needed. I don't want couples to give each other the self-sacrificing willingness of Givers. I want the enthusiastic willingness of Takers.

A Tale of Three Couples

How does this policy work out in real life? First, let's consider three alternatives to the Policy of Joint Agreement.

Couple A: Tom and Mary do not even discuss their plans with each other, much less agree. They just go ahead and plan their days with no consideration whatsoever for each other's feelings. If Tom wants to stop for a drink on the way home from work, he does, without asking Mary how she would feel about it. She never knows when he'll be home. If she wants to go shopping after he comes home from work, she says good-bye to the kids, and out the door she goes, hardly noticing Tom, let alone asking him if he'd watch their children.

Tom and Mary have adopted a strategy common among those in the state of Withdrawal. I'm sure you recognize it as the Taker's strategy. They have become terribly incompatible, developing a lifestyle and personal habits that ignore each other's feelings. When they argue, it's about who spends the money or who watches the children. For them, just asking the question, "How would you feel if I did this?" would be a vast improvement.

Couple B: Rick and Janet use a somewhat better decision-making strategy. They discuss their plans with each other. Each partner even thinks about how his or her plans would affect the other. But they both reserve the right to make the final decision, and each of them regularly does things that the other doesn't like.

For instance, there is an optional business trip that Rick could take, but it coincides with Janet's birthday. He talks it over with her, registers her wishes, but decides to go anyway. Janet is offered a community leadership position that will take her away from home several nights a week. Rick explains how it would complicate his life, but she accepts the offer anyway.

To the extent that they disregard each other's feelings, they are building an incompatible lifestyle.

This couple is often in the state of Conflict, because once in a while their decision-making strategy causes one to gain at the other's expense. Discussing their plans helps them understand each other, and they often accommodate each other with that understanding. For example, when Rick learned that Janet objected to a certain after-shave lotion that he bought, he stopped using it. Truth was, he didn't care much for it either. But every time he did not yield to her wishes, he hurt her feelings twice: He hurt her by going on the business trip and leaving her alone on her birthday and he hurt her a second time by going on the trip when he knew it would make her unhappy.

Couple C: Dan and Carla go one step further: They do not go ahead with most decisions unless there is agreement. But they are willing to accept *reluctant* agreement. Their Givers make a valiant effort to override the concerns of their Takers, and even though their hearts are in the right place, their unselfish approach actually encourages some incompatibility.

One Monday night, Dan wanted to watch football with one of his friends and invited Carla to go with him. She not only refused to go with him, but she let him know that she didn't even want him to go. He reluctantly agreed to stay at home that evening, but he resented her for ruining what could have been fun. All night he was quiet, thinking about the game. By the time they went to bed, Carla wished she had let him go, because he was so ugly to be around.

Dan's Giver was strong enough to override his Taker's wishes to watch football, but not strong enough to keep his Taker from vigorously protesting. And Dan got (and delivered) his Taker's message loud and clear. Before the evening was over, he flew into a rage over some little thing. (Three days later when he was telling me about the incident, he had forgotten what had made him lose his temper but he sure remembered having given up *Monday Night Football*.)

Reluctant agreement *seems* like a satisfactory solution to many couples. Most of us view personal sacrifice as a noble thing, giving up our well-being for the good of others—but it's really very risky in a marital relationship. When you reluctantly agree to some course of action with your spouse, it means that he or she is gaining at your expense. And that can tip the delicate balance of your marriage. If a decision is not in the best interest of both of you, it is not in the best interest of the relationship.

That's not to say that you should never sacrifice. We have all sacrificed our own short-term interests for a long-term interest. Not every decision we make can, or should, be viewed as benefiting us immediately. For example, I went through quite a bit of self-sacrifice when I earned a Ph.D. in psychology. It was no fun, I assure you. Yet my Taker was with me in this plan because it could see future value in my decision.

The same is true in my relationship with my wife, Joyce. I am willing to sacrifice my immediate pleasure for something that will give us both long-term pleasure. Having children probably fits into that category. I knew that Joyce and I would not be able to give each other the same attention after Jennifer and Steve were born. Still, my Taker (like Joyce's) was enthusiastic about the future fulfillment involved in having children.

What I'm saying is that your Taker can be enthusiastic about sacrifice, if it's in your long-term interest. When you agree to something reluctantly, you are sacrificing your own best interest even though you see no short-term or long-term benefits. That's why reluctant agreements usually get sabotaged later by your Taker.

Occasionally a strategy of reluctant agreement can work—at least for a while. Joan and Mike used it during their courtship and, as long as their Takers did not interfere, their Givers could freely give in to each other. As a result, Joan and Mike thought they were much more compatible than they really were. Many of the activities that Joan agreed to were unpleasant to her, and the same was true for Mike. In general, they were developing too many habits that were good for one and bad for the other. It was only a matter of time before one Taker or the other would emerge and put an end to all this rampant giving.

So let's evaluate the three alternatives to the Policy of Joint Agreement. I think we all agree that Tom and Mary, our first couple, are in deep trouble as they pass each other like ships in the night. Their strategy of self-centeredness doesn't work at all in marriage, and couples that follow it usually divorce.

Rick and Janet, couple B, have taken a step in the right direction, but they're in trouble, too. They still allow thoughtlessness to come between them, robbing them of the intimacy that they want in marriage.

Most of us can best relate to our third couple, Dan and Carla, with their reluctant agreement. You can probably think of many instances of the sacrifices you've made to accommodate your spouse. (Incidentally, although your spouse has also made sacrifices for you, I'll bet you can't think of nearly as many examples of his or her reluctant agreement to accommodate you.)

Dan and Carla's marriage will survive, but their habit of reluctant agreement will allow stubborn pockets of incompatibility to remain. Their Takers will feel left out and will occasionally cause a ruckus.

It's only when a couple takes the final step, where they continue to negotiate about every conflict until there's *enthusiastic* agreement between them, that martial compatibility flourishes. Then a couple creates a lifestyle that benefits both of them simultaneously. When that happens, it can truly be said that they "live in harmony" with each other.

Is the Policy of Joint Agreement Unrealistic?

You're crazy, Harley!

Is that what you're thinking now? If so, I don't blame you.

This "policy" may sound good in theory, you may be thinking, *but you've never met my spouse. It's all we can do to reach any agreement at all, and you want us to be enthusiastic! Yeah, right. If you want enthusiasm, you've come to the wrong place.*

That's the sort of reaction I get from many couples I counsel, and I understand the despair they're feeling. The Policy of Joint Agreement must seem like a distant fantasy.

I advise these couples to take it one day at a time. The policy will prove its value almost from the start. Try it. What do you have to lose?

I hear another voice saying, *Why should I clear all my plans with my spouse? I did not marry to have someone tell me what to do with my life. I'll do what I choose, thank you, and if my spouse doesn't like it, we both know where the door is. You'd turn me into a slave if I took this stuff seriously.*

Hello, Taker. I'm used to talking to those who have come to the same conclusion. They're the ones who have tried to be accommodating only to find that it leads to painful sacrifices. Sometimes it takes a while, but I usually show them that my policy doesn't hurt them a bit. When they see that they have nothing to be afraid of, their Givers peek out from behind the curtain and I find caring and considerate spouses under layers of resentment and anger.

Rather than engaging my clients in lengthy philosophical discussions about the nature of consideration, I simply tell them that the policy is a practical solution to the misery they have been experiencing. While it may be difficult to follow at first, when it is followed, they will see improvement in their relationship almost immediately. In fact, for some couples it has helped create miraclelike solutions to a host of their marital conflicts within weeks or sometimes even days.

Compatibility doesn't just happen. It's made to happen because couples choose to live together in harmony. The Policy of Joint Agreement is simply a way to express how people treat each other when they choose to be compatible.

Joan and Mike's First Efforts

Joan and Mike needed the Policy of Joint Agreement very badly. Except for a few fleeting moments of peace, since their honeymoon disaster all they had seen in each other were the thoughtless, selfish Takers who weren't interested in meeting anybody's needs but their own.

In my first session with them, I introduced them to the Policy of Joint Agreement, *Never do anything without the enthusiastic agreement of both you and your spouse.* I recommended that, from that moment on, they follow it.

When people's Takers call the shots, it's hard to sell them on the Policy of Joint Agreement. Your Taker will find it hard to believe that it's in your best interest to seek your spouse's enthusiastic agreement on every decision. *Think of everything you'll be missing if you always need your spouse's permission to do anything,* your Taker whispers.

But that's just the point. You'll be missing the pain that you and your spouse are inflicting on each other. This policy helps put the perspective of both spouses back into the decisions you make. It helps balance every choice so that the interests of both of you are considered simultaneously.

I encouraged Joan and Mike to try it for just three days, until their next appointment with me. What would they have to lose?

After they had been so mean to each other, neither of them felt the other deserved their consideration, but they knew they needed help. Willing to try just about anything, they both agreed to try the Policy of Joint Agreement.

Before they left the office, I explained that the policy also applied to their conversation. They could not even talk to each other in ways that were disagreeable or unpleasant. Everything they did and said had to meet with each other's agreement. No abusive, angry outbursts. No nagging and nit-picking. No judgmental and disrespectful remarks. In other words, they were to stop talking to each other in ways that made their marriage a nightmare.

Since their feelings were so negative toward each other, I suggested they avoid talking about those feelings altogether, limiting their conversation to pleasant topics. Sure, it seemed phony at first, but it helped them avoid some of the most painful moments they would spend with each other. It would also help them learn to be more positive in their conversation.

But the most important part of the policy, of course, was that neither could do anything without taking the other's feelings into account. If Mike wanted to do something that his Taker was encouraging him to do, he had to check with Joan (Joan's Taker) to be sure it would be in her best interest, too. Joan had to do the same thing: Check with Mike (Mike's Taker) to see how he would feel. They needed enthusiastic agreement, which usually comes only when one's own interests are being served. No halfhearted, shrugging, self-sacrificing murmurs of "All right, I guess." Mike and Joan need to learn to pound out compromises that they both felt great about.

When they met with me three days later, they had both made an effort to stop hurting each other, allowing their Givers a chance to breathe once again. But their Takers were not sure that this was going to work.

Without Mike's knowledge, Joan had scheduled an evening out with her friends. She had planned it weeks earlier and even had a baby-sitter lined up just in case Mike wasn't home. If he was home, she figured, she would tell him about her outing fifteen minutes before she left. That way, he wouldn't be able to argue much, and it would be too late for her to change plans anyway. (Her Taker had worked out every detail with brilliant precision.) But the Policy of Joint Agreement changed everything, forcing Joan to ask Mike if her plans were all right with him.

Mike was not enthusiastic, to say the least—especially when he discovered that this group of her friends included women and men from the restaurant where she worked part-time. "No way!" he demanded. So she didn't go. He offered to take her out to dinner instead, but she didn't want to go with him. She was very angry (something her Taker prodded her to feel) and came very close to canceling her appointment with me. So far, the policy sure hadn't proved its value.

She phoned me for clarification. "I had already made plans with my friends before I agreed to your policy," she explained. "If I cancel my plans, I will be doing something that I do not agree with enthusiastically. So I should be able to go out with my friends, right?"

I reminded her that the agreement covered what she did, not what she had planned to do. The policy simply says you cannot do anything without each other's enthusiastic agreement. In the worst case, the two of them would sit at home doing nothing because they would be unable to agree to even get up out of their chairs.

She remembered that her agreement was only for three days and she made it through the conflict without saying anything to upset Mike. Her Taker was not pleased, to say the least, but she kept her part of the bargain.

Mike's behavior was much improved during those three days and that was an encouragement to Joan. He managed to get through the entire period without criticizing her once. Well, he started a few critical comments but cut himself off and then apologized for what he would have said. Actually, Mike and Joan didn't say very much to each other at all and they didn't do anything together but at least they had made an initial effort to stop doing things that had made them incompatible.

Overcoming Incompatible Lifestyles

At their next appointment I asked them how many years they had been married. "During all that time," I pointed out, "you've been developing incompatible lifestyles. It will take more than a few days to undo that, but this is a good start."

Since their honeymoon, Mike and Joan had been making choices at each other's expense. They were even going beyond mere selfishness and acting with contempt toward each other. No couple can survive a relationship that is based on rude and disrespectful behavior.

"This whole process would be a lot easier," I said, "if you were in love with each other again." Mike and Joan almost smiled at the absurdity of this thought. In love? They were just hoping to coexist.

"But wouldn't you like to be taken back to the days before your marriage," I went on, "those days when you couldn't get enough of each other, when you cared about each other?"

But restoring love is inconceivable when you hate someone. For Joan and Mike, their courtship was a distant memory. They just wanted to stay together until the kids grew up, and then *Sayonara, baby.* They had no dream of a restored love, no hope of a real marriage.

"My goal in counseling you is to help you rediscover romantic love by helping you become compatible," I told them. "Or, if you prefer, I'll help you become compatible by helping you rediscover romantic love. Either way you look at it, if you do what I recommend, compatibility and romantic love will be the outcome. The Policy of Joint Agreement is the key, even though it may go against your instincts. But trust me, trust this policy, and give it a chance to work."

Joan and Mike had their doubts about what I was suggesting but they had run out of options. They were imprisoned in the hole they had started digging during their honeymoon. True, they were considering divorce as an escape from that hole but they knew that divorce is an emotional, financial, and spiritual disaster to almost everyone involved. In a divorce children often feel as though they've been tossed off a cliff by their parents. Even in their desperate state, Joan and Mike wanted to avoid divorce because they both loved their children.

Yet they saw no way back. The love they shared in their courtship was long ago and far away. Their Givers hardly recognized each other. Their Love Bank accounts were insolvent. By now they had developed ways of thinking and feeling about each other that just tore them further apart. They were miserable with each other and expected to stay miserable until the kids were grown. The stage of Withdrawal was their only sanctuary.

I was offering them a way out. I was pointing to the first few footholds on the long climb out of their misery. They needed just enough hope to grab on to that first foothold and start climbing. Maybe, just maybe, they could turn this thing around and have the marriage they were looking forward to the day they married.

Chapter Six

It's Okay to Make a Deal

How to Negotiate for Compatibility

My grandmother had the ultimate Giver, at least in her relationship with me. I was regularly the recipient of her generosity. Among the gifts I received were pennies from her purse whenever she came to visit. On one occasion, I devised a plan that would give me more than pennies. I negotiated a better deal for myself.

After she gave me fifteen pennies, I asked, "Grandma, would you give me a nickel and a dime for these fifteen pennies?"

"Of course," she responded, exchanging those coins for my pennies.

Then came the most brilliant part of my plan. "Grandma, can I have your pennies now?"

Within a few minutes I had all the change in her purse. If I had thought it through more carefully, I probably could have received all her dollars as well. Maybe even her entire bank account!

Couples in the stage of Intimacy bargain the way my grandmother bargained. They give each other whatever is requested.

But by the time they come to see me, most couples I counsel are nothing like my grandmother. They're more like the child I was—getting whatever I could at my grandmother's expense. Each spouse wants to come out ahead, even if it means that the other spouse loses.

When they have a disagreement, they don't negotiate; they grab for all they can get. To make matters worse, they often do and say angry, vindictive things that make it impossible to resolve the problem.

I was not negotiating with my grandmother. She was giving and I was taking. When couples come to see me with their Takers in full battle dress, they are not negotiating either. Neither one of them is giving.

Though couples desperately need to negotiate fair solutions to their problems, many don't know how. True negotiation takes place only when a deal is struck that simultaneously takes the interest of *both* parties into account—and that means that both of the Givers and Takers must be involved.

When you marry, your feelings are as important as those of your spouse. Your Giver doesn't want you to believe this, but it's true. You're a team, and your decisions should make both of you happy, not one or the other. Neither of you should gain at the other's expense, even if it's voluntary. I should not want Joyce to do something for me if she must suffer to do it. She should not want me to suffer for her, either.

There's nothing wrong with negotiation in marriage. In fact, through negotiation we come to understand each other best and meet each other's needs most effectively. Through negotiation we know precisely what our spouse values the most, and our spouse learns what we value the most. When we give what's most important to our spouse in return for what's most important to us, we have the most caring relationship possible.

Marital negotiation is simply putting your needs on the table and figuring out how you'll work together to meet them. When you reach an enthusiastic agreement, you feel that your bargain is fair, and you value your relationship even more. Both of you get what you need, and neither of you suffers.

Successful Negotiations Build Strong Relationships

Joan and Mike needed to learn how to negotiate. Each knew how to meet the other's needs, because they both had done it so successfully prior to marriage. Though they had a few disagreements during their courtship, these were never serious enough to threaten the relationship. So one or the other always gave in. As their love grew, they were willing to walk barefoot over broken glass to make each other happy.

Mike and Joan's tendency to give in built a serious weakness into their relationship. They had never learned how to take both of their interests into account at the same time. In other words, they didn't know how to negotiate.

Givers don't know how to negotiate. Givers just want to give, give, give, without getting anything in return. In fact, Givers believe it's wrong to expect anything in return. Imagine a labor union sending little Mary Sunshine into a contract dispute. "Oh, all right! We'll work sixty-hour weeks for lower pay and less benefits. We're here to help the company succeed and we're willing to do whatever it takes." Smiles cross the faces of the management, and a deal has been struck. But at what price?

Takers don't know how to negotiate, either. They have one goal in mind. Get as much as possible for as little as possible. Unchecked, they will accept the generous offer of the Givers the way I accepted my grandmother's pennies: "Can't you give me even more?" By their very nature our Takers have no interest in providing care for others, only care for themselves.

If you're not skilled in marital negotiations, your efforts may seem superficial and strained. Remember, neither your Giver nor your Taker knows how to negotiate, and you may be in the habit of letting one or the other control your life. But if you develop the skill of negotiation, eventually it will become an art to you—it will become second nature. You will not only be successful in solving a host of problems but you will also become each other's best friend.

From this perspective, you can see why I feel that negotiation is so important in marriage. It represents the most effective way to satisfy the interests of both spouses. Successful negotiation can create continual improvement in your ability to meet each other's needs and avoid hurting each other. Without it, your marriage is likely to become increasingly unfulfilling. With it, you will become compatible.

The Policy of Joint Agreement: The Cornerstone in Negotiation

When Joan and Mike returned for their second appointment with me, they had already been trying out the Policy of Joint Agreement.

Though they found it difficult to follow, they seemed much more relaxed with each other than they had been in their first session. The Policy of Joint Agreement had helped them lower their defenses a bit.

But if I had asked them at that point to begin discussing their conflicts, they would have been embroiled in a fight within seconds. It would have been, "You never . . ." and "I always have to . . ." and "Why are you so . . . ?"

Before we got down to specifics, I had to teach them how to negotiate.

As you might guess, my approach to successful negotiation follows directly from the Policy of Joint Agreement: *Never do anything without an enthusiastic agreement between you and your spouse.*

The fact is, if you do not follow this policy, there's not much to negotiate. You're either doing your own thing, ignoring each other's feelings, or you're selling yourselves into slavery. There's no point to negotiating unless you care about each other's feelings.

But if you follow the policy, you will be negotiating with fairness. You will try to understand and meet each other's needs and, when there are conflicts, look for solutions about which you can both be enthusiastic.

Joan had already raised a good issue. Remember, she had planned to go out with friends from work but could not get Mike's enthusiastic agreement. Why should Mike have veto power over something she had already planned? She was not enthusiastic about canceling her plans, so shouldn't she be allowed to go ahead and meet her friends?

Though she did, in fact, cancel her plans after phoning me, she wasn't happy about it. Yet if Joan had known more about negotiating, she might have won Mike's enthusiastic agreement for her outing by accepting something he wanted to do. Or they might have agreed to an activity that both of them were willing to do together. But they weren't ready for that yet. They soon would be, because in the second session they would learn how to negotiate.

Four Guidelines for Successful Negotiation

Let's begin with the assumption that you and your spouse do not agree about something. It can be about an unmet need, and one of you wants the other to do a better job meeting it. Or it can be about a thoughtless habit, and one of you is hurting the other. It can be about anything where it is important for you both to be in agreement.

Chances are you have been responding to this issue in one of two ways: ignoring your spouse's feelings or downplaying your own feelings. Negotiation requires you to do something entirely different: Take your feelings *and* your spouse's feelings into account.

To help couples like Joan and Mike negotiate fairly, I've suggested four guidelines for successful negotiation.

Guideline 1: ***Set ground rules to make negotiations pleasant and safe.***

Joan and Mike viewed negotiation as a trip to the torture chamber. Not only were their efforts fruitless, but they would come away battered and bruised. Who wants to negotiate when you have nothing but pain and disappointment to look forward to?

So before you begin to negotiate, you should set some basic ground rules to be sure that you'll both enjoy the experience. Why? Because you tend to repeat activities that you like. Since marital negotiation should be a regular part of married life, it should be at least as enjoyable as breakfast.

I'm sure you can think of several ground rules that will help insure a pleasant and safe environment, but here are three that you should include:

Ground Rule 1: ***Try to be pleasant and cheerful throughout negotiations.***

It's fairly easy to start the process in a good mood. But negotiations can open a can of worms, and you must be prepared for negative emotional reactions. Your spouse may begin to feel uncomfortable about something you say. In fact, out of the clear blue, he or she may inform you that the deal's off and there will be no more negotiating.

I know how upset and defensive couples can get when they first tell each other how they feel about the way they're being treated. That's why I often see them individually to prepare them. I simply tell them what I'm telling you: Be as positive and cheerful as you can be.

Ground Rule 2: ***Put safety first—do not threaten to cause pain or suffering when you negotiate, even if your spouse makes threatening remarks or if the negotiations fail.***

Once the cat's out of the bag, once you've told each other what you want, you've entered one of the most dangerous parts of this entire process. Couples are tempted to retaliate when their feelings have been hurt. If you can keep each other safe beyond this point, you're in a good position to make the changes you both need.

Don't threaten your spouse and don't express anger or resentment. I know that negotiation can be a frustrating effort. At times, it seems as if there will never be a satisfactory solution. But if you use threats, your negotiation will end in failure. Threats not only prove how uncaring you can really be, but they encourage your spouse to be just as uncaring. As a result, your marriage becomes a place of suffering rather than safety, pain rather than protection.

What if you intend to divorce your spouse if the negotiations fail? Should you mention that while you're negotiating? Wouldn't that make your spouse more serious about the negotiations?

Think for a moment. How would you feel if your spouse were to lay that on you? If you felt that divorce was likely, would you want to invest more love and attention in your spouse, or less?

And how would the threat of divorce affect your own balance between the Giver and Taker? At first, your Taker might panic and agree to anything, but after recovering, it would encourage you to prepare for divorce yourself. Your Giver would have little opportunity to care as your Taker prepared you for war. Then, angry and resentful, you'd be planning your divorce, while giving your spouse the impression you were trying to cooperate. Demands and threats don't change our behavior in the long term—they just make us angry.

When your negotiations hit a roadblock—and they will—be patient. I know the problem sometimes seems impossible. But do not let your frustration lead you to threats, demands, and insults. You will find, as many couples do, further thought leads to a breakthrough, and eventually an agreement is reached.

Ground Rule 3: ***If you reach an impasse, stop for a while and come back to the issue later.***

Just because you cannot resolve a problem at a particular point in time doesn't mean that you will not resolve it in the future. Don't let an impasse prevent you from using your creativity and intelligence to overcome it at a later date.

What do you do when the negotiations turn into pain and sorrow? I recommend that you end the discussion gracefully and try to change the subject to something more pleasant. After a brief pause, your spouse may be willing to return to the subject that was so upsetting. Without such willingness, you should let the subject drop and return to it at some other time.

Ground Rules for Negotiations

1. Try to be pleasant and cheerful throughout negotiations.
2. Put safety first—do not threaten to cause pain or suffering when you negotiate, even if your spouse makes threatening remarks or if the negotiations fail.
3. If you reach an impasse, stop for a while and come back to the issue later.

Even in the unpleasant situation I just described, if you try to maintain a cheerful attitude, you can turn disaster into victory. After all, what is your alternative? An ugly response can only ruin future opportunities to negotiate.

There is a solution to almost every problem. The question is *Can you discover it?* If after giving it serious consideration, you find yourself stumped, you may simply need more time to think about it.

Remember, a solution is possible only when you can both enthusiastically agree to it. If you feel you need help finding that solution, perhaps a friend, clergyman, or marriage counselor can help you think of alternatives you may not have considered.

But your minds are much more powerful and imaginative than you probably give them credit for. If you discuss the problem one day and come back to it the next, you will be surprised how many new solutions you will have identified in that brief time. Your brain works on your problems when you're not even thinking about them and has solutions ready for you when you come back to them later. Try it—you'll discover something very remarkable about the most valuable part of yourself, your mind.

Guideline 2: ***Identify the problem from both perspectives.***

Once you have set ground rules, you're ready to negotiate. But where do you begin? First, you should understand the problem, and it should be understood from the perspectives of both you and your spouse.

Most couples go into marital negotiation without doing their homework. They don't fully understand the conflict itself, nor do they understand each other's perspectives. In many cases, they're not even sure what they really want.

One of the jobs of a marriage counselor is to help couples clarify the issues that separate them. I'm amazed at how often the clarification itself solves the problem. "Oh, that's what we're fighting about!" Once they understand the issue and each other's opinions, they realize the conflict is not as serious as they thought. Or when the issue is clarified, the solution is immediately apparent and the conflict is resolved.

Maybe you don't need a counselor to do that for you. Sit down and talk about it. What is the issue? What do you want? What does your spouse want? Get your cards out on the table.

I know, sometimes you've been in the trenches so long, you've forgotten what the war is all about. You may need some help putting your finger on the problem. If you've read some of the other books I've written, you know that I use questionnaires to help couples clarify issues that need to be resolved. For example, the Love Busters Questionnaire (appendix A) helps identify harmful habits that you and your spouse have, habits that cause each other unhappiness and should be overcome. The Emotional Needs Questionnaire (appendix B) helps to identify each other's most important emotional needs so that you can care for each other in the most meaningful ways. The use of these questionnaires is explained in chapters 7–10. Other questionnaires you may find useful are in a workbook I've written, *Five Steps to Romantic Love* (Revell, 1993).

These tools (and others) can help you identify and communicate your unmet needs. But whether or not you use them, you should know enough about the issue so that you can state it clearly to your spouse. You should also be able to state your position on the issue (your opinion) and the position of your spouse (your spouse's opinion). So before you actually begin thinking of a solution, be certain you've identified the problem and understand it from each other's perspective.

Guideline 3: *Brainstorm with abandon.*

You've set the ground rules. You've identified the problem. Now you're ready for the creative part—looking for solutions that you think will make both of you happy. I know that can seem impossible if you and your spouse have drifted into incompatibility. But the climb back to Intimacy has to start somewhere, and when you put your minds to it, you'll think of options that please you both.

The secret to understanding your spouse is to think like your spouse's Taker. It's easy to appeal to your spouse's Giver. "If she really loves me, she'll let me do this." "He'll be thoughtful enough to agree with that, I'm sure." But any lasting peace must be forged with your spouse's Giver *and* Taker, so your solutions must appeal to your spouse's most selfish instincts. At the same time, it must appeal to your own selfish instincts.

For example, let's take the conflict that arose between Mike and Joan right after their first appointment with me. Joan wanted to go out with her friends from work that night. Mike didn't want her to party with the men from work. She had planned to spring her outing on him just before she left, so he could not stop her, but her appointment with me wrecked it all. Since they had not yet learned to negotiate, she simply did not go. She was angry and Mike felt guilty. (Yet they did the right thing: If she had gone, she would have violated the Policy of Joint Agreement. She would have gained at Mike's expense.) But if they had negotiated successfully, they would have found a way to make them both happy. And this process would have started with brainstorming.

When you brainstorm, quantity is more important than quality. Let your minds run wild; go with just about *any* thought. You won't end up *doing* everything you think of, but if you let your creative side run free, you're more likely to find a solution.

Let's do a little brainstorming about alternatives to Joan's evening out.

- *Joan goes to the party but agrees to return at 10:00.* She avoids the embarrassment of not attending an office party, and Mike is comfortable with her relatively short showing.
- *They go to the party together.* She enjoys the company of her friends, and he is witness to the fact that she is not flirting with her male colleagues.
- *She does not go to the party, but Mike agrees that they'll host a party for her coworkers next month.* She feels that having an opportunity to host the party in her home is well worth skipping the current outing. And this way Mike can get to know her

coworkers better. Mike likes the idea of having a party in their home.

- *She does not go to the party, and in return, Mike cleans the kitchen and washes the dishes for a month.* Mike does not mind doing this, and Joan doesn't feel guilty when she watches TV after dinner.

These barely scratch the surface. There are many options that could meet with their approval, and it should only be a matter of time before they find one that generates mutual enthusiasm.

Guideline 4: ***Choose the solution that is the most appealing to both of you.***

After brainstorming, you will have created some good and bad solutions. Now you need to sort through them.

Good solutions are those that both you and your spouse consider desirable. In other words, they meet the conditions of the Policy of Joint Agreement. Bad solutions, on the other hand, only take the feelings of one spouse into account at the expense of the other. The best solution is the one that both you and your spouse are the *most* enthusiastic about.

If Mike and Joan had had another chance to resolve this conflict, they might have chosen an alternative that would have eased Joan's resentment. For example, Mike might have agreed to let Joan shop with her sister at the mall, while he stayed home with the kids. He would be enthusiastic because she would be shopping for gifts for their son's birthday, which he values. She would enjoy shopping with her sister as much as she would have enjoyed the office party.

Many problems are relatively easy to solve. You will be amazed at how quickly you can find agreement when you've decided to take each other's feelings into account. Of course, other problems are very difficult to resolve, involving many steps. In the rest of this book, I'll be addressing some of those.

Each time you negotiate, it should be done with friendship and encouragement in mind. That way you'll negotiate with each other the rest of your lives. If it ever becomes unpleasant, you're not likely to continue negotiating with each other.

The skill you develop as negotiators will enhance your marital compatibility. You will learn to meet each other's emotional needs and avoid being the cause of each other's unhappiness. Before long, your Love Banks will be overflowing, and you'll be crazy about each other again.

Done right, negotiation can be an enjoyable way to learn about each other. If you avoid unpleasant scenes and if you negotiate to an enthusiastic agreement, you'll resolve with relative ease all of the many conflicts you'll have throughout life.

A word of caution: Be sure that your spouse isn't in a state of emotional Withdrawal when you suggest negotiating. Withdrawal makes negotiating impossible.

Those in Withdrawal are not unable to negotiate, just unwilling. They are emotionally divorced. They do not want to meet their spouse's needs, and they don't want their own needs met either. Negotiations require a willingness to create a better relationship. Beware of the car salesman in his last day on the job.

If your spouse is in the state of Withdrawal, you must first restore trust. Defenses need to be lowered. Be sensitive to the fact that you've inflicted pain, and your spouse is in Withdrawal to avoid it. When you stop hurting your spouse, he or she will eventually come out of emotional Withdrawal. Only then will you witness a willingness to negotiate.

Where to Start?

So much to resolve, so little time. Where should you begin to negotiate?

At this moment, there are probably several conflicts in your marriage you would like to resolve. You may consider some of them trivial, while others may be creating a great deal of distress for both of you.

Perhaps, like Joan and Mike, you and your spouse have some conflicts you don't believe you can ever overcome. Where do you start?

Simply put, marital conflict is created in one of two ways: (1) Couples make each other unhappy, or (2) couples fail to make each other happy. In the first case, couples are hurting each other, intentionally or unintentionally. In the second case, they are frustrated because their needs are not being met. I call the first cause of conflict *failure to protect* and the second *failure to care.*

I believe that conflicts have an order of importance. Those caused by a couple's failure to protect are more important than conflicts caused by a failure to care. Why? Because a failure to protect changes your spouse's attitude about your care. If you are causing me pain, I do not want to care for you, nor will I receive care from you. I certainly do not want care from someone who is failing to protect me from his or her own actions. Most of us will not allow those who hurt us to try to make up for it by meeting our needs.

So the conflicts that I encouraged Joan and Mike to resolve first were conflicts that arose from their *failure to protect.* In the next several chapters, I will show you how Joan and Mike identified and then overcame behavior that made each other unhappy.

Whenever you do something that hurts your spouse, you are withdrawing love units from your account in his or her Love Bank. For that reason, I call those inconsiderate acts Love Busters, because they destroy romantic love.

After we see how Joan and Mike overcame Love Busters, we'll look at that second cause of conflict, *failure to care.* In chapters 11–17, we'll see how Mike and Joan learned to recognize and meet each other's needs.

But I'm getting ahead of myself, first we should take a look at how Joan and Mike—and perhaps you and your spouse—can eliminate Love Busters.

Learning *to* Protect

Part Two

Chapter Seven

Become a Jerk in Five Easy Lessons

How Love Busters Destroy Compatibility

"The road to hell is paved with good intentions," the saying goes, and we've seen the truth in that proverb. If all we needed in marriage was good intentions—a desire to do the right thing—most of us would be in good shape. What is true about heaven and hell is also true about good marriages and bad marriages. Good intentions are not enough.

Joan and Mike had absolutely no desire to wreck their marriage. Yet the way they behaved, you'd think they had taken advanced courses on the subject. As much as they wanted to have a great marriage, they felt compelled to ruin it.

Almost everyone I've seen feels that he or she has put 150 percent into the marriage. These people are downright proud of the fact that, even though it's failing, they've done their part—it isn't their fault. After two sessions with me, however, they (like Joan and Mike) discover that "their part" is part of the problem.

The Policy of Joint Agreement helped Joan and Mike bring each of their parts of the problem to light. Then they began to see how their instincts were destroying their marriage and themselves. Though they didn't feel comfortable following this rule, they knew it was the right thing to do. After their first session, they both tried to apply it to each decision they made. With each application of the policy, they were building compatibility.

In their second session, they saw how negotiation would help them resolve conflicts in a more thoughtful way. After I gave them my guidelines, they agreed to give negotiation a try. They were certainly getting off to a good start, but it was just the beginning.

Both the Policy of Joint Agreement and the guidelines for negotiation help couples avoid new problems, but most couples have a host of existing problems that make their marriages intolerable. Mike and Joan were no exception: They were often hurting each other without even knowing it or thinking about it.

Over the years they'd been married, each had learned habits that made the other miserable. They had created an incompatible lifestyle. So what was our next step? Identifying these troublesome habits—these Love Busters—and then overcoming them.

Busting the Love Bank

In the simplest terms, Love Busters are those things you do regularly that make your spouse unhappy. They rob love units from your account in your spouse's Love Bank and destroy romantic love.

From my work with couples over the years, I have identified five categories of Love Busters: (1) Angry outbursts, (2) Disrespectful judgments, (3) Annoying behavior, (4) Selfish demands, and (5) Dishonesty. You may already be familiar with them if you've read my book *Love Busters* (Revell, 1992). Chances are, you and your spouse are guilty of some of these. Whenever you do them, you're destroying the feeling of love you have for each other.

The Love Busters
Angry outbursts
Disrespectful judgments
Annoying behavior
Selfish demands
Dishonesty

So why do we do these things? It's really quite easy to understand. While all of these habits make our spouses feel bad, they make *us* feel good. In every Love Buster there is something that's in our own best interest—so we do them because we like to do them. Love

Busters give us pleasure, and we have a difficult time resisting them, even when we know they are at our spouse's expense.

When our spouse complains about Love Busters, we try to rationalize our behavior. We're not the selfish ones, we protest, our spouse just doesn't want us to be happy. Of course, that's a Taker's argument. Takers love the Love Busters, and Givers are horrified by them. Our Givers go to great lengths to avoid Love Busters, but our Takers see nothing wrong with them. All our excuses for Love Busters represent very sound reasoning to our Takers, because they consciously and deliberately ignore the feelings of our spouse.

Technically, a Love Buster should not exist in marriage. It should be a foregone conclusion that one spouse would not hurt the other to gain pleasure for himself or herself. If we all followed the Policy of Joint Agreement, there would be no Love Busters.

But most couples do not follow the policy, and they don't negotiate well. They fall in love and let their Givers call the shots—as long as they're in the state of Intimacy, that is. Intimacy is ruled by the Givers, so Love Busters need not apply. The very thought of taking advantage of your lover, of hurting your sweetheart, of gaining at your spouse's expense, would instantly be vetoed by your Giver.

But the state of Conflict is inevitable, and eventually Takers do their thing. This is where the Love Busters breed and multiply, with both spouses' Takers grabbing all they can get. If couples are in this state very long, their self-centered behavior hardens into habits, locking Love Busters into place.

Once Love Busters become the norm, when a couple creates a lifestyle of hurting each other, it is very difficult for them ever to return to the state of Intimacy. Marriage turns into a war between Takers, with the thoughtfulness of Givers becoming a distant memory.

So let's look at these dangerous behaviors. The five categories of Love Busters deserve a very close scrutiny.

Angry Outbursts

What makes you angry?

Anger usually occurs when you feel (a) that someone is making you unhappy, and (b) that what that person's doing just isn't fair. In your angry state, you're convinced that reasoning won't work, and the offender will keep upsetting you until he or she is taught a lesson. *The only thing such people understand is punishment,* you assume. *Then they'll think twice about making me unhappy again!*

Your Taker uses anger to protect you and it offers a simple solution to your problem—destroy the troublemaker. If your spouse turns out to be the troublemaker, your Taker urges you to hurt the one you've promised to cherish and protect. It does not care about your spouse's feelings and is willing to scorch the culprit if it prevents you from being hurt again.

But in the end, you have nothing to gain from anger. Punishment does not solve marital problems; it only makes your punished spouse want to inflict punishment on you. When you become angry with your spouse, you threaten your spouse's safety and security, you fail to provide protection. Your spouse's Taker rises to the challenge and tries to destroy you in retaliation. When anger wins, love loses.

Each of us has an arsenal of weapons we use when we're angry. If we think someone deserves to be punished, we unlock the gate and select an appropriate weapon. Sometimes the weapons are verbal (ridicule and sarcasm), sometimes they're devious plots to cause suffering, and sometimes they're physical. But they all have one thing in common: the ability to hurt people. Since our spouses are at such close range, we can use our weapons to hurt them the most.

Some of the husbands and wives I've counseled have fairly harmless arsenals, maybe just a few awkward efforts at ridicule. Others are armed to nuclear proportions; the very life of their spouse is in danger. The more dangerous your weapons are, the more important it is to control your temper. If you've ever lost your temper in a way that has caused your spouse great pain and suffering, you know you cannot afford to lose your temper again. You must go to extreme lengths to protect your spouse from yourself.

Remember, in marriage you can be your spouse's greatest source of pleasure, but you can also be your spouse's greatest source of pain, particularly if your anger is directed toward him or her.

Disrespectful Judgments

Have you ever tried to "straighten out" your spouse? We're all occasionally tempted to do that sort of thing. At the time we think we're doing our spouse a big favor, to lift him or her from the darkness of confusion into the light of our "superior perspective." If they would only follow our advice, we assume, they could avoid many of life's pitfalls.

Yet if we're not careful, our effort to keep our spouse from making mistakes can lead to a much bigger mistake, one that withdraws love units and destroys romantic love. The mistake is called disrespectful judgments.

A disrespectful judgment occurs whenever someone tries to impose a system of values and beliefs on someone else. When a husband tries to force his point of view on his wife, he's just asking for trouble. When a wife assumes that her own views are right and her husband is woefully misguided—and tells him so—she enters a minefield.

This is a problem that's painfully easy to slip into—and hard to escape. Most of us feel that our opinions are correct. But when someone expresses an opposing idea, we sometimes feel that their "incorrect" opinion will get them into trouble someday. When we try to "correct" that person, we're just trying to help, aren't we? If that someone is a spouse, we're motivated by our love. We want to save that person from the consequences of error.

So why is it such a problem?

The trouble starts when we think we have the right—even the responsibility—to impose our views on our spouse. Almost invariably, our spouse will regard such imposition as personally threatening, arrogant, rude, and incredibly disrespectful. That's when we lose units in our Love Bank accounts.

When we impose our opinions on our spouse, we imply that he or she has poor judgment. That's disrespectful. We may not say this in so many words, but it's the clear message that they hear. If we valued their judgment more, we might question our own opinions. What if they're right, and we're wrong? That seldom occurs to us, because we trust our own judgment more than we trust our spouse's judgment.

I'm not saying that you can't disagree with your spouse. But respectfully disagree. Try to understand your spouse's reasoning. Present the information that brought you to your opinion and listen to the information your spouse brings. Entertain the possibility that you might change your own mind, instead of just pointing out how wrong your spouse is.

That's how respectful persuasion works. You see, each of us brings two things into a marriage—wisdom and foolishness. A marriage thrives when a husband and wife can blend their value systems, with each one's wisdom overriding the other's foolishness. By sharing their ideas, sorting through the pros and cons, a couple can create a belief system superior to what either partner had alone. But unless they approach the task with mutual respect, the process won't work, and they'll destroy their love for each other in the process.

Annoying Behavior

When was the last time your spouse did something that annoyed you? Last week? Yesterday? An hour ago? Maybe your mate is humming that irritating tune this very minute!

One of the most annoying things about annoying behavior is that it doesn't seem all that important—but it still drives you bananas! It's not abuse or abandonment, just annoyance. You should be able to shrug it off but you can't. It's like the steady drip-drip of water torture. Annoying behavior will nickel and dime your Love Bank into bankruptcy.

"If Sam loved me, he'd let our cats sleep with us at night."

"If Ellen were not so self-centered, she'd encourage me to go bowling with my friends every Thursday."

When we're annoyed, we usually consider others inconsiderate, particularly when we've explained that their behavior bothers us and they continue to do it. It's not just the behavior itself, but the thought behind it—the idea that they just don't care.

But when our behavior annoys others, we soft sell the whole problem. It's just a little thing, why make a federal case out of it? Why can't other people adjust?

As a counselor, I try to help couples become more empathetic, to see through each other's eyes. Of course, no one can fully imagine what someone else feels, and that's a great part of the problem. I often wish I could switch a couple's minds: Joe becomes Jane for a day and Jane becomes Joe. If they could only know what it felt like to experience their own insensitive behavior, they would change their ways in a hurry.

I've found it helpful to divide annoying behavior into two categories. If behavior is repeated without much thought, I call it an annoying habit. If it's usually scheduled and requires thought to complete, I call it an annoying activity. Annoying habits include personal mannerisms such as the way you eat, the way you clean up after yourself (or don't!), and the way you talk. Annoying activities, on the other hand, may include sporting events you attend, your choice of church, or your personal exercise program.

Every annoying habit or activity drives a wedge between you and your spouse, creating and sustaining incompatibility. If you want compatibility in your marriage, you must get rid of your annoying behavior.

Selfish Demands

Our parents made demands on us when we were children, teachers made demands in school, and employers make demands at work. Most of us didn't like them as children, and we still don't.

Demands carry a threat of punishment. *If you refuse me, you'll regret it.* In other words, *You may dislike doing what I want, but if you don't do it, I'll see to it that you suffer even greater pain.* In the godfather's terms, a demand is "an offer you can't refuse."

People who make demands don't seem to care how others feel. They think only of their own needs. *If you find it unpleasant to do what I want, tough! And if you refuse, I'll make it even tougher.*

Demands depend on power. They don't work unless the demanding one has the power to make good on his threats. The godfather in the movie had the power to make those "unrefusable" offers. A four year old who demands a new toy does not have power—unless you count the ability to embarrass you by screaming bloody murder in the middle of a crowded store.

But who has power in marriage? Ideally there is shared power, the husband and wife working together to accomplish mutual objectives. But when one spouse starts making demands—along with threats that are at least implied—it's a power play. The threatened spouse often strikes back, fighting fire with fire, power with power. Suddenly, the marriage is a tug-of-war instead of a bicycle built for two. It's a test of power—*who will win?*

If the demanding partner doesn't have enough power to follow through with the threat, he or she often receives punishment, at least in the form of ridicule. But if power is held fairly equally between a husband and wife, a battle rages until one or the other surrenders. In the end, the one meeting the demand feels deep resentment and is less likely to meet the need in the future. When the demand is not met, both spouses feel resentment.

Does this mean that you should never ask your spouse for a favor? Isn't it good to communicate your needs?

Yes, communicate—but don't demand. You may make requests, but not threats. When I ask my wife, Joyce, to do something for me, she may cheerfully agree to it—or she may express her reluctance. This reluctance may be due to any number of things—her own needs, her comfort level, or her sense of what's wise or fair.

Now if I push my request, making it a demand, what am I doing? I'm overriding her reluctance. I am declaring that my wishes are more important than her feelings. And I'm threatening to cause her some distress if she doesn't do what I want.

She now must choose the lesser of two evils—my "punishment," on the one hand, or whatever made her reluctant, on the other. She may ultimately agree to my demand, but she won't be happy about it. I may get my way, but I'm gaining at her expense. My gain is her loss. I guarantee you, she will feel used.

"But you don't know my husband!" some wife might say. "He lies around the house all night, and I can't get him to do a thing. The only time he lifts a finger is to press the remote control. If I don't demand that he get up and help me, nothing would get done."

"You can't be talking about my wife," a husband might say. "She only thinks about herself! She spends her whole life shopping and going out with her girlfriends. If I didn't demand that she stay at home once in a while, I'd never see her."

There are some major conflicts in these brief examples, but I still maintain that demands hurt more than they help. If you force your spouse to meet your needs, it becomes a temporary solution at best, and resentment is sure to rear its ugly head. Threats, lectures, and other forms of manipulation do not build compatibility; they build resentment.

Dishonesty

If your spouse had an affair, a brief indiscretion that was over ten years ago, would you want to know about it?

If you had an affair ten years ago that you ended because you knew it was wrong, should you tell your spouse about it?

These are tough questions, that go to the heart of our fifth Love Buster—dishonesty.

Dishonesty is the strangest of the five Love Busters. Obviously, no one likes dishonesty, but sometimes honesty seems more damaging. What if the truth is more painful than a lie?

When a wife first learns that her husband has been unfaithful, the pain is often so great that she wishes she had been left ignorant. When a husband discovers his wife's affair, it's like a knife in his heart. *Maybe I would have been better off not knowing,* he wonders. In fact, many marriage counselors advise clients to avoid telling spouses about past infidelity, because it's too painful for people to handle. Besides, if it's over and done with, why dredge up the sewage of the past?

This sort of confusion leads some of the most well-intentioned husbands and wives to lie to each other or at least give each other false impressions. They feel that dishonesty will help them protect each other's feelings.

But what kind of a relationship is that? The lie is a wall that comes between the two partners, something hidden, a secret that cannot be mentioned, though it's right under the surface of every conversation.

And dishonesty can be as addictive as a drug. One secret leads to another. If you start using dishonesty to protect each other's feelings, where will it end?

That's why dishonesty is a strange Love Buster. Lies clearly hurt a relationship over the long term, but truth can also hurt, especially in the short term. That's why many couples continue in dishonesty—because they feel they can't take the shock of facing the truth, at least right now. As a result, the marriage dies a slow death.

Honesty is like a flu shot. It may give you a short, sharp pain, but it keeps you healthier over the following months.

In the case of infidelity, don't you think that your own affair would be one of the most important pieces of information about you? How could you ever expect to have an intimate relationship with someone to whom you cannot reveal your innermost feelings?

This is certainly an extreme example. There are many other issues in marriage that are less serious, but I wanted to use this extreme case to underscore the curious nature of this Love Buster.

I draw a distinction between the pain of a thoughtless act and the pain of knowing about a thoughtless act. Honesty sometimes creates some pain, the pain of knowing. But it is really the thoughtless act itself that causes the pain. Dishonesty may defer some of that pain, but often it compounds the pain. The truth often comes out eventually, and the months or years of hiding it make everything worse.

Dishonesty strangles compatibility. To create and sustain compatibility, you must lay your cards on the table: You must be honest about your thoughts, feelings, habits, likes, dislikes, personal history, daily activities, and plans for the future. When misinformation is part of the mix, you have little hope of making successful adjustments to each other. Dishonesty not only makes solutions hard to find, but it often leaves couples ignorant of the problems themselves.

There's another very important reason to be honest. Honesty makes our behavior more thoughtful. If we knew that everything we did and said would be televised and reviewed by all our friends, we would be far less likely to engage in thoughtless acts. Criminals would not steal and commit violent acts if they knew they would be caught each time they did. Honesty is the television camera in our lives. We know what we do, and if we are honest about what we do, we tend not to engage in thoughtless acts because we know that we, ourselves, will reveal those acts.

In an honest relationship, thoughtless acts are revealed, forgiven, and corrected. Bad habits are nipped in the bud. Honesty keeps a couple from drifting into incompatibility: As incompatible attitudes and behavior are revealed, they can become targets for elimination. But if these attitudes and behavior remain hidden, they are left to grow out of control.

How to Bust the Love Busters

Love Busters should not exist. They just don't belong in a marriage. Every Love Buster is an instance of one spouse gaining at the expense of the other. In order to feel good, one spouse makes the other feel bad, in obvious violation of the Policy of Joint Agreement. It simply should not be this way.

But it is.

Love Busters are destroying marriages at an unprecedented rate. Unless you and your spouse agree to eliminate the Love Busters in your marriage, you can kiss good-bye any hope for compatibility, romantic love, or happiness.

Joan and Mike had too many Love Busters to count. They needed to eliminate them as quickly as possible, but there were so many of them. Where would they begin?

I recommended a four-step process.

Step 1: ***Identify Love Busters.***

Before you go to battle, you need to know your enemy. And if you're battling Love Busters, you need to know what they are. We have identified five broad types of Love Busters that can turn us all into jerks. But which of these are especially troubling in your marriage, and what specific behavior is involved?

Often one partner is ignorant of the things he or she does to hurt the other. Love Busters can become second nature, habits we don't even think about. In these cases, the spouse on the receiving end of these Love Busters has to identify them, because he or she is the only one who feels the pain. Joan had to tell Mike what he was doing that she couldn't stand, and vice versa.

So at the end of my second session with Mike and Joan, I gave each of them a questionnaire to complete before I saw them again four days later. (This Love Busters Questionnaire is available for you and your spouse in appendix A of this book. You may want to refer to it occasionally as you read on.)

The questionnaire analyzes each type of Love Buster to see: (1) whether this type is, in fact, present in your marriage; (2) how often it occurs; (3) the form(s) it takes; (4) the worst form(s) it takes; (5) when the behavior started; and (6) how it has developed.

Exactly one week from their first appointment with me, Joan and Mike were seeing me for the third time. They brought with them their completed Love Busters Questionnaires, and I saw them individually to review their answers.

Joan confessed that their week had gone more smoothly than any week she could remember since they'd been married. Each day they had taken a few minutes to talk about how their day had gone and they made a point to avoid any unpleasant topics. They were also discussing their plans with each other and—following the Policy of Joint Agreement—they canceled plans on which they could not agree.

One side effect: They were becoming a bit more generous with each other. For instance, Joan planned to leave the kids with Mike Saturday morning while she did some grocery shopping. Though she feared that he might snap at her for this, he actually responded favorably, agreeing that this arrangement made sense. As a result, she made a special effort to return earlier than she had promised, to rescue Mike from the kids. When Mike had to work late on Friday night, he consulted Joan in advance, and she did not object.

"Were you enthusiastic about Mike's working late?" I asked Joan.

"He had already agreed to let me go shopping without the kids the next morning," Joan replied, "so I was comfortable with his working late."

"But were you *enthusiastic?*" I pressed.

"About as enthusiastic as I get about anything these days," she answered, handing me her Love Busters Questionnaire.

For the moment, I had to be content with her feeling "comfortable." But that was much better than she'd felt for years. The enthusiasm would come later.

Step 2: ***Identify Love Busters that cause the greatest pain.***

In some marriages, all five types of Love Busters are ruining the relationship. But for most, only two or three cause most of the problems. Whether all five are present, or only two, you should begin by focusing most of your attention on the one that's the worst. Once you have a handle on it, you can then turn to the next most troublesome Love Buster. To help couples know which ones should be tackled first, on the last page of the questionnaire I ask them to rank the Love Busters in terms of their impact on the marriage.

Joan ranked angry outbursts number 1 and disrespectful judgments number 2. These Love Busters caused her the greatest unhappiness. Her total list looked like this:

Rank	*Love Buster*
1	Angry outbursts
2	Disrespectful judgments
4	Annoying behavior
3	Selfish demands
5	Dishonesty

Generally, I suggest that clients work on only one or possibly two Love Busters at a time, but if the others are seriously affecting the marriage, they may deserve attention as well. So I don't just look at the ranking, but also the scale of unhappiness for each of the Love Busters (which appears earlier in the questionnaire).

Dishonesty was not a problem for Joan. Ranked last, it earned a 0 on the unhappiness scale. Mike never lied to her.

Annoying behavior, which Joan ranked fourth, got a 2 (out of 6) on the unhappiness scale. Apparently Mike did a few annoying things that made Joan mildly unhappy, but with three other Love Busters ahead of it, annoying behavior did not need our attention just yet.

But selfish demands, which Joan ranked third, had a higher unhappiness rating of 4, which caused me some concern. Still, the top two Love Busters, angry outbursts and disrespectful judgments, were crying out for attention, each with a perfect (perfectly awful) unhappiness rating of 6. We had to work on these first, since they were both so painful to Joan. The others could wait.

So before Joan left my office, we had decided to overcome Mike's angry outbursts and disrespectful judgments. Mike had his work cut out for him!

Then it was Mike's turn.

"Yes, life has seemed more peaceful this past week," Mike reported, echoing his wife's sentiments. "I haven't fallen head over heels in love, but things are just less . . . stressful."

When I asked for his Love Busters Questionnaire, Mike replied, "Oh, yeah, I filled it out, but I don't think it will do you much good. The problem doesn't have much to do with what's on that form. The problem is that Joan's a lousy housekeeper, she hardly ever talks to me, we have nothing in common, and sex died out years ago. Everything a guy would want in a wife, she's not. Besides that," he smiled, "everything's fine."

I looked at Mike's questionnaire anyway. He ranked the Love Busters as follows:

Rank	*Love Buster*
4	Angry outbursts
5	Disrespectful judgments
3	Annoying behavior
1	Selfish demands
2	Dishonesty

But when I looked at the unhappiness scale for each Love Buster, I saw that the highest rating was a 4 (out of 6) for selfish demands.

In other words, according to his own analysis, Joan wasn't doing much to hurt him—she just wasn't doing much to *help* him. She wasn't meeting his emotional needs.

As we have said, the two main obligations of a spouse are to protect (avoid hurting) and to care (meet emotional needs). While Joan felt that Mike was failing to protect her (from the pain of his angry outbursts and disrespectful judgments), Mike felt that Joan was failing to provide care for him.

The failure to protect is a greater disaster in marriage than the failure to care. This is largely due to the fact that once you unleash pain on your partner, his or her desire to meet your needs evaporates. There's no point in discussing emotional needs as long as Love Busters dominate a relationship, because when you're in pain, you don't want to meet needs or have your own needs met.

Joan and I had yet to discuss her emotional needs. All she wanted was for Mike to leave her alone. To help avoid the pain, she built a defensive wall. She was in the state of Withdrawal and had no interest in discussing ways they could care for each other. Mike had to eliminate his angry outbursts and disrespectful judgments before Joan would feel safe enough to come out from behind her defensive wall.

So I explained to Mike that we would be getting to the care issue after we had resolved the protection issue. As long as Mike was hurting Joan, they would not be able to improve their care for each other.

Step 3: ***Agree to eliminate Love Busters for each other.***

I had a problem. The situation was unbalanced. Our analysis of the Love Busters clearly showed that Mike was at fault. He needed to change before we could move on to the next step, which was helping them meet each other's needs. His angry outbursts and disrespectful judgments were preventing them from caring for each other.

But let's look at it from Mike's perspective. In fact, let's try to get inside the mind of Mike's Taker: "All right, I admit it. I get angry with Joan, and I am disrespectful sometimes. But how would you feel if you came home to a pigsty every night? I never hear, 'How was your day, dear?' She never says anything unless she has a job for me to do. And she hasn't slept with me for over a year. Wouldn't that make you angry? Don't I have a right to show some disrespect?

"I've come to you for help, and you're telling me that it's all my fault? I've got to change? What about her? She needs to give me a reason to change, all right? I can't be a better husband until she starts being a better wife!"

There was no point in arguing with Mike. Mike's Giver already agreed that he should protect Joan from his anger and disrespect, but any agreement had to satisfy his Taker, too. Somehow, I had to make the assignment more evenhanded. Joan had to make changes too, even though it could not yet be in the area of care. The only area I could consider was her Love Busters, even though they were not rated very high by Mike.

"If Joan worked on eliminating her selfish demands," I asked Mike, "would you be willing to eliminate two Love Busters, angry outbursts and disrespectful judgments?"

Fortunately, Joan and Mike had spent the week trying to follow the Policy of Joint Agreement, and Mike had begun to recognize his role in wrecking their relationship. A few glimpses of thoughtful behavior from Joan had allowed Mike's Giver to see how much he had been hurting her. His Taker recognized that whatever they had been doing that week was making Mike happier, and it approved of the idea that they'd both be working on Love Busters.

"Yes," he answered, "I think that's fair."

Joan readily agreed to this as well, and the next step was taken. Nothing had changed yet, but they both knew what they needed to do.

Joan and Mike might have completed this step without professional help if they had been armed with the Policy of Joint Agreement. But many couples cannot get past this step without encouragement, especially if there's an imbalance in the relationship. It's easy to tell your spouse, "You need to change!" but it's hard for your spouse to see it that way. If you find yourself stuck at this point, be sure to offer something in return to make the arrangement seem fair. If you still can't seem to make progress, find a professional counselor to help you. It helps to have a neutral and objective party help you negotiate when you're still at war with each other.

But I also encourage couples to try to resolve conflicts on their own before seeking the help of a counselor. In most cases, couples can solve their problems without outside intervention if they simply follow the Policy of Joint Agreement. With that in place, both spouses usually recognize the need to work on their Love Busters.

Step 4: ***Overcome the Love Busters.***

You know what you need to do, now do it!

For some couples, it really is that easy.

Love Busters are inspired by your Takers, and your Takers will only cooperate in stopping the love busting if it is in your best interest to do so. Takers do not listen to logic, fair play, or pity but they do take bribes. "What will I get out of this deal?" is the question they raise. That's why both partners must make a pact to lay down their weapons, treat each other with respect, avoid annoying each other, stop making demands, and commit themselves to honesty. Their Takers will agree to disarm only if there is no threat from the other side.

When you and your spouse agree to protect each other, the Takers and their self-centered Love Busters tend to step back and give you an opportunity to enter the state of Intimacy. Then the influence of the Givers kicks in: Care and thoughtfulness become instinctive.

How to Bust Love Busters

1. Identify Love Busters.
2. Determine which cause the most pain.
3. Agree to eliminate the most painful ones first.
4. Overcome them.

For some couples I've seen, it's simply a matter of agreement. The details of how the Love Busters are overcome are left to each spouse, and they eliminate the bad habits just as they promised.

For other couples, it isn't quite that simple. They need a plan to follow and someone to hold them accountable to complete the plan.

Marriage support groups sponsored by churches or community organizations enable couples to overcome Love Busters by being accountable to others in the group. The group will check up on you, holding you to your promises.

Or you might ask a marriage counselor to hold you accountable. With Joan and Mike, I was the one who monitored their progress and reminded them of their commitments. They couldn't afford to spend years working on each other's list of Love Busters. If their marriage was to survive, they had to make considerable progress in a short time. So we went right to work eliminating their Love Busters as quickly as possible.How did they do this? In the next three chapters, we'll see how Joan and Mike tackled the three Love Busters that were causing their greatest pain: angry outbursts, disrespectful judgments, and selfish demands.

Chapter Eight

Mine Sweeping

How to Overcome Angry Outbursts

"You stupid idiot! How could anyone be so incompetent? You just make me sick."

With these and other expletives, Mike often expressed his rage. For what? Some slow driver who pulled out in front of him. A sales clerk who ignored him when he needed help. A colleague at work who didn't have a report ready when he wanted it.

And when Joan irritated him, she became the target of an even more blistering attack.

Mike knew he had a bad temper. He'd had trouble with it since childhood. But when he dated Joan, Mike managed to keep his temper under lock and key. Oh, once in a while he'd yell obscenities at a football game but he tried not to express his anger when he was with Joan. He knew it upset her whenever he did. And he never expressed anger *toward* Joan before they were married.

The first time Joan saw his anger directed toward her was on their honeymoon, when she refused to go to the Mayan ruins with him. After that episode, whenever she didn't do what he wanted, he got steamed.

He had never hit her, but just two weeks before their first session with me, he came dangerously close. That close call helped propel them to make an appointment with me.

What Causes Angry Outbursts?

Why do some people get so angry?

There are bad drivers everywhere, salespeople who ignore us, reports that are not written in time, and annoying spouses. Some people manage to shrug these off, but others choose anger as a response. Why?

After we had identified Mike's problem with this Love Buster, angry outbursts, we began to investigate the underlying causes in his life. Whenever Mike lost his temper with Joan, he felt she was the cause of his unhappiness and that she would continue to upset him unless she was punished. For Mike, anger was a strategy for dealing with his unhappiness.

It had worked when he was a child. His bad temper helped him get his way. His teachers gave him special privileges to avoid the ugly scenes he could create in school, and classmates would try not to upset him, for fear of his retaliation. Even his parents seemed to show more respect for him when he was in a bad mood.

But as Mike grew up, he became painfully aware of how few friends he had. His temper may have given him what he wanted at the time, but if he wanted a friend, he had to shield that person from his temper. That's how he was able to keep Joan from experiencing his rage for such a long time—she didn't see his temper because he kept it locked away.

He knew that if he wanted Joan as a friend and lover, he could not afford to be angry. But after he was married, he must have figured that she was stuck with him, for better or for worse. So he unleashed his anger, assuming that this was one friend who would not get away, regardless of his attacks.

So from his childhood, Mike learned that his anger helped him get his way. But if he'd given it much thought, he would have seen that punishment doesn't change people. It might have given him what he wanted in the short run, but in the long run, people learned to resist his demands.

It was certainly true in Joan's case. He wanted a better housekeeper, and his anger helped create a lazy, sloppy boarder. She wanted things neat and clean but she would rather live in filth than give in to Mike's rude treatment of her. He wanted to make love more often, and his anger made her sleep in another room. (She was not as disinterested in sex as he thought, but his anger completely turned her off. As a result, she wouldn't make love to him if he were the last man on earth.)

If Mike had taken a good look at the situation, he would have seen that his anger was totally ineffective in changing Joan's behavior. In fact, it did the opposite of what he wanted.

This is the case with most people who try to punish others. Most parents know how ineffective punishment is at changing long-term behavior. When our kids turn out okay, it's not because we punished them, but because we taught them effective ways to live that they appreciated and found rewarding.

Most of those in prison today had plenty of punishment when they were growing up. What they lacked was sensible and rewarding guidance. Many people told them what not to do, but no one encouraged them in what to do. Prison simply keeps these people from continuing to hurt others; it doesn't teach them to help others.

But changing Joan's behavior was not the only purpose Mike had when he punished her with his anger. *He also did it to balance the books.* He felt Joan had hurt him—and she needed to know how it felt. An eye for an eye. He just wanted to get even.

Often, after losing his temper with Joan, Mike wanted to make love. How outrageous: rage to romance in the blink of an eye! How was that possible? Was it yet another way to be abusive?

No, it was because he had balanced the books *and closed them.* Justice had been served, the penalty paid, and now Mike genuinely felt affection for her.

Of course, at these moments lovemaking was the last thing Joan felt like doing. She still harbored the humiliation of Mike's angry tirade. To her, his sudden amorous attention seemed like rape.

What Can Be Done about Angry Outbursts?

Some people are born angry. No, I'm not talking about an infant's reaction to the doctor's first slap, I'm just saying that temper is part of the personality that you're born with. Some people are naturally hot-headed, others aren't.

But even among the most mild-mannered, anger rears its ugly head once in a while. Instinctive reactions take over, and people do things they later regret.

Only when the anger has subsided can people see the foolishness of it. Maybe they "punished" the wrong person, or their outburst was out of proportion to the "crime." In their attempts to uphold justice, they often create more injustice. In many cases they see this after the fact, but *in the moment of rage* they're out of control. In the midst of an angry outburst, it's impossible to discuss the issue intelligently. When they see red, they see nothing else.

Can anything be done about angry outbursts?

Yes. If, in your moment of serenity, you agree that you should never punish your spouse with an angry outburst, and if your spouse has indicated on the Love Busters Questionnaire that you are guilty of angry outbursts, I've got a plan that may help you avoid using this Love Buster as a weapon of destruction. The plan worked successfully for Mike and many others I've counseled.

It cannot undo nature. Those "born" angry will still feel anger, but even they can learn how to protect their spouses from this cruel Love Buster. As I met with Mike and Joan, I showed them this simple plan:

Step 1: ***Identify instances of angry outbursts.***

You'd think it would be easy to know if you're losing your temper. But I've worked with many angry people who honestly don't recognize when this happens. Mike was that way.

As we reviewed Joan's Love Busters Questionnaire, we came to the second question, *Indicate how often your spouse tends to engage in angry outbursts toward you.*

"Five times a week," Joan read from what she had written.

Mike looked at her in amazement. "Five times a week? I don't think it happens five times a year! When was the last time I lost my temper?"

"Well," Joan thought a while and answered, "you've been good this last week because we've both been trying so hard. But before we saw Dr. Harley, you lost your temper almost every day."

He had honestly forgotten how often he lost his temper because losing it didn't make him feel bad. It made him feel better. Joan was the one who got hurt whenever it happened, so she was the one who remembered it best.

"Okay." Mike sighed. "If you say so. Five times a week. Let's go to the next question."

The third question asked, *When your spouse engages in angry outbursts toward you, what does he/she typically do?*

Joan read her answer: "He raises his voice, throws things like pillows around, calls me names, tells the children I'm lazy, paces around the house, and drives off in the middle of the night without telling me where he's going."

"I leave the house to avoid losing my temper!" Mike shot back. "Can't I even leave the house when I'm angry?"

"Yes," I intervened. "You can leave the house if you feel you can't control your temper. But let's save that discussion for later. In our next session we'll talk about what you can do to control angry outbursts. But is Joan right? Have you done these things when you were angry?"

"If she says it, it must be true, right?" Mike responded.

The fourth question asked which expression of anger caused the greatest unhappiness. "They all upset me," Joan had written. "Whenever he is angry I become very nervous and then depressed."

Mike needed to hear this. Up to this point, he still wasn't entirely convinced that he had a problem with anger. But here, in the safety of my office, he was hearing the honest cry of her heart: *This is what you do to me; this is how I feel.*

There's nothing magical about the Love Busters Questionnaire, of course, but it may help you get to this point, as it helped Mike and Joan. If you decide to use it on your own, without a counselor's assistance, you may need to give each other absolute assurance that your answers about angry outbursts will not lead to yet another angry outburst.

Joan would have been very reluctant to communicate these things to Mike if she had not felt the safety of a counseling office. If you want honest answers, you must not make any effort to intimidate your spouse or try to change his or her answers.

Maybe you think your spouse is dead wrong. True, your spouse may be misinterpreting your intentions (as Joan may have misread Mike's reasons for leaving the house), but your partner is an expert on his or her own feelings. The fact remains that something you do makes your spouse feel "punished." To conquer this Love Buster, you must listen carefully.

As soon as Mike understood Joan's responses to the questionnaire, her estimate of the frequency and nature of his angry outbursts, they were ready for the second step.

Step 2: ***Try to understand why and when you use angry outbursts to punish your spouse.***

As Joan and Mike left my office after their third session with me, I gave Mike some homework. (We were working simultaneously with Mike's disrespectful judgments and Joan's selfish demands, and I also gave them homework for those issues, but we'll discuss all of that in the next two chapters.) We needed to analyze Mike's anger process. He had not given it much thought in the past but now he was willing to try to figure out what set him off. The assignment was designed to turn the emotional reactions of anger and vengeance into a thoughtful analysis of the problems they create.

I gave him eight questions to answer before his next visit:

1. What are the most important reasons that you use angry outbursts to punish your spouse?
2. When you use angry outbursts to punish your spouse, what do you typically do?
3. When you use angry outbursts to punish your spouse, what hurts your spouse the most?
4. After you use angry outbursts to punish your spouse, do you usually feel better about the situation than before you used them? Why or why not?
5. Do you feel that punishment evens the score and that without it your spouse wins and you lose?
6. Do you ever try to control or avoid using angry outbursts to punish your spouse? If so, why do you do it? How do you do it?
7. If you were to decide never to use angry outbursts to punish your spouse again, would you be able to stop? Why or why not?
8. Are you willing to stop using angry outbursts to punish your spouse? Why or why not?

When Mike returned three days later, we spent a good part of the session discussing his answers.

Fairness lay at the root of the problem, Mike explained. It seemed unfair to him that Joan, who had so much to offer before marriage, had not kept up her part of the bargain. She was making no effort at all to meet his needs.

Mike's attitude was fairly common. People often get angry because they perceive some injustice, and they want to set things right. Some couples are forever trying to settle the score with each other. You know how this goes, don't you? You don't think that your spouse has been fair, so you use punishment to even the score. After a fight, you may feel you have evened the score—but you're not even. Now your spouse must think of some way to punish you for what you've done. This cycle goes on and on.

Joan wasn't exactly punishing Mike, but what she did hurt him even more. She completely withdrew from him emotionally, wanting as little as possible to do with him. Reeling from her rejection, Mike regularly lashed back in anger.

That's the *why* of his anger, and it leads us to the *when.* Mike had angry outbursts when he felt taken advantage of. When Joan failed to meet his expectations—for a clean house, quiet kids, a listening ear, or eager lovemaking—he felt that he was giving more than he was getting. The unfairness of the situation galled him, and he exploded in anger.

Sure, he lived every hour in a state of unfairness (or so he thought), but the outbursts usually occurred when he felt some snub from Joan that reminded him of his ordeal. With this in mind, Mike could pinpoint the dangerous moments of his marriage. Like the weather service that issues a tornado watch when the conditions are favorable for a twister, Mike could now recognize when conditions were leading to a storm of his own.

But was he willing to change? Did he agree that his angry outbursts were an inappropriate way to express his frustration? The answer depended on Mike's view of fairness, and he and I spent quite some time discussing it.

Is it fair to forgive your spouse? Is it fair to offer the gift of peace to stop the hatred and pain? Is it fair to put your weapons of destruction down right after your spouse has let you have it with one of his or hers? Is it fair to be generous when you feel your spouse has done nothing to deserve generosity?

It's all a matter of perspective. I've counseled very few couples where one admits that the other deserves to be treated with kindness. It seems that most people I counsel feel that *they've* done the most for the marriage, and now it's time for their spouse to do something. And a little punishment helps get them moving. But it's certain that your angry outburst will not get your spouse moving in the right direction; it will not even the score; it will not bring fairness to your marriage; and you will never solve marital conflicts with it.

Those who are physically and verbally abusive to their spouse usually express deep remorse for their destructive acts, promise it will never happen again, and beg forgiveness. But it's their Giver doing all the begging. Their Taker is sitting in the corner, momentarily satisfied that the score's been settled but waiting for the next reason to attack.

Every time you're angry with your spouse about anything (and that's sure to happen), your Taker will try to punish him or her. For you to effectively prevent that from happening, you must first come to the practical decision to renounce angry outbursts once and for all.

That's what Mike did. He agreed that his anger hurt his chances of ever being happy with Joan, and she would never meet his needs as long as he used it to punish her. He would no longer tolerate his own angry outbursts toward Joan, regardless of his sense of fairness and regardless of her behavior. He was ready for the next step.

Step 3: ***Try to avoid the conditions under which you tend to use angry outbursts to punish your spouse.***

Let's say you routinely yell at your spouse after you mow the lawn. The logical solution is to have someone else mow the lawn—pay for it, if you have to.

Married life usually isn't that simple, but you may still find conditions triggering your anger that you can easily avoid.

To help Mike identify those conditions, I gave him more homework—a new batch of questions to answer before his next session:

1. In the instances of angry outbursts that you identified, describe the conditions that seemed to trigger them. Include your physical condition (amount of sleep, physical health, etc.), setting, people present, behavior of those people, your mental state, and any other relevant information.
2. What changes in any of those conditions or efforts to avoid them might help you avoid using angry outbursts in the future?
3. What changes identified in question 2 can be made with your spouse's enthusiastic agreement?
4. Describe your plan to change or avoid the conditions that can be made with your spouse's enthusiastic agreement. Include a deadline that also meets with his or her enthusiastic agreement.

When Mike came home from work, Joan would sometimes have country music playing loudly in the background. He didn't like country music and had told her many times never to play it in the house. Whenever he heard it, it immediately put him in a bad mood that would sometimes last the rest of the evening.

It's just music, right? Wrong. The music itself just grated Mike's ears; what grated on his soul was the idea that his wife didn't seem to care at all about his feelings. *If she doesn't care enough to turn it off, no wonder she won't make love to me,* Mike thought. *I'm just a paycheck to her; she doesn't really care about me at all!* When he had to tell her for the bezillionth time to turn it off, he did so with deep disappointment.

Actually Joan knew that he didn't like country music and she tried to have it turned off before he got home. But she listened to it throughout the day and often forgot that it was on when he came home. When he barked at her to turn it off, she was forcibly reminded that he didn't seem to share her taste in music or anything else and that they were totally incompatible. This made her withdraw even further.

Country music was not really an issue, but a condition. When the music was playing, it brought all their old issues to the surface, and they both reacted—for him, explosion; for her, withdrawal.

Fortunately, this was a condition that Joan was willing to change. She agreed to turn it off around 3:00 so that there would be less risk of her forgetting to have it off by 5:00. But if country music was on when Mike came home, he would not rant and rave, just say, "I'll be back in a minute." That would be Joan's cue to turn off the music, and Mike would reenter his home in peace.

Granted, this was a little thing, but Joan's willingness to accommodate Mike on this one issue gave him a great deal of encouragement.

If you can change or avoid the conditions that tend to trigger angry outbursts, you should find it much easier to control those outbursts. And the more you can eliminate, the more margin of safety you'll have.

Some of the conditions we're talking about concern health—your sleep, your diet, or your exercise. If you are not taking care of yourself, you may find yourself more irritable.

The time of day can also be a factor—when you first wake up or when you get home from work, just before dinner may be the most difficult. Obviously you can't avoid these times but you can tread lightly. If you and your spouse both identify those danger zones in your schedule and avoid other anger-causing conditions, it will be much easier to live peacefully.

Sometimes other people can create conditions for angry outbursts. Visiting your parents or in-laws can dig up old issues or cause resentment. Even if your relationship with them is pleasant, you may still find yourself irritable afterward—and your spouse may become an innocent victim. Coworkers and neighbors can also lower your tolerance for frustration.

Of course it may be that your spouse just does things that upset you. This may be as trivial as playing country music or as insensitive as inviting a former lover over for the afternoon. Regardless of the issue, you and your spouse should find a way to avoid anything that does not bring comfort to both of you. If your lifestyle meets with your mutual enthusiastic agreement, you will have eliminated most of the conditions that trigger angry outbursts.

A word of caution: Avoid an attitude that says, "You are causing my angry outbursts, therefore you need to change before I can change." Instead, say, "I have a problem with my temper, and I'd like your help."

Joan's willingness to change something as simple as country music brought them closer together. You may discover the same thing as you begin to accommodate each other. But be prepared for occasional failure. Your spouse may intend to change conditions for you and fail. Don't use it as an excuse to get angry. Have a backup plan, just in case the conditions that usually make you angry catch you by surprise.

Step 4: ***When you cannot avoid conditions that trigger angry outbursts, find an individual or support group to encourage you.***

What could Mike have done to avoid an angry outburst if Joan had refused to turn off the country music?

We can't always control conditions that make us angry. Bad drivers will cut in front of us, legislators we voted against will raise our taxes, and our spouses will forget to pick us up after work. Most of us learn to control our tempers in spite of those conditions.

Once he set his mind to it, Mike actually did a good job controlling his temper, without much encouragement from me. But let me tell you about someone who did not do so well on his own.

George was referred to me by the courts because he had been convicted of physically abusing his wife, Linda. After a brief analysis of the problem, George and I realized that Linda would not cooperate with his efforts to control his temper. Her thoughtless and irresponsible behavior, which often triggered his outbursts, would continue unabated.

For instance, during the first two weeks that he was coming to me for counseling, Linda dragged a metal chair over his newly painted car to get back at him for the way he had treated her in the past; she got into his coin collection and sold all his silver dollars; then she went to a bar, had sex with one of the patrons, and came home, drunk, to tell him about it.

If he had hit her then, he would have gone to prison for a year. The threat of imprisonment certainly helped him put a lid on his temper—but it wasn't enough. What he needed was almost daily support for what seemed to be impossible conditions.

Each time Linda did something to upset him, George called me to tell me about it. We discussed his alternatives, and I helped him get through the worst of the storm. For two months he was able to control his temper and, by then, Linda's thoughtlessness had decreased considerably. Her Giver was finally having an impact on her behavior, and she put a stop to her own abusive behavior.

During those months, George came very close to divorcing his wife; he probably would have if her behavior had not improved. But he came to recognize that physical abuse in particular, and angry outbursts in general, were not an option for him—*regardless of how she behaved.* His only rational response to her abuse was to try to protect her from his abuse or to be separated from her.

In many cases angry outbursts are incited by something a spouse does or says that's annoying or inflammatory. First, you ask your spouse politely to stop doing or saying whatever it is, but it keeps right on happening. Then your Taker steps in, suggesting that you've been polite long enough, and now it's time for the strong medicine of an angry outburst.

When George would call me after Linda had upset him, his Taker had a chance to explain its predicament to a supportive person. It asked a reasonable question, *What alternatives do I have when my spouse does something to annoy me?*

Your Taker is not as committed to your spouse's punishment as it is to your happiness. (Remember what the plaque on its wall says? *"What's in It for Me?"*) A supportive person can remind your Taker that (a) punishment does not help matters, but makes things worse;

(b) what goes around comes around, so you're likely to be the target of your spouse's punishment; (c) there are more productive ways to cope with someone who annoys you—at the very least, get out of his or her way; and (d) don't let someone's insensitivity lower you to their standards—rise above it all!

Think of the most anger-inducing situation you can imagine.

Now, is there anything that would help keep you from losing your temper? How about the Irish Sweepstakes? Could you control your temper for a year if you were paid $10 million?

Well, if you can control it for $10 million, you can control it, period.

If you have trouble controlling your temper, consider seriously the support of a counselor, a friend, or a group. They not only give you encouragement but they also hold you accountable for your commitment to overcome this bad habit.

An anger support group is a good alternative to the support of a professional counselor. Members of such a group understand your frustrations and congratulate you for controlling your temper. They know what you're going through, and they understand how much effort and creativity it takes to keep from punishing others (especially your spouse). And when you're right on the edge, you can call one of them for support on the spot.

With the help of others, you can learn to overcome one of the cruelest and most destructive Love Busters. That will carry you a long way toward making your marriage safe for your spouse and restoring compatibility.

Step 5: ***Measure your progress.***

Good marriage counselors are notorious for measuring whether or not a goal has been achieved. They won't dismiss you from therapy until there is solid evidence that your presenting problem has been overcome.

Whether or not you see a counselor, you should do the same thing: Measure your progress toward the elimination of angry outbursts.

Since the angry spouse often forgets details of the outbursts (and sometimes forgets them entirely), the best witness is the spouse who *endures* the outbursts. His or her memory of the event should be taken as the most reliable.

On that basis, I had Joan complete a form I call the Angry Outbursts Worksheet. (This worksheet is not in the appendix. Copy the instructions in italics to make your own worksheet.) With this form, she could chart each of Mike's angry outbursts, following these instructions:

Please list all instances of your spouse's angry outbursts and other acts that you consider punishment for something you did. These include verbal and physical acts of anger and threatened acts of anger toward you, cursing you, and making disrespectful or belittling comments about you. Include the day, date, time, and circumstances, along with the description of each angry outburst.

Each time Mike and Joan came for their appointment, Joan would hand me her worksheet, which described each of Mike's angry outbursts. As I've said, Mike did a good job controlling his temper. After he committed himself to eliminating his outbursts, Joan reported only two instances of angry behavior.

Overcoming Angry Outbursts

1. Identify instances of angry outbursts.
2. Understand why you use them.
3. Avoid conditions that trigger angry outbursts.
4. Get support when you can't avoid the triggering conditions.
5. Measure your progress.

The first came as they left my office after their third session, when I had just given Joan the Angry Outbursts Worksheet. As they were going to the car, Mike asked, "What do you think? Do you think counseling can help us?"

"I don't know," Joan replied. "I've been disappointed so many times before, I just don't want to get my hopes up."

Mike felt blindsided. He should have guessed that her answer would reflect her state of emotional withdrawal, but he was encouraged by the counseling session and thought she was too. Her pessimism irked him.

"You always have to ruin everything, don't you?" he barked. "Why do you insist on dragging me down all the time?"

It was Mike's Taker elbowing its way into the conversation. Fortunately he recognized it as soon as it happened, and he apologized—but it was too late; the cat was out of the bag. Joan already had her first instance of anger to document, and it hadn't even been fifteen minutes!

Even with that rocky start, Mike got through the entire week without another incident, and Joan came to their next session with only one entry on her worksheet.

The second time he had an angry outburst was three months later, long after they had assumed that he had finally controlled it once and for all. In fact Joan wasn't even keeping the worksheet anymore—there had been nothing to report!

But it happened, and it illustrated a very important point. The state of Conflict, which every married couple experiences from time to time, makes all the Love Busters seem almost instinctive. Whenever Mike was in that state of marriage, he had to make an effort to overcome angry outbursts.

After two months, Joan and Mike's marriage was much improved, and Mike had reentered the state of Intimacy, where he thought his problem with anger had been completely overcome. Remember, in the state of Intimacy the Giver takes charge, and the Giver wants no part of angry outbursts.

Although I warned him that they would return once in a while to the state of Conflict, Mike was unprepared when it happened. Joan had just begun to meet his need for sex, and he was in love again. But she had not yet reached the state of Intimacy herself, and her Taker was still very protective of her. It brought to her mind memories of how Mike had treated her in the past.

Right in the middle of making love, Joan pushed Mike away. "What? What's wrong?" Mike stammered.

Joan didn't want to talk about it. For a moment, she was in Withdrawal again. She wanted to be alone.

You can imagine how Mike's feelings were hurt. In an instant, he tripped into the state of Conflict, rediscovering his penchant for angry outbursts. He flew into a rage.

As with his first slipup, he gained control and apologized almost immediately, but the damage had already been done. It took Joan almost a week to recover from his anger long enough to emerge from Withdrawal. Then she resumed progress back toward Intimacy.

Six months after I first saw them, I was convinced that Mike understood his anger well enough to protect Joan from it for the rest of their married lives. I'm not saying that he has never lost his temper to this very day, because I simply don't know. He might slip up now and then, but it's no longer a habit.

Mike recognized the seriousness of this Love Buster and did what he had to do to overcome it. If you and your spouse follow the same plan that I used for Mike, you will probably experience the same success.

On the other hand, if you find yourselves in serious disagreement regarding any part of the plan and cannot create one that works for you, please find a counselor specializing in anger and violence to help mediate. No one should be made to endure angry outbursts from a spouse. It's a problem that destroys marriages.

While Mike was overcoming angry outbursts, Joan was also trying to overcome a Love Buster. In the next chapter, I will show you how I helped her overcome selfish demands.

Chapter Nine

I Want It Done Now!

How to Overcome Selfish Demands

Not long after Joan was born, her father stopped loving her mother. Though he managed to pay the bills, he had as little as possible to do with the family, carrying on one affair after another. Joan's mother wanted a divorce but was afraid to be on her own. They finally split up when Joan was fifteen.

For fifteen years Joan received special education from her mother. The subject: how to cope with a bad marriage. Her mother's favorite coping strategy was selfish demands.

This was the only way she seemed to be able to get anything from Joan's father. Mother would muster up her courage, look him in the eye, shake her finger at him, and tell him what to do. Amazingly, he would do it . . . once in a while.

Joan didn't understand her father's motives. (I suspect it had something to do with guilt his Giver repeatedly foisted on him for being such a lousy father and husband.) All Joan knew was this: If you want a man to face up to his responsibilities, you *demand* it.

Imagine her confusion when, years later, trying to save her own struggling marriage, she saw Mike name selfish demands as the Love Buster he wanted her to overcome. She didn't know what to think. It was like asking her to sweep the floor without a broom.

"If I can't demand anything, he won't do anything," she complained to me. "He'll do as little as possible."

It's always difficult to unlearn an ingrained behavior, especially one you picked up in childhood from a parent you respect. In addition, Joan had used this tactic regularly in her marriage and she thought it worked fairly well.

I had to explain that her mother, admittedly in a tough situation, had not made the best choices in dealing with Joan's father. While his lack of care for his family was absolutely disgraceful, her way of resolving the problem was selfish. She was not taking his feelings into account because she didn't care how he felt; she simply wanted something done and wanted it done *now.*

Demands are not only selfish, I told Joan, but also ineffective and shortsighted. Caring behavior arises from a spirit of love and compassion, but selfish demands choke this spirit with the threat of punishment: *If you refuse me, you'll regret it.*

In the last chapter, on angry outbursts, we saw how ineffective punishment is. It doesn't create permanent changes in behavior, it simply changes behavior while the punishment is imminent. As soon as the punisher leaves the room, you're back to your old habits again. Demands work the same way. Take away the threat, and the desired behavior goes with it.

How would Joan's father ever learn to care for his family if his wife only communicated with demands and threats? These demands achieved a short-term response—something the father needed to do for the family—but they did nothing to restore the relationship. In fact, the demands drove Joan's parents further apart.

I wasn't blaming Joan's mother for the breakup of that marriage. Her father also bore his share of responsibility. I was simply showing Joan that neither parent had made choices that could save their marriage, and I was offering her a new choice that would work.

Years earlier, Joan had given up on Mike's caring for her. And she had no interest in caring for him. But what did she have to lose? If he stopped losing his temper and making disparaging remarks, it would be well worth giving up her selfish demands—at least for a while. So she agreed to the program, and I suggested a four-step process.

Step 1: ***Identify instances of selfish demands.***

Mike's Love Busters Questionnaire helped us understand the problem. How often did Joan make selfish demands? Twice a day, Mike said. This surprised Joan, who actually thought she must have done this *more* often. But apparently Mike interpreted some of her demands as simple requests.

What did Joan do when she made selfish demands? "She tells me what to do, instead of asking me," Mike had written. "If I don't get right up and do what she wants, she continues to bug me until I do it."

Joan agreed with his analysis, but she had an excuse. "*Asking* him had no effect whatsoever," she laughed. "I tried that. Whatever it was I asked him to do, I would always end up doing it myself!"

The questionnaire also asked which form of selfish demands caused Mike the greatest unhappiness. His answer brought a smile to my face: "When she asks me to do something in the middle of a football game." (Oh, how many marriages suffer during football season!)

As Joan and I talked about this, we found a fascinating train of thought that occurred whenever she saw Mike watching a game. That image—the man of the house relaxing in the recliner, eyes riveted on the TV—brought up memories of her father. She remembered how little he had done for his family. That made her think of items that needed fixing. By the end of the first quarter, she would have a list of repairs needing immediate attention—a list that would take the rest of the game to complete. If he didn't get up to do these chores, she would sometimes turn off the television.

The next question on Mike's questionnaire concerned the onset of Joan's selfish demands. "She's been making demands ever since I first knew her," Mike had answered.

You might be asking, "Then why did he marry her?" But it made sense when you consider the roles of the Giver and Taker. In the early days of their relationship, Mike's Giver was more than willing to oblige any request Joan made, regardless of the cost. What she was giving him in return was more than enough to compensate for her requests. At the time, he didn't regard them as demands at all. As far as his Giver was concerned, they were requests.

It was only when she stopped meeting his needs that his Taker reinterpreted her requests as demands. And her Taker gave the requests the added punch of a demand. When they were dating, he could have refused her requests, and her Giver would have understood. But not now. Now any refusal was met with consequences. The television would be turned off, or worse!

Answering the final question—how the problem developed—Mike said that Joan had become more demanding, going to greater lengths to force him to obey her demands.

"I had to!" Joan protested. "He wouldn't respond anymore. If I didn't push him harder and harder, he wouldn't get anything done around the house. But I'm not asking him to do anything that isn't already his responsibility. So they're not really selfish demands, just reasonable reminders."

Actually, as it became more difficult to get Mike's attention, she demanded fewer things of him. But instead of doing them herself, she just left them undone. Whenever Mike complained about her housekeeping, she consoled herself with the thought that he wasn't doing his fair share either.

Clearly Joan had an interpretation of the situation that justified her behavior. But at least in this first step, she got a glimpse of what Mike was thinking. Even though she offered excuses for her selfish demands, she realized that she was doing something that bothered Mike. This understanding was a good start.

Step 2: ***Try to understand why and when you make selfish demands.***

I didn't respond to Joan's excuses right away. Instead, I gave her the following questions to answer for her next session with me.

1. What are the most important reasons that you make demands of your spouse?
2. When you make demands of your spouse, how do you usually do it?
3. When you make demands of your spouse, how does it make him or her feel?
4. After you make demands of your spouse, do you usually feel better about the situation than before you made them? Why or why not?
5. Do you feel that your demands give you more control and without them you would be powerless?
6. Do you ever try to avoid making demands on your spouse? If so, why? How do you do it?
7. If you were to decide never to make another demand on your spouse again, would you be able to stop? Why or why not?

8. Are you willing to stop making demands on your spouse? Why or why not?

Joan made selfish demands because they worked. Or so she thought. Like many others, she considered this an effective way to get things done. But how effective is this method? Joan needed to evaluate her strategy to see if it worked as well as she thought.

In Joan's next session, we reviewed the questions I had given her. I tried to explain that demands do not take into account the feelings of their recipient. While they may get the job done in the short term, they hurt a relationship over the long term. And the health of a marital relationship is infinitely more valuable than any individual chore.

The problem for Joan was that selfish demands didn't *seem* selfish. If they had, she would not have disagreed so vehemently. "But I'm not being selfish," Joan said. "I'm just asking Mike to fulfill his responsibilities."

That's a key word: *responsibility*. I have borrowed money from a bank on the condition that I repay it. I accept the responsibility for paying the debt. When the bank expects to be paid, I may not want to pay up, but I accept my responsibility to do so.

In marriage, however, the issue of responsibility is not as clear-cut. Did Mike ever make an agreement with Joan to sweep the front porch during the football game? I asked Joan about this.

"No, he didn't."

"Well, then, how is sweeping the porch his responsibility?"

"Someone has to do it, and I'm tired of doing everything around the house," Joan blurted out. "Once in a while he should help."

"But you never came to an agreement about the work you do or the work he does around the house," I replied. "You can't hold him responsible for something that he never agreed to in the first place."

That's what's selfish about selfish demands. Joan was perfectly reasonable in assuming that Mike would help around the house—*but she imposed her own view of what Mike needed to do and when he needed to do it.*

Mike had a different view of his household responsibilities. He thought sweeping the porch was Joan's job. But even if he had accepted the job, he would not have chosen to do it during the football game.

But Joan gave him no choice in the matter. "Do this *now*—or I'll turn off the TV."

Why didn't Mike refuse? Why didn't he just stay in the chair and sweep the porch later? Obviously if Mike had never responded to Joan's demands she would have eventually given up on them. But he did respond, sometimes. Occasionally Joan's selfish demands did get the job done. Why? When selfish demands worked, why did they work?

It's a Giver-Taker transaction. If Joan wants Mike to do something, her Taker may choose the *guilt trip* card. She appeals to Mike's Giver by explaining that it's his *responsibility.* His Giver bites on the bait, and the rest is history. Givers, of course, feel responsible about everything and everyone, so if Mike's Giver is paying attention, it may leap into action.

But if Mike's Taker is in charge at the time, Joan's Taker will choose the *threat* card, promising to make Mike's life miserable if he doesn't sweep the porch. Mike's Taker weighs the pros and cons. It may decide that missing the whole game is too much of a sacrifice, so he rushes out to sweep the porch during a commercial. It's not much of a job, and he's back in time for the second quarter.

Selfish demands get the job done often enough to keep Joan using them, but what else do they do? They alert Mike's Taker to Joan's selfish tactics. Two can play that game, you know, and Mike's Taker has more than selfish demands up its sleeve. Angry outbursts, for example. Sooner or later, Mike fights fire with fire and makes Joan pay for her selfish demands. But not right now, because the game isn't over yet. Revenge can wait.

"Then what can I do?" Joan asked. When she finally realized that her chosen method of motivation courted disaster down the road, she was at a loss. "How can I get Mike to do anything?"

I reintroduced the Policy of Joint Agreement. *Never do anything without an enthusiastic agreement between you and your spouse.* Whenever Joan made a demand, she violated the policy, because she wanted Mike to do something that he would not have agreed to enthusiastically.

As it turns out, there is an alternative to selfish demands that follows the Policy of Joint Agreement. I call it thoughtful requests.

A thoughtful request begins, *How would you feel about . . .* and then you make your request. This question makes all the difference in the world. For one thing, it reflects consideration of your spouse's feelings, something that a selfish demand blatantly ignores. But there's more to it than that.

A thoughtful request is withdrawn if a spouse indicates that it would be unpleasant to fulfill. Thoughtfulness is more than choosing the right *words.* It is also taking the right *action.* A thoughtful person will not accept the help of a friend unless the friend would enjoy helping.

Joan just shook her head. "You men are all the same," she sneered, "you just don't understand how much women are expected to do. It's just not fair."

"But that's not where thoughtful requests end," I quickly explained. "If a request is withdrawn, a caring couple will then discuss alternative ways to accomplish the same objective with mutual enthusiasm."

The Policy of Joint Agreement does not leave a couple high and dry. It points them to alternatives that lead to effective and permanent solutions to their problems. Thoughtful requests do the same thing. It isn't what you want, it's how you go about trying to get it. Unless you take your spouse's feelings into account, you're being selfish and shortsighted. It's just that simple.

To make it a little easier to remember, I gave Joan the three conditions for thoughtful requests:

1. Explain what you would like and ask how your spouse would feel fulfilling your request.
2. If your spouse indicates the request will be unpleasant to fulfill, withdraw the request.
3. Discuss alternative ways your spouse could fulfill your request and feel good about it.

"I'm willing to try anything for a while," Joan sighed, "but I don't think this will work."

Step 3: ***Replace selfish demands with thoughtful requests.***

At the end of the session I gave Joan new questions to answer for her next appointment with me.

1. Describe your demands. Include a description of your feelings, your thoughts and attitudes, and the way you make demands on your spouse.

2. Describe the conditions that seem to trigger your demands. Include physical setting, people present, behavior of those people, and any other relevant conditions.
3. What changes in the conditions described in question 2 would help you replace demands with requests?
4. Which of the changes in question 3 can be made with your spouse's enthusiastic agreement?
5. Describe your plan to change these conditions. Include a deadline to make the change complete. Be certain you have your spouse's enthusiastic agreement.
6. Which of the changes described in question 3 cannot be made with your spouse's enthusiastic agreement or cannot be made at all?
7. Describe your plan to replace demands with requests when the conditions described in question 6 exist. Include a deadline for successful completion of the plan. Be certain it has your spouse's enthusiastic agreement.
8. How will you measure the success of your plan to replace demands with requests? Does this measure have your spouse's enthusiastic agreement?

Much ado about nothing. That's how Joan saw these questions. If I wanted her to stop making demands, she would simply stop. Why go through all these questions?

But what she had in mind was to stop asking Mike for anything. She was not planning to change her demands to requests; she was planning to not go to him for help. She would do everything herself.

It was easy for Joan to stop asking Mike for favors. All she needed to do was leave the Conflict state of marriage and enter the Withdrawal state. Whenever Joan made a demand of Mike, she did it from the Conflict state, because in Conflict couples are willing to have their needs met. They do it with the insensitivity of their Takers, but at least they are approachable in that state. In Withdrawal, however, they cannot risk the vulnerability of dependency and therefore avoid asking for anything.

So I had to encourage Joan to make requests.

"What would you like Mike to do for you?" I asked.

"He wouldn't be doing it for *me*," she snapped, "he would just be doing what he's supposed to do."

Joan was flirting with the state of Withdrawal. She wanted to deny needing Mike for anything, and I didn't want to upset her. Besides, being male, I was already at a disadvantage. Joan expected me to take Mike's side. She didn't trust me to champion her cause. She feared that Mike would get what he wanted, more sex, and she would be left with nothing. I didn't want to get bogged down in all that, so I asked my question again: "All right, but what would you like him to do?"

We came up with a list of things that Mike could do around the house. Take out the garbage, sweep the porch and driveway, mow the lawn, help clean up the kitchen after dinner, keep kitchen surfaces free of dishes and boxes of food when he came in for snacks, pick up his clothes after he changed, and so forth.

After we listed about ten items, I asked her to request each of them that week and try to follow the three conditions for thoughtful requests when she made them.

Step 4: ***Measure your progress.***

You'll remember that the one who is in the best position to judge the presence or absence of Love Busters is the spouse who suffers their effect. So Mike was best suited to measure Joan's progress in changing selfish demands to thoughtful requests. I asked him to complete a Selfish Demands Worksheet, which had these instructions:

Please list all instances of your spouse's demands. These are orders to obey a directive without willingness to accept no for an answer. Failure to comply with a demand usually causes threatened or actual punishment. Include the day, date, time, and circumstances along with the description of each demand.

I also gave Mike a Thoughtful Requests Worksheet with these instructions:

Please list all instances of your spouse's thoughtful requests. These are requests for assistance that follow three conditions: (1) You are to be asked how you would feel fulfilling the request; (2) if you indicate that the request would be unpleasant to fulfill, it is withdrawn; and (3) you both discuss alternative ways you could fulfill the request and feel good about it.

When Joan and Mike returned the following week, he had entries on both worksheets. (These worksheets are not in the appendix. Copy the instructions in italics to make your own worksheets.)

Joan had determined within herself that she would ask Mike for nothing except the ten chores on the list we had made the previous week. And even then, she did not expect him to want to do any of them.

But as it turned out, she made many demands of him without even thinking. She was so accustomed to getting what she wanted with demands that she could hardly talk to him without making one.

The trick was to begin with, "How would you feel about . . ." She was in the habit of just telling him what to do, like a drill sergeant. So whenever she would tell Mike to do something without asking first how he felt about it, he rushed to the Selfish Demands Worksheet to write it down. By the end of the week he had several pages of entries.

Overcoming Selfish Demands

1. Identify selfish demands.
2. Understand why you make them.
3. Replace selfish demands with thoughtful requests.
4. Measure your progress.

Yet Joan did make a genuine effort. Not only did she request the ten tasks on the list, but she also caught herself a few times in mid-demand, quickly converting to request mode. So Mike had several pages of thoughtful requests to report too.

Several of Joan's requests were tasks that Mike had no objection to, and he did them immediately. That was the easy part.

The hard part was when he told her it would be unpleasant for him to meet her request. Then they had to discuss alternative ways he could help her while feeling good about it.

Negotiation. This is an art they had never mastered. Their Takers had been battling it out for so many years, they knew little about listening and negotiating.

Their first efforts were frustrating. As soon as the discussion would begin, with both partners announcing their differing positions, Joan would declare an impasse and refuse to discuss it further.

Joan was still being lured into the state of Withdrawal. She lacked the motivation to work out a compromise and wasn't sure she wanted the marriage to work anyway. She was being asked to open doors that had been closed for a long time.

I encouraged Mike and Joan with the fact that their discussions would become more fruitful as their relationship improved. As they defeated their Love Busters, one at a time, they would have more to give each other.

And that's exactly what happened. As Joan saw the effort Mike made in eliminating his Love Busters, she became more motivated to attack hers. (Besides, with his angry outbursts under control, discussion was much less threatening to Joan.)

Over the following weeks, not only was Joan able to catch herself before she made demands, but her requests were accompanied by a willingness to consider alternatives. This gave them a greater opportunity to practice the Policy of Joint Agreement, since they developed patience waiting for mutually acceptable solutions to their problems.

At the end of the six months that I saw them, Joan (and Mike too) had learned to replace demands with requests. Oh, once in a while a demand would slip into a conversation, but by that time they both recognized demands for what they were, selfish and ineffective.

Another reason for Joan's success was that Mike was able to overcome disrespectful judgments, the other Love Buster that threatened the marriage. With his angry outbursts tamed, they could have safe discussions. But once disrespectful judgments were cast aside, their conversation became downright enjoyable!

How did Mike learn to overcome disrespectful judgments? Read on.

Chapter Ten

Let Me Ridicule Your Shallow Opinions

How to Overcome Disrespectful Judgments

In 1907 German astronomer Karl Schwarzschild helped predict the existence of black holes. The scientific community wasn't ready for his theory. In fact the term *black hole* wasn't even used until sixty years later. Schwarzschild died long before anyone could demonstrate that there really were black holes in space.

I wonder if Schwarzschild discussed black holes with his wife. What would her reaction have been to such a bizarre idea?

"Come in and help with the dishes, Karl!"

"Just a moment, dear, I've almost proven it."

"Proven what?"

"The existence of black holes."

"Black what? It sounded as if you said black holes."

"I did. Black holes. In space. That's what I'm proving."

"Karl, we already know that space is a huge black hole. Why prove something everybody knows?"

"No, dear, I'm not talking about space, I'm talking about an object in space that is so dense and yet so huge that its gravity won't let even light escape. Whatever goes into a black hole never escapes, including light. That's why it's black to any observer."

"Say what?"

"Yes, some are bigger than a billion of our suns, yet we can't see them. And there are little ones too. Anything that gets too close gets sucked in—whoosh!"

"You're beginning to scare me, dear. Where do you come up with these crazy ideas?"

"Someday you'll be proud to be my wife. *Schwarzschild* will be a household word. Like Columbus. Like Galileo. The man who discovered—"

"Nothing! Look honey, *dishes* is the household word I care about right now. I'll have a black hole in this sink if any more dishes accumulate, so why don't you help me out here before *I* get sucked in."

We all may not be brilliant scientists but we feel that our beliefs and attitudes are true, even if we can't prove them. And even if no one else believes us, we'd like our spouse simply to trust us, without challenging us at every turn. We'd like him or her to take our word for it, to give us the benefit of the doubt, instead of insisting that we prove everything we believe. We think that if our spouse respects us, he or she will agree with us.

Karl would have wanted his wife to find his new theory fascinating—a discovery that would revolutionize science.

"Oh, Karl! You're so brilliant. Your friend Albert will be so excited when you tell him about it. Don't bother with the dishes, I'll do them myself so you'll have more time to think."

But what happens when your spouse disagrees with you? *She doesn't trust me. He thinks I'm stupid. She's just trying to upset me. He must not like me.* We tend to see disagreement as an attack on our very character, judgment, and intelligence.

Disagreement, while inevitable in marriage, is hard enough for most of us to handle. But in many marriages, it turns *disrespectful.* All your worst apprehensions come true. Your character is attacked. Your judgment and intelligence are questioned. And you get the distinct impression that you're not liked. It is no longer simple disagreement, it is *disrespectful* disagreement.

Disrespectful disagreement is bad enough, but your spouse can go one step further. He or she not only disrespectfully disagrees with you but then tries to make you change your mind. He or she tries to *straighten you out.* I call this common but tragic method *disrespectful judgments.*

When we first think of disrespectful judgments, images of sarcasm, ridicule, and contempt come to mind. Mike used all of these when he tried to motivate Joan to go to the Mayan ruins with him on their honeymoon. He disagreed with her plans for the day and was trying to convert her to his plans, but the method he chose (disrespectful judgments) backfired.

If Mike had simply disagreed with her, I would have considered it disrespectful disagreement, which is bad enough. Or if his disrespect had simply been a way to punish her for lack of cooperation, I would have considered his ridicule an angry outburst, which is designed to punish, not to persuade.

For spouses to engage in disrespectful judgments, one must be making an effort to force his or her way of thinking on the other, changing that person's attitudes, beliefs, and/or behavior. And the persuasive effort must be disrespectful, using lectures, ridicule, threats, or other means.

In marriage, respect is the key to a host of doors that lead to Intimacy. Disrespect, on the other hand, leads to Conflict and defensive reactions. Marriage partners come together with different mind-sets, different backgrounds, and different emotional makeups. They must learn to accommodate each other through mutual understanding and care, not by bullying, intimidating, or trying to control each other. As is the case with all Love Busters, disrespectful judgments make marital compatibility impossible. After all, how can they lead to an "enthusiastic agreement"?

How Does It Feel to Be on the Receiving End?

We've all been buttonholed by someone, cornered by a person who won't let us go until we've agreed with him or her. Salespeople are most notorious for this kind of thing, but well-meaning friends and relatives can also do it.

How does it feel? Are we grateful that they care so much about us that they persist until we're exhausted? Are we happy to have the opportunity to gain new insights that we've thought through and rejected in the past? Are we pleased that we're forced to defend our own position with the threat of disrespect and humiliation?

Hardly.

During the Spanish Inquisition, church leaders felt that if a person was tortured to a point of expressing faith in Jesus Christ, that person would go to heaven. The end justifies the means, the inquisitors reasoned. Since the person's soul was saved, any manner of physical punishment was justified.

But think about those tortured into reciting certain words of faith. Did they actually change their point of view? Wasn't it more likely that they wondered what kind of God was willing to torture them to death? He'd be the last person they'd want to be with for eternity.

Your disrespectful judgments are not at the level of the Spanish Inquisition, I'm sure. But we all can learn a few things from this historical example. First, even if you win the argument, you may take an even greater loss. You may win the fight and lose your marriage.

But you may not even win the argument. Your spouse may say the words of agreement just to put an end to your disrespectful judgments. A true agreement is a *meeting* of the minds, not a *beating* of the minds.

If people want to convince us of their way of thinking, they must begin with respect for us and our way of thinking. Once they show that respect, we're usually willing to respect their point of view in return and perhaps be persuaded that they're right and we're wrong.

Respect means that they will never try to force their way of thinking on us. They will not try to punish us until we change our mind and they will not persist in their arguments long after we've indicated our unwillingness to continue the discussion. Whenever someone tries, we don't like it, and we resist their ideas, regardless of their merits.

When Mike tried to force his opinion on Joan, he was saying that her opinion had no merit whatsoever. What's more, he maintained that the reasoning process that led her to such a stupid conclusion was so inferior that she should simply accept his point of view without even trying to analyze it. Those implications, predictably, infuriated Joan and led her to stop discussing anything with Mike.

In their marriage his disrespectful judgments had devastating consequences. Not only was this strategy an ineffective way to change Joan's mind, but it left her feeling very upset. Love units disappeared by the hundreds, and the desire to talk about anything disappeared with them. Even though Joan wanted to talk to Mike, that wasn't the kind of conversation she wanted, and she eventually initiated very little conversation.

How Do You Know If You're Being Disrespectful?

When Mike tried to force Joan to agree with him, he was obviously being disrespectful. But he didn't realize it, because he was using habits that had been around for quite a while. It almost felt instinctive to Mike. He really wasn't trying to be disrespectful, though it certainly turned out that way.

Joan's Love Busters Questionnaire brought the problem to his attention. Not only was he surprised at how often he resorted to this tactic, he also gained insight into how Joan felt about it.

But just in case he still didn't quite get it, I've developed another short questionnaire that I use to make the point. Ask your spouse to answer the following questions, and if any of them are answered in the affirmative, it's evidence that you use disrespectful judgments.

1. Do I ever try to "straighten you out"?
2. Do I ever lecture you instead of respectfully discussing issues?
3. Do I ever view my opinion as superior to yours?
4. Whenever we discuss an issue, do I ever prevent you from having a chance to explain your position?
5. Are you ever afraid to discuss your point of view with me?
6. Do I ever ridicule your point of view?

All of these questions reflect an effort to force your way of thinking on your spouse. You do not agree, so you try to *make* your spouse agree with you.

What's the answer, then? How should you deal with those inevitable disagreements?

The only appropriate way to persuade a spouse, or anyone else for that matter, is to show respect. Respectful persuasion is the only effective alternative. When couples use this method, it is not offensive. It actually feels good to the person on the receiving end. It uses methods that are enjoyable to both parties of a conversation.

Remember how Joan had thought that her selfish demands were the only effective way to motivate Mike? As she analyzed this strategy with me, she found her demands to be counterproductive, and she eventually adopted thoughtful requests as a better strategy.

In the same way, Mike had been using disrespectful judgments because this seemed to be the right way to approach disagreements. Even though he never really changed her mind this way, he couldn't think of another way to get his point across.

But as Mike and I talked about it, he came to see how useless this strategy was in changing Joan's mind and how upset she became whenever he tried. Love units were disappearing by the hundreds, and their attempts to understand each other were brief and infrequent.

Mike had enough evidence to know he had a problem and he was willing to do something about it. He desperately needed an alternative way to express his opinion. He agreed to work on developing a new habit—respectful persuasion.

While disrespectful judgments make marital compatibility impossible, respectful persuasion can restore compatibility, depositing love units in both partners' Love Banks—*even when they disagree.*

Since both Mike and Joan were willing to try this new method, I gave them this six-step plan.

Step 1: *Practice disagreeing with respect.*

If you are learning CPR, you don't wait to practice until you find people dying. You practice on healthy people first. In the same way, I didn't want Joan and Mike to wait for a real disagreement to practice disagreeing with respect. I expected them to fail for a while before their new habits were formed—and Mike could not afford to fail in something as important as respect.

In the meantime, I told them to put off resolution of any important issues until Joan was satisfied that Mike had learned to avoid being disrespectful.

We set convenient times and relatively private, distraction-free places for them to practice during the following week. I recommended avoiding a restaurant or some other public place, or their mistakes might have become entertainment for others.

The total time for each practice session was to grow as Mike's skills developed. I recommended beginning with only five minutes of practice and building their time to an hour. They were to add five minutes to each practice session only if Joan agreed that Mike made *no* effort to force his opinion on her. They scheduled ten practice sessions for the first week. (Since they began as five-minute sessions, it was not too difficult to engineer.)

Under no circumstances were they to discuss any serious issue outside the practice sessions. And they could not go over their time limit. It was tempting, especially for Mike, to continue the conversation once the five minutes was over, but I warned Joan not to yield. When the practice was over, they had to wait for the next practice session to begin the discussion again.

Step 2: ***Clearly state your conflicting opinions to each other.*** Which is better, red or green?

"It doesn't matter," you might say. Then that's what I want as the subject of your practice session. I encouraged Joan and Mike to pick subjects they didn't care about. Should we celebrate birthdays once a month? Is Disneyland more fun than the Grand Canyon? Which are more attractive, frogs or toads?

If Mike had wanted to, he could have inspired fiery arguments over even these issues. But since he seriously wanted to learn to avoid such arguments, he chose subjects that made it easier for him to develop good conversational habits. They chose the frog and toad issue for their first session.

Each practice session began with a statement of the conflicting opinions. Since they only had five minutes at first, there wasn't much time to explain themselves. But in spite of the brief time, Mike made some mistakes. (I gave Joan a pad of paper and instructions to write down anything Mike did in these practice sessions that made her feel disrespected or any instance where he tried to force his opinion.)

According to Joan's report, Mike laughed at her opinion about why frogs were more attractive and he interrupted her. While Joan was explaining her opinion, he broke in and tried to clarify his own opinion. He needed to learn to let her talk, saving his questions until she was finished.

Another mistake was nonverbal gestures. Frowns, groans, looking at the ceiling in disgust, clearing his throat, and other condescending reactions communicated disrespect not only for Joan's opinion but also for Joan herself. Mike had to learn to show interest, not as a prosecuting attorney shows interest in a defense witness, but as lovers show interest in each other's attitudes and feelings.

I encouraged Mike to ask questions but to avoid making them argumentative. "How on earth did you ever come up with that idea?"—*not* a good question. But there are more subtle argumentative questions that convey the same meaning. He was to ask questions that would help him understand Joan's opinion, not give him ammunition to destroy it.

If Mike made any mistakes, Joan was not to add any time to their next practice session. By the time they saw me the following week, they were still practicing for five minutes at a time and had barely started step number 3 because they had to begin with step number 2 each time they practiced.

Step 3: ***State each other's opinion.***

In order to respect your spouse's opinion, you need to understand it. One of the best tests of your understanding is your ability to explain your spouse's opinion to him or her. Once you've done it, ask, "Is that what you're saying?" If you're not accurately stating your spouse's ideas, listen to them again.

Mike listened as Joan explained her position on the beauty of frogs. When he thought he understood it, he repeated the essential aspects of her argument back to her until it met with her satisfaction. Then she did the same with his arguments for the beauty of toads. And it had to be done with respect and conviction. They tried to put themselves in each other's shoes.

Joan continued writing down instances of Mike's failure to show respect and his efforts to force opinions. And they both took notes regarding each other's basic arguments so they could get them right. I've found that, when couples write their opposing viewpoints, they tend to be less emotional and more rational about the issues. Furthermore, once their viewpoints are in writing, couples understand the issues more clearly, and misunderstandings are more obvious.

Many couples I've counseled have had violent relationships. In most cases, the violence grows from a simple disagreement. When I see a couple with a history of verbal or physical abuse, I often encourage them to disagree in writing only. They bring the written arguments to each counseling session for review and analysis.

At first, their writing contains the same abusive language found in their speech, but as they make an effort to understand each other's positions with respect, the anger diminishes—and the abuse along with it. If they can understand each other and respect each other's opinion, many of the misunderstandings leading to anger are overcome.

In many cases, conflicts are based on incorrect assumptions. When spouses clearly explain what they think, it often turns out there is no conflict.

As Mike and Joan wrote down each other's arguments, it became clear that they were talking about more than frogs and toads. Even in this silly exercise, deep emotional issues emerged.

For instance, Joan felt frogs were better looking because they had fewer lumps on their skin, and lumps make anything ugly. Mike, on the other hand, argued that lumps had character. Smooth was boring, but lumps represented distinctiveness. Besides, he argued, toads do what they do with purpose and patience, making their personalities more attractive. And in the end, he argued, character makes us all appear attractive, regardless of our physical blemishes.

As you can see, they were getting down to some of their beliefs about life, character, and personality. You, too, will find that your spouse's arguments help you understand his or her basic beliefs, those that determine your spouse's approach to many issues. You may not find these arguments logical, but that's because you have a different system of beliefs. The more you understand your spouse's beliefs, the more logical his or her reasoning becomes.

Although my Ph.D. is in psychology, in college I majored in philosophy. My education (particularly a course on Plato) taught me how to argue. At least it taught me how to drive fellow philosophers crazy.

Begin by asking someone to describe a belief that is supported by reason. If they answer you with one of their beliefs, then ask the question of the typical four-year-old: *Why?* The person may respond with other reasonable beliefs. Again, ask why. *Why are these other beliefs true?* By then you may be hearing another set of beliefs, even more basic. Like a toddler, ask it again: *Why?*

Sooner or later, you come to a belief that is not supported by a more basic belief at all, but rather by a leap of faith, a conviction, a feeling of certainty. And that, in turn, is supported by emotion.

Then, you say, "See, your belief is not supported by reason at all, it is supported only by your feeling that it's true. You feel one way, I feel another, and neither of us can prove the other wrong."

It turns out that feelings are important, after all. Fundamental beliefs are based on a feeling of conviction, a leap of faith. From those beliefs, all our other values and attitudes follow logically (for some it's more logical than for others). We believe what we do because it feels better than alternative beliefs. So it's easy to see why so many of us don't understand each other. We don't share the same emotional reactions, so we don't understand how we could possibly believe differently. In other words, we *think* differently because we *feel* differently.

For Mike, lumps add character. To Joan, they are disgusting. Their emotional reactions to lumps help define their beliefs about the beauty of lumps and, ultimately, the relative beauty of frogs and toads.

As Joan and Mike discussed their attitudes about amphibians and lumps, they focused more and more attention on their emotional reactions instead of their beliefs and attitudes. They became aware of a very basic principle of mutual understanding: *Opinions are more emotional than they are rational.*

Joan and Mike had different emotional reactions to frogs and toads, and they made up rational arguments to support their emotional reactions. But by the time they understood each other more clearly, their emotional reactions were seen as the basic elements of their argument.

Of course, I encouraged Mike and Joan to accept emotional reactions with the same respect as attitudes or beliefs. Mike, at first, had some difficulty accepting the idea that Joan could argue in terms of her emotional reactions. He wanted her to use logic and reason to explain how her frogs were more beautiful than his toads. But eventually he accepted as legitimate her argument that she found toads disgusting because of their lumps. He learned that he needed to take Joan's feelings into account if he would ever win the argument. At that point, they were ready for the next step.

Step 4: ***Explain how your opinion is in your spouse's best interest.***

Takers tend to fight. Your Taker wants you to feel good, and your spouse's Taker wants your spouse to feel good—and they don't care how it's done. Each is more than willing to sacrifice the other person's feelings to get what it needs. When Takers battle each other, they take no prisoners, and that's why an argument can be so destructive.

Your Takers will play tug-of-war for decades if you let them. But if you want to resolve conflicts, your Givers need to get into the act. Your Giver needs to find a way to express your opinion in terms that your spouse's Taker will accept. Meanwhile, your spouse's Giver needs to sell your Taker on your spouse's opinion. When that happens, you're on your way to a solution.

You need to ask the question, *How is my opinion in my spouse's best interest?*

But then make sure your Giver answers, not your Taker.

Your Taker will say to your spouse, "It's in your best interest to agree with me because if you do, I'll agree with you next time."

Or, "If you agree with me, I won't lose my temper."

Or, "I'll be nicer to you."

Or, "Someday you'll see that I've been right all along, and you won't make such a fool of yourself with your opinion."

Takers are masters of the threat, the bribe, the insult, the scare tactic. But of course, these are not very effective in finding a solution acceptable to your spouse. It's not too difficult to see that your Taker isn't really interested in the welfare of your spouse. Your spouse's Taker will see right through it.

Your Giver, on the other hand, *is* committed to your spouse's happiness. Let your Giver brainstorm a little, seeking ways that your opinions will meet your spouse's needs.

Of course, Givers tend to give in. Mike's Giver may whisper to him, "Agree with Joan's perspective on toads and lumps. You'll eventually get used to it, and it will make Joan happy."

But that isn't what we want from your Giver (eventually your Taker would step in and sabotage the process). We want your Giver to take a close look at your opinion and find elements in it that can serve your spouse. After such an examination, it may say to you, "Your opinion simply isn't in your spouse's best interest, it's only in *your* best interest." Or, "It would be in your spouse's best interest if you compromised a little."

Whatever your Giver concludes, the process of seeking ways to please your spouse can only draw you closer together. As you let your Giver explore creative options, you are caring for your spouse's feelings. You are not just trying to win the argument; you're trying to reach a win-win solution.

"If we were to have a pet toad," Mike suggests to Joan, "I think you'd really come to like it."

"I might," she replies. "But then, maybe you'd like a pet frog."

They go on to present their reasoning, whatever that might be. But notice the change in their wording. It's no longer, "*I* like toads better." Now it's focused on the other person: "I think *you* would like toads better."

After you've explained to your spouse why you think it's in his or her best interest to adopt your opinion, you're ready for the next step in respectful persuasion, proving that you're right.

Step 5: ***Suggest a test of your opinion.***

How do you know who's right?

Sometimes you don't. Oh, sure, occasionally there's a disagreement over some fact. Those are easy. My wife, Joyce, says we've run out of milk. I think we still have some. A look in the refrigerator proves she's right again!

But most marital conflicts involve a difference in personal preference. The preferences can be recreational, social, political, artistic, religious, sexual, or medical. Couples can disagree about how to raise their children, what friends to choose, what car to buy, what flowers to plant, and how to treat their aging parents. One spouse likes doing something one way, and the other likes doing it another way.

In these disputes, there is usually no right or wrong. Regardless of the issue, a couple's conflict is ultimately based on conflicting emotional reactions. You feel comfortable with your way and uncomfortable with your spouse's. *Should we have helium-filled balloons at Junior's birthday party?* Your spouse likes them, you don't. Who's right? It's not a question of correctness. It's a matter of finding a course of action you both like.

> Success in resolving marital conflict depends on a couple's ability to create new options that make them both comfortable.

The most sensible way to make decisions is to use the Policy of Joint Agreement. Be certain that you both feel good about the outcome of each decision you make.

But how can you be certain that your spouse will feel good about doing things your way or that you will feel good about doing things your spouse's way?

If you want to buy the Ford Taurus and your spouse likes the Buick Regal, what do you do? You take a test drive in each. You could argue for days about the relative merits of the two vehicles, but you won't know much until you get behind the wheel.

Success in resolving marital conflict depends on a couple's ability to create new options that make them both comfortable.

The same thing is true in marital conflicts. You need to take some test drives. If you are truly interested in your spouse's comfort, if you are convinced that your idea is in your spouse's best interest, the best way to prove your point is to ask your spouse to test it out.

So one of the best arguments in defense of your opinion is "Try it, you'll like it."

In the case of the frogs and toads, Joan considered changing her attitude about toads and lumps. But actually having a toad in the house was way too unpleasant. She wanted some evidence that she might like toads without actually having them move in. So she and Mike struck a deal and visited a pet store (one that happened to have frogs and toads).

After looking at several species of frogs and toads, they came to realize that they liked each other's preferences more than they first realized. Mike thought frogs had much more character than he first imagined, and Joan saw toads as having their own special beauty. After looking at the frogs and toads, they agreed that both were beautiful after all.

Of course, this was only a test. Mike and Joan weren't actually arguing about which creature to take home as a pet, so their exercise ended here, at the pet store, with both of them expanding their opinions to accept the other's point of view.

Amphibians, balloons, cars, division of household chores, when and how often to have sex—no matter how serious your disagreement is, you can probably find some way to test out a solution. If your spouse finds that your proposal is in his or her best interest after all, you've just won yourself a convert.

But this method cuts both ways. Don't be surprised if, in the process of testing, you become converted to your spouse's way of thinking. In fact, you may both come to appreciate each other's preferences much more.

But what do you do if the effort to persuade your spouse doesn't work? What if neither preference or opinion sits well with the other spouse. Well, then you're ready for the next step.

Step 6: ***If your test fails, abandon your opinion and search for mutually appealing alternatives.***

Let's change the scene at the pet store. Instead of accepting each other's point of view, let's say Mike continued to hate frogs and Joan became physically ill at the sight of a toad. And, upping the ante, let's say they were choosing a pet for their home. What then?

Get a cat.

If Mike were to take the position that a toad was the only pet that would make him happy and that sooner or later he'd get Joan to agree with him, he would be in for war. It's incredibly annoying to have someone pestering you about something you've already rejected. You come to feel that if you ever agree, it will simply reward the person for his or her insensitivity. So Joan would lock on to her bias toward frogs, and Mike would stick to toads; they'd keep trying to force their opinions on each other, and they'd never get a pet.

But there are plenty of other fish in the sea. When you are at loggerheads and neither partner will budge, find a third option you can both get excited about. Abandon both frogs and toads and look into mammals.

Overcoming Disrespectful Judgments

1. Practice disagreeing with respect.
2. Express conflicting opinions to each other.
3. State each other's opinion.
4. Explain how your opinion is in your spouse's best interest.
5. Test the opinions.
6. Find mutually appealing alternatives.

The Policy of Joint Agreement is fundamental in this approach to problem solving: *Never do anything without an enthusiastic agreement between you and your spouse.* This policy has well served the couples I've counseled over the years, because it guarantees that, whatever they do, they will be taking each other's feelings into account when they do it.

If your test to prove your opinion actually fails, back away from it entirely. Don't suggest that you try it again or try another test. Your preference had a chance, it didn't work, now look for other alternatives.

Let's consider a more serious example. How can you convince your spouse that you should both go to church A, rather than church B?

You could argue about differences in theology, but that probably won't get you anywhere. You need to experience both churches. Does your spouse enjoy the service at church A, the one you prefer? Is this church meeting the spiritual needs of your spouse? Perhaps you may end up liking church B, the one your spouse prefers.

But what should you do if the test fails, if neither of you feels comfortable in the other's favored church? You should then look for other churches until you find the one you both like.

This issue can get thorny, because religious convictions are often deeply felt. One person *must* go to a Catholic church, another *must* go to a Baptist church—it's unthinkable to go elsewhere. And it has nothing to do with how padded the pews are or how friendly the members seem. It's often a deeply held sense of conviction. There is no compromise.

The same can be said for political opinions. My mother is a political liberal, and my father is conservative. She is as left of center as he is right of center. She barely believes in the right of people to own property, strongly believes in big government, and has no objection to high taxes to pay for the comforts of those with less. My father is an individualist, hates big government, and believes that welfare encourages laziness. They cancel out each other's vote at every election.

Will my mother and father ever be comfortable with each other's political opinion? Never! Then how can they have such a good marriage? Because they never try to persuade each other. Each respects the other's opinions, even though they don't agree.

Having been influenced both by my mother and father, I've also come to respect both political liberals and conservatives, and I've developed insight into why one position is comfortable for some and the other is comfortable for others.

As far as I'm concerned, my mother was born to be a liberal, and my father was born to be a conservative. Conservative opinion makes my mother go berserk. She hates it when people advocate conservative thought, yet she loves my father. My father would make a terrible mistake to try to persuade her to his way of thinking. Such an effort would have made their marriage miserable. He was very smart not to have tried.

When your first efforts to persuade your spouse fail, my advice to you is to give up. Don't use disrespectful judgments to force agreement to your way of thinking. For one thing, it won't work. For another, it'll mess up your marriage.

Don't make the mistake of winning the battle only to lose the war. If you force your spouse to agree with you—and lose a bunch of love units from your Love Bank—it will be a hollow victory. On the other hand, if you take your spouse's feelings into account in your discussions, you will never try to force your spouse to do anything. You will discuss alternatives, and if they cannot be agreed upon, you'll drop the issue. When the discussion is over, you will still be in love with each other.

Can you imagine the effect overcoming Love Busters had on Joan and Mike's relationship? Mike's angry outbursts were a thing of the past. Joan made thoughtful requests instead of selfish demands, and mutual respect punctuated their conversations. They had learned to stop hurting each other.

Now they were willing to have their emotional needs met by each other. This was a major step for Joan, who started from the state of Withdrawal. She managed to return to the state of Conflict—to test the marital waters, so to speak. Since they had learned to protect instead of punish each other, they discovered that the water was warm. They had convinced their Takers to lay down their weapons.

Earlier I said that there were two causes of marital incompatibility: (1) failure to protect; and (2) failure to care. When Mike and Joan overcame Love Busters, they had overcome the first cause, failure to protect. Each had become committed to protecting the other from his or her own selfishness.

Now they were ready to learn to avoid the other cause of incompatibility, the *failure to care.*

To create compatibility, they had to do more than avoid hurting each other; they had to learn to care for each other. Their protection of each other got them out of the state of Withdrawal and into the state of Conflict, but if they wanted to rise to the state of Intimacy, they had to learn to deposit the most love units possible by meeting each other's most important emotional needs. The next phase of my marriage counseling was designed to help them do just that.

LEARNING *to* CARE

PART THREE

Chapter Eleven

I Need You!

What Are the Most Important Emotional Needs?

Imagine walking into a grocery store and having a cheerful employee greet you. Another worker rolls up a shopping cart for you, while a third offers to answer any questions.

What a change from the impersonal, often surly service you have been getting! This store is festooned with banners that say, "We Are in Business to Serve You," "The Customer Is Always Right," and "Glad to Have You Shopping with Us." What a great store! No more rude clerks, confusing price labels, or check-cashing hassles.

One problem, though. The shelves are empty. The store has nothing to sell.

"Excuse me," you say to the thoughtful employee at your side, "where's the produce section?"

"Terribly sorry, but we don't have any produce. But thank you for asking!"

"Then what about the dairy section? I need some milk and butter."

"Another good question." The woman smiles. "But I'm afraid we don't have any dairy products either."

"Bakery? Canned goods? Frozen foods?"

The woman keeps smiling. "No, no, and no. Actually we have nothing at all in the store—but you have to admit *we treat you right!*"

She's right. There are no angry outbursts and no disrespectful judgments. In fact, all of the employees have learned to avoid doing anything that would make customers like you and me unhappy. Why, then, are we so unhappy?

Because they cannot meet our needs. You come in for milk and butter, and they have neither. Helpful, courteous employees are only relevant when they can sell you what you need.

The same thing is true in a marriage. While thoughtfulness is essential to a good marriage, couples must also deliver the goods—they must meet each other's needs.

That's where we started this book. I explained, in chapter 1, what it would take for Joan and Mike to straighten out their marriage: "When spouses communicate their emotional needs to each other and meet them simultaneously, they've discovered the formula for lasting love and a fulfilling marriage. So there you have it, Mike and Joan. Just return to the days when you were meeting each other's emotional needs, and your marriage will be fine!"

But it's never that easy. Joan and Mike had spent their marriage developing hurtful habits. That's why our first few sessions of counseling focused on eliminating their Love Busters. These behaviors—angry outbursts, selfish demands, and disrespectful judgments—were forcing them apart.

It was as if the grocery store had all the best products lining the shelves, but the employees had become so rowdy that no customers would dare to enter. Joan and Mike could not meet each other's needs because they didn't trust each other to get close enough to do so.

But they worked on their Love Busters and overcame them. By dropping their weapons, Mike and Joan had reached a point where they could finally *consider* each other's needs. Now they were ready to communicate their emotional needs to each other and learn to meet them. They were ready to stock the shelves in their store.

Great Expectations

Like most couples, Mike and Joan entered marriage with high expectations. They committed themselves to meeting certain intense and intimate needs in each other with the assurance that their own needs would be met as well.

Joan assumed Mike would continue to talk with her the way he had when they were dating—giving her undivided attention and showing an interest in her favorite topics of conversation. She also assumed that he would express the same affection for her after marriage that he had expressed so eloquently before marriage. Mike expected Joan to continue to admire him and to become a passionate sex partner. They actually discussed these expectations prior to marriage, and they never doubted that they could fulfill them.

They married each other because they were effective—or at least expected each other to be effective—in meeting each other's emotional needs. Shock and disillusionment came after marriage, when these expectations were not realized.

What is an emotional need? It's a craving that, when satisfied, leaves you feeling happy and content. When it's unsatisfied, you feel unhappy and frustrated. There are probably thousands of emotional needs—a need for birthday parties (or at least birthday *presents*), peanut butter sandwiches, *Monday Night Football*. . . . I could go on and on.

> An emotional need is a craving that, when satisfied, leaves you feeling happy and content. When it's unsatisfied, you feel unhappy and frustrated.

But there are very few emotional needs that, when met, make us so happy that we fall in love with the person who meets them. I call these our *important* emotional needs. These were the needs Joan and Mike expected each other to meet after they were married.

Ten Important Emotional Needs

In my counseling I have identified ten basic emotional needs that are usually expected to be met in marriage: affection, sexual fulfillment, conversation, recreational companionship, honesty and openness, physical attractiveness, financial support, domestic support, family commitment, and admiration. We experience pleasure when they're met and frustration when they're not.

While almost everyone has these ten emotional needs to some extent, people vary greatly in the way they prioritize them. For some, the need for sex is the most important of the ten, while others place the greatest priority on admiration. Whichever need is considered most important, that's the one that deposits the most love units when it's met (and withdraws the most when it's unmet).

It isn't necessary for couples to meet all of these needs. If a couple simply learns to meet each other's most important emotional needs, they can have a fulfilling marriage.

What are your spouse's emotional needs? I listed ten basic needs common to most of us. But one of the most important discoveries I made early in my counseling career was that men and women tend to put these needs in a very different order.

Men tend to give highest priority to:

1. Sexual fulfillment
2. Recreational companionship
3. Physical attractiveness
4. Domestic support
5. Admiration

Women, on the other hand, tend to give the highest priority to:

1. Affection
2. Conversation
3. Honesty and openness
4. Financial support
5. Family commitment

Of course not every man or woman prioritizes the needs the same way. Many men make affection or conversation one of their top five needs, and many women rank admiration and sexual fulfillment among their most important needs. But on average, men and women rank these needs in the ways I've listed.

Since the emotional needs of men and women are so different, no wonder they have difficulty adjusting in marriage! A man can set out to meet his wife's needs, but he will fail miserably if he assumes her needs are the same as his. Women will also fail if they assume their husbands have the same needs women have.

I have seen this simple error threaten many a marriage. A husband and wife fail to meet each other's needs—not because they're selfish or uncaring, but because they are ignorant of what those needs are.

He may think he is doing her a big favor by inviting her to play golf with him (recreational companionship, a high-priority need for him), but she'll come home thoroughly frustrated because he didn't talk with her most of the time (conversation, one of her top needs). She hopes to please him by showering him with affection (which meets her need), but ends up frustrating him because her affection revs up his sexual engines (his need for sex), and she's not in the mood. Both partners think they are valiantly trying to meet the other's needs, but they are aiming at the wrong target.

I'm reminded of an insurance ad I saw a few years ago. A husband and wife are pleased with their financial position, despite college costs, business struggles, and a death in the family—all due to the foresight of their insurance agent.

"How did our agent know we'd need this?" one of them wonders.

"He asked."

The two-word punch line applies to marriages as well. How do you know what your spouse needs? You ask.

His Needs and Her Needs

Admiration
Affection
Conversation
Domestic support
Family commitment
Financial support
Honesty and openness
Physical attractiveness
Recreational companionship
Sexual fulfillment

You cannot assume that your spouse's needs are in the same order of priority as yours. As we have seen, if you are like most couples, your most important emotional needs are probably quite different. But whether or not you're like most couples, you are the only one who can identify your most important emotional needs. Only you know what your spouse can do to give you the best feelings possible. In the same way, your spouse is the best expert on his or her needs, so you have to ask.

But before you ask, I'd like you to become more familiar with the choices. Let's begin by taking a closer look at the ten categories of need. Later we'll discuss how to negotiate to get these needs met. (If you've read my book *His Needs, Her Needs* [Revell, 1986], you're already somewhat familiar with them; this will be a refresher.)

I describe these as "his needs" or "her needs," according to the sex of those who tend to give them high priority. But don't let that box you in, and please don't let it offend you. Each person is different, and many men and women do not fit the average expectations. In fact, almost everyone crosses over to the list of the opposite sex when identifying at least one or two of his or her own priorities.

Affection: The Cement of a Relationship

To most women, physical affection symbolizes security, protection, comfort, and approval, vitally important ingredients in any relationship. When a husband shows his wife affection, he sends the following messages:

1. You are important to me, and I will care for you and protect you.
2. I'm concerned about the problems you face and will be there for you when you need me.
3. I am very attracted to you.

A simple hug can say any and all of the above. Men need to understand how strongly women need these affirmations. For most women, there can hardly be enough of them. They hug other women, children, and animals, even stuffed animals. I'm not saying that women automatically throw themselves into the arms of just anyone. They can become quite inhibited about hugging if they think it could be misinterpreted in a sexual way. But in safe situations, this holds true throughout most countries and cultures. Women hug and like to be hugged.

I emphasize hugging here because I believe it is a skill most men need to develop to show their wives affection. It is also a simple but effective way to build accounts in a wife's Love Bank.

Of course there are other ways to express affection, too. A greeting card or an "I love you" note can communicate a great deal. Don't forget that all-time favorite—a bouquet of flowers. Almost universally, women see flowers as a powerful message of love and appreciation.

Holding hands is another time-honored and effective sign of affection. Walks after dinner, back rubs, phone calls, and conversations with thoughtful and loving expressions all add units to the Love Bank. As more than one song has said, "There are a thousand ways to say 'I love you.'"

For most women, affection is the essential cement of a relationship with a man. Without it, a wife usually feels alienated from her husband. With it, she becomes emotionally bonded to him.

Sexual Fulfillment: The First Thing He Can't Do Without

When a man chooses a wife, he promises to remain faithful to her for life. He vows that his wife will be his only sexual partner "until death do us part." He makes this commitment because he trusts her to be as sexually interested in him as he is in her. He trusts her to meet his sexual needs, being sexually available to him whenever he needs to make love, just as she trusts him to meet her emotional needs.

Unfortunately many men see this total trust in their wives for sexual fulfillment as one of the biggest mistakes of their lives. They have agreed to limit their sexual experience to their wives, but for some reason their wives are unwilling to meet that vital need. Mike was in that boat, trying hard to remain faithful to Joan though she had stopped sleeping with him. Such men find themselves up the proverbial creek without a paddle.

Just as many men don't seem to need affection as much as their wives, many women don't seem to need sex as much as their husbands. Where both sex and affection are concerned, if a spouse is not an enthusiastic and frequent participant, the need goes unmet.

Sexual compatibility is usually a mark of a good marriage. I rarely come across a couple contemplating divorce who report having a great sexual relationship. When a marriage starts to have trouble, the sexual relationship is one of the first aspects affected, especially for women.

But great relationships don't always translate into wonderful sex. Many couples love each other deeply but still don't have a fulfilling sexual relationship. Their problem is often ignorance about sex.

In some cases, the wife just doesn't understand or accept her husband's need for sex. "I love my husband, but it seems like he's always 'in the mood.' How can I be enthusiastic about something I don't need or want?" And some husbands make sex so unpleasant that their wives try to avoid it whenever possible. "Why should I force myself to do something that I find painful, disgusting, and demeaning?" these women ask.

Another problem is that husbands and wives are often out of sync sexually, making the experience less than satisfying for one or the other or both. While men and women experience the same five stages of sex (desire, arousal, plateau, climax, and recovery), they experience them in very different ways.

These and other sexual difficulties can be conquered when a couple takes two important steps:

1. Overcome sexual ignorance. A husband and wife must each understand their own sexuality and their own sexual response.
2. Communicate sexual understanding to each other. A husband and wife must share what they have learned about their own sexual responses so that they can each achieve sexual pleasure and fulfillment together.

Sexual problems cause tension and unhappiness in most marriages. In many cases, this is merely a reflection of a couple's sexual ignorance, but sometimes it indicates a breakdown of the relationship itself. The partners know how to meet each other's sexual needs, they just don't want to. They can't bear the thought of having sex with someone they have grown to hate.

I have counseled many couples with serious sexual problems, but after we rooted out the Love Busters that had grown up between husband and wife, sex was no longer a problem. This was the case with Mike and Joan, who saw their sexual relationship come back to life as they dropped their weapons. Nowadays I hardly mention sexual conflicts in a counseling session until I'm convinced a couple has learned to stop hurting each other. Once that occurs, sexual problems seem to melt away.

Conversation: She Needs to Talk with Him

Just as most men find sex enjoyable in its own right, most women enjoy conversation simply because they like to converse. Men usually see conversation as a means to an end, often a way to discover the solution to a problem. Women also use conversation for practical purposes, but they also tend to get together "just to talk." They especially enjoy conversation that helps bond them together with others—conversation that communicates their care for one another.

While some men also have an emotional need for conversation, this need is usually rated higher by women. The difference is often a source of great frustration.

"I don't understand why my husband never talks to me anymore. When we were dating, we were always chatting about the details of our lives, but now he just reads the paper or watches TV."

It's true, men and women don't have too much difficulty talking to each other during courtship. That's a time of information gathering for both partners. Both are highly motivated to discover each other's likes and dislikes, personal background, current interests, and plans for the future.

But after marriage, many a woman finds that the man who once spent hours talking to her on the telephone now seems to have lost all interest in talking with her and spends his spare time watching television or reading.

Foolish men! Don't they realize that the man who takes time to talk to a woman will have an inside track to her heart?

Recreational Companionship: He Needs Her to Be His Playmate

During courtship, it's not uncommon for women to join men in hunting, fishing, watching football, or other activities they would never choose on their own. They want to spend as much time as possible with the men they like, and that means going where the men like to go. If a woman finds that she just can't tolerate the man's favorite activities, they generally break up. But if she can hang on and become his recreational companion, that friendship is likely to lead to marriage. Without recreational companionship, few couples would ever fall in love.

So, before marriage, a man and woman often become each other's favorite recreational companion, though they're usually doing what the man enjoys most.

After marriage, wives often try to interest their husbands in activities more to their own liking. If the wife fails in her attempts, she usually encourages her husband to continue his own recreational activities without her and she begins other activities. Within a few years, a husband and wife often find themselves in completely different activities, with new recreational companions. I consider this a very dangerous trend.

I won't deny that marriage changes a relationship considerably. But does it have to end the activities that helped make the relationship so compatible? Can a husband's best friend be his wife—and vice versa? I think so, and I encourage every husband and wife I counsel to become each other's best friend by becoming each other's favorite recreational companion.

Let's think about this for a moment in terms of the Love Bank. It's generally not easy to deposit a large number of love units all at once. For that to happen, the person you're with must be having a smashing good time. But what if you just happen to be there when your spouse is having a smashing good time, doing whatever he or she enjoys most? You would then get credit for all the pleasure experienced—and you really don't have to do much to earn that credit. You could be depositing love units simply by associating yourself with whatever event gives him or her the greatest happiness.

That's precisely why I encourage couples to be each other's favorite recreational companions. It's one of the easiest ways to deposit love units.

Honesty and Openness: She Needs to Trust Him

Woven through the most important emotional needs of most women is a single golden thread: a sense of security.

To feel secure, a wife must trust her husband to give her accurate information about his thoughts, feelings, habits, likes, dislikes, personal history, daily activities, and plans for the future. What has he done? What is he thinking or doing right now? What plans does he have?

If a husband does not have honest and open communication with his wife, he undermines her trust and eventually destroys that essential feeling of security. If she can't trust the signals he sends, she has no foundation on which to build a solid relationship. Instead of adjusting to him, she always feels off balance; instead of growing with him, she grows away from him.

If a wife can't trust her husband to give her the information she needs, she also lacks a means of negotiating with him. Suppose, for example, a wife wants to plan the family's next vacation. "Where would you like to go?" she asks her husband. "Would you like to go camping, or should we go to a resort?" (She is not fond of camping, but will do it because her husband and their two sons love it so much).

"It doesn't make any difference to me," her husband replies.

So they go to the resort, and he sits around grumpy for two weeks, muttering about how they could have bought a camping trailer for the same amount they are spending on these fancy accommodations.

This scenario is the stuff of sitcoms. Why? Because it's repeated so often in the lives of the viewers! But in reality there's no laugh track. The conflict is not very amusing.

A woman *needs* to trust her husband. Whatever advantage a man may gain in being secretive, closed, or even dishonest, he wins it at the expense of his wife's security and marital fulfillment. She must find him predictable. She needs to blend her thinking with his to the point where she can almost read his mind. When a woman reaches that level of trust, she is able to relax and let love units flow into her Love Bank without reservation.

An Attractive Spouse: He Needs a Good-Looking Wife

It's embarrassing to have this need.

We shouldn't judge people according to their appearance, right? We should appreciate inner qualities such as intelligence and thoughtfulness. I know, I know.

Yet, for many—if not most—men, a woman's physical appearance can be one of the greatest sources of love units. Many women also find a man's physical appearance to be equally important. As a counselor trying to help couples re-create romantic love, I cannot overlook the importance of physical attractiveness.

If a husband reluctantly admits that one of the most important ways his wife can meet his needs is to be physically attractive to him, can I afford to overlook it? Why not encourage his wife to meet that need by improving her appearance to him? If a wife complains that her husband has just stopped trying to look good for her, shouldn't that be addressed in counseling?

This is hard for some couples to talk about, because they recognize that they aren't "supposed to" put such stock in superficial characteristics. But they do! It's completely normal to be affected by the physical appearance of a spouse.

Among the various aspects of physical attractiveness, weight generally gets the most attention. Most men do not find their wives attractive when they are overweight. Many women feel the same way about their overweight husbands. Since physical fitness and a normal weight have so many health and social implications (besides their marital impact), I feel that overweight spouses should place physical fitness among their highest priorities. It not only helps restore romantic love, but it adds greatly to a person's overall quality of life.

However, weight is not the only important consideration in developing attractiveness. Choice of clothing, hairstyle, makeup, and personal hygiene all come together to make a person attractive. Since attractiveness is usually in the eyes of the beholder, let your spouse tell you what he or she finds attractive.

Like it or not, physical attractiveness is often a vital ingredient to the success of marriage, and those who ignore this notion risk disaster.

Financial Support: She Needs Enough Money to Live Comfortably

With dual-career couples on the rise, you'd think that the emotional need for financial support would be shrinking. After all, if both spouses earn an income, would either feel the need for financial support? But I have not seen much of a change in this need over the past twenty-five years.

Financial support is an emotional need felt almost exclusively by women. While not all women feel this need, hardly any men do.

Is this an important need for you? Sometimes it's hard to tell, especially if your spouse has always been gainfully employed. But what if, before marriage, your spouse had told you not to expect any income from him or her? Would it have affected your decision to marry? Or what if your spouse could not find work, and you had to financially support him or her throughout life? How would you feel about that?

If you would have been reluctant or resentful in these scenarios, you probably have an emotional need for financial support.

But what constitutes financial support? Earning enough to buy everything you could possibly desire or earning just enough to get by? Different couples would answer this differently, and the same couples might change their answer through the various stages of life.

But like many of these emotional needs, financial support is sometimes hard to talk about. As a result, many couples have hidden expectations, assumptions, and resentments. At one point, for instance, Mike felt pressured to work overtime to provide for Joan and the kids, even though that kept him away from his growing family. How important was the need for extra money, compared to the need to have him home, helping with parental duties? Many couples face similar dilemmas.

If you have a need for financial support, talk it over with your spouse. Express your needs clearly and work together to see them fulfilled. You both need to know when this need is being met and when it's not being met.

Domestic Support: He Needs Peace and Quiet

The need for domestic support is a time bomb. At first it seems irrelevant, a throwback to more primitive times. But for many couples, the need explodes after a few years of marriage, surprising both of them.

Domestic support involves the creation of a peaceful and well-managed home environment. It includes cooking meals, washing dishes, washing and ironing clothes, housecleaning, and child care.

In earlier generations, it was assumed that all husbands had this need and all wives would naturally meet it. Times have changed, and many people have changed along with them. Now, many of the men I counsel would rather have their wives meet their needs for affection or conversation, needs that have traditionally been more characteristic of women. But many men still have an emotional need for domestic support, and it should not be overlooked.

Marriage usually begins with the willingness of both spouses to share domestic responsibilities. Newlyweds commonly wash dishes together, make the bed together, and divide many household tasks. The groom welcomes the help he gets from his wife, since she's sharing tasks he's been doing alone as a bachelor. At this point in marriage, neither of them would identify domestic support as an important emotional need. But the time bomb is ticking.

When does a man's need for domestic support explode? When the children arrive! Children create huge needs—both a greater need for income and greater domestic responsibilities. The previous division of labor is now obsolete. Both spouses must take on new responsibilities—and which ones will they take?

Characteristically, the mother focuses on the baby's immediate needs—food, diapers, sleep, and a healthy environment. The father characteristically reacts with a desire to provide support, by earning more money. His focus of attention, then, is work and money. He puts in for overtime and hopes for a raise. He worries about the ever-increasing bills and how they'll get paid. He frets that he might lose his job.

Domestic responsibilities, never a high priority for most men, usually become a very low priority when they have new families. After fighting freeways and pacifying their cranky bosses all day, they often resent having to pitch in with household chores. This was the case with Mike, who included among his biggest complaints that Joan never did any housework. As we saw in their case, this can create considerable friction in many homes, especially if the wives also work and therefore experience the same pressures. Unless a couple can act on all this with honesty and intelligence, Love Bank balances are sure to suffer.

For dual-career couples the arrival of children is a tragic but well-documented cause of divorce. I believe that much of the problem stems from the failure to meet these emotional needs that surface for the first time: domestic support for men and family commitment for women (we'll discuss that emotional need next).

Most husbands simply don't do much housework, whether or not their wives work. In most cases, working wives come home exhausted to tend to their children and clean up as best they can, but much of the housework is left undone. Weekends aren't spent resting; working women spend this "free time" watching their children, cleaning the house, and washing clothes. These women learn soon enough that they, too, have a need for domestic support. When both husband and wife work, more and more couples are using outside domestic services to meet this emotional need.

I feel that anyone with a full-time job and children has some need for domestic support. Most working women will agree with me on that one. But I still feel that, for many men, it's one of their most important needs; they feel the *greatest* pleasure when the need is met. If that's the case, managing the home can be one of the best ways for a wife to deposit love units in her husband's Love Bank.

Family Commitment: She Needs Him to Be a Good Father

Women seem to know instinctively what we psychologists have discovered in research and practice: *A father has a profound influence on his children.*

My own father exerted a powerful influence on my education and moral development, though he may not have known it at the time, because I often disagreed with him on many issues. On reaching adulthood, however, more often than not I found myself leaning toward his point of view. This development of my moral values was extremely important to my mother, and I am certain she gives my father a great deal of credit for training me properly.

In families where the father takes little interest in his children's development, the mother usually tries desperately to motivate him to change. She buys him books on parenting and leaves them in conspicuous places. She coaches him to attend seminars sponsored by the church or PTA. She may even ask him to talk with a family counselor in the hope that he can be inspired to show greater interest and commitment. Such efforts usually meet with only partial success.

When a woman says she wants her children to have a good father, what does she really mean? Obviously she expects her husband to fulfill certain responsibilities. Ironically, though, the fulfillment of these responsibilities often conflicts with his need for domestic support. He needs peace and quiet; she needs to see him rasslin' with the kids on the rec-room floor. They are at cross-purposes.

To deal effectively with such conflicts, each couple must reach enthusiastic agreement about how to go about achieving good parenting without sacrificing tranquility.

Family commitment requires time and training. I recommend that a father spend fifteen hours a week in Quality Family Time—providing his children with moral and educational development. This does not include basic child care—feeding, clothing, or watching over children to keep them safe. Quality Family Time is when the family is together for the express purpose of teaching the children the value of cooperation and care for each other. While it should be in the context of family recreational activities, its primary purpose is educational.

But fathers also need training themselves. If you wish to parent your children well, you need to face the fact that you need some extra education in this skill. No one automatically knows how to care for a child.

While both men and women benefit from parenting classes, in my experience men seem to need the training more. Parent-instruction manuals, books, and courses abound with information on everything from toilet training to enforcing bedtimes, but one of the most significant areas of training regards how to discipline children properly.

As you might expect, I encourage couples to follow the Policy of Joint Agreement when it comes to discipline. Punishment should never be decided by one parent alone. Both parents should agree on how and when to punish their children. When a father punishes the children without such agreement, it can withdraw scores of love units from his wife's Love Bank.

Many men view this need for family commitment as a very demanding role—sometimes too demanding. Not only must they act as good husbands, providing their wife with affection, conversation, honesty, and financial support; now they must become good fathers too. Some, feeling overwhelmed by the time and training involved, choose to abdicate their role as father, turning all the parenting over to their wife. By neglecting this important role, they risk not only their children's future but also the respect and love of their wife.

On the other hand, men who accept the challenge of good fathering report that they come away with increased marital fulfillment. Their wife responds to their efforts on behalf of their children with deeper respect and romantic love.

Admiration: He Needs Her to Appreciate Him

I don't believe the popular notion that you must love yourself before you can love anyone else. Nor do I believe that you must be loved by others before you can love yourself.

The truth is, there's a part of us that always loves ourselves and another part that always loves others. Your Taker loves you and never does care for anyone else. Your Giver, on the other hand, loves everyone but you. When your Giver is in charge of your life, you love others, but you risk neglecting your own needs. When your Taker is in charge, you love yourself at everyone else's expense.

The secret to a well-balanced and successful life is learning to love ourselves and others simultaneously. We must learn to care for others without sacrificing our own happiness and care for ourselves without sacrificing the happiness of others.

Having said all of this, however, I do recognize a very strong need to be affirmed by others, validating our own Taker's instinctive judgment that we're okay. I call this a need for admiration. I think men, especially, sense this need.

Most of the men I counsel express a deep desire to be respected, valued, and appreciated by their spouses. They need to be affirmed clearly and often.

I don't think it's a sign of a weak ego to need appreciation. (Even God wants us to appreciate him!) It comes, instead, from our Taker's desire to be sure we get credit for the difference we make in the lives of others. And our Giver also wants to know whether or not we are doing enough for others.

Appreciation is simply the feedback we need in order to fine-tune our care for others. It tells us we are on the right track. Without appreciation, we are likely to abandon efforts we make on others' behalf.

Appreciation is one of the easiest ways to deposit love units into a man's Love Bank. Just a word of appreciation and, presto, you've made your spouse's day.

On the other hand, criticism usually does exactly the opposite. A trivial word of rebuke can set some people on their heels, ruining their day and withdrawing love units at an alarming rate. Some become depressed because their Giver is told that their efforts have been inadequate. Others become angry because their Taker realizes they've received no credit for all their work. Some people express both reactions at once.

We all need criticism from time to time, but unless it is balanced with words of admiration, we'll become discouraged.

If your spouse has a need for admiration, you should find ways to express how much you value him or her. Be sensitive to the times and situations when your spouse needs your admiration most. When you must criticize, balance your comments with praise and affirmation.

You have the power to build up or deplete your account in your spouse's Love Bank with just a few words. Will you choose supportive words that bring you closer together or critical words that pull you apart?

Most of our happiness in life comes from our relationships with others. For those who marry, the relationship with a spouse is the greatest source of happiness—or sadness.

Why, then, don't more people try to understand how to maximize marital happiness and minimize marital sadness? Why is there so little training in the skills of being a husband or wife?

It's not really that difficult. In fact, the secrets to a happy marriage are fairly easy to discover, if people would simply educate themselves a little. Couples need to view marriage as an important profession, one that requires skill in order to succeed. People take courses all the time to learn computer programming or business management or hairstyling. Why not take the initiative to learn how to meet your spouse's needs and get your own needs met at the same time?

We've already discussed how to avoid being the cause of your spouse's unhappiness by systematically eliminating Love Busters, when you gain at your spouse's expense. I've suggested steps that eliminate these destructive habits. Now I'm ready to show you how to become professional in identifying and learning to meet each other's most important emotional needs.

Chapter Twelve

Let's Get Real

How False Assumptions Create Incompatibility

Imagine for a moment that you are seated in a sunlit church at the wedding ceremony of two friends. The minister faces the bridegroom, before this audience of witnesses, and asks:

Will you take this woman to be your wife, to live together in the holy covenant of marriage? Will you love her, comfort her, honor and keep her, in sickness and in health, and forsaking all others, be faithful to her so long as you both shall live?

The groom responds, "I will." The bride also agrees to this same declaration of consent.

Now let's fast-forward to another scene, several years later, in divorce court. Suppose the judge digs up a video of their marriage ceremony and plays it for them, pausing just after the vows. "What happened?" the judge asks.

In a flurry of recrimination, the once happy couple point fingers and cast blame.

"You didn't live up to your promises!"

"That's because you gave up on the marriage!"

"But you were supposed to 'honor and keep' me. You promised!"

"You just changed so much, I couldn't recognize you anymore."

It's a sad scene, but the judge's question is a good one: "What happened?"

As powerful and inspiring as the marital promises are, they do not keep good, loving, well-intentioned men and women from winding up at the office of a divorce attorney. In fact, those vows tend to create false illusions about marriage. When we expect our lives together to be just as those wedding vows describe, we fail to protect ourselves from some of the most common causes of divorce.

Compatibility is what makes marriages thrive. And the truth is, attaining compatibility can be hard work. We are not born to be compatible in marriage, but incompatible. The forces at work within us that ruin marriages seem to be stronger than those that build marriages.

You might think that marriage counseling is a matter of calling out the natural instincts of love and care from within the marriage partners. But over the years, I've found the exact opposite to be true. As I try to help restore broken marriages, I fight people's destructive instincts. Left to their natural tendencies, most couples would tear their marriages apart.

I believe we have many attitudes and beliefs that also contribute to broken marriages. These lie buried, like seeds, in almost every one of us. If allowed to grow, they can create the behavior that destroys a marriage.

These attitudes and beliefs that threaten compatibility are actually written into many of the vows we made when we were married. It's no wonder we enter marriage so unprotected—we begin with false assumptions.

The Illusions and Realities of Marriage

Over the years many couples have told me how disillusioned they are with marriage. It all began with a false understanding, an illusion, of what marriage would be. Then, when they had to face the realities of marriage, they began to feel terribly hurt and angry.

"It's not supposed to be this way," they protest to me. "What are we doing wrong?"

But that question quickly turns into: "What is my spouse doing wrong?"

Couples are so quick to point the accusing finger because their illusions encourage them to do so. Let's examine two of these illusions of marriage.

The First Illusion and Reality

The Illusion: ***Care and protection in marriage should be given unconditionally. They should be given even when they are not***

received. I want to believe that my wife will care for me unconditionally. The understanding that, if I treat her badly, she'll end her commitment to me and divorce me makes me feel insecure. Instead I want her to tell me that she'll always care for me, even if I don't care for her.

But is this true? Is it realistic? Can I expect my wife to cherish me until we are parted by death, no matter how I treat her? Would that be a wise choice for her?

We have already discussed the importance of balance. If you are to be happily married, your Giver and Taker and your spouse's Giver and Taker must balance all their interests. Unconditional love sounds like a great plan, but it makes balance impossible. It actually encourages Givers and Takers to struggle for domination instead of balance.

Women who practice unconditional love are sometimes beaten, verbally abused, and victims of infidelity. Men who make this commitment are similarly mistreated. These people may think they are bearing these indignities for a good cause. They expect unconditional love to save their marriage. But in most cases it helps throw the relationship out of balance and into chaos.

The truth is, I should not want unconditional love from my wife. I should not want her to remain married to me if I did not prevent myself from hurting her. If I truly care for her, as I promised to do in my wedding vows, I would want her to leave me if I no longer treated her as I should.

Occasionally I hear someone attribute the rising divorce rate to the lack of unconditional love. This comment reflects a misunderstanding about divorce. Marriage commitments are broken when men and women come to recognize that their efforts to stay married are ruining their lives. Most divorces are not the result of two people simply drifting apart. A drift into incompatibility is an early sign of a bad marriage. But by the time a couple is ready for divorce, they are hurting each other so badly that one or both cannot endure the relationship any longer. Many of these marriages began with the belief that care would be unconditional, but that belief led to self-indulgence and laziness. It would have been far better to face reality from the start.

The Reality: ***Care and protection in marriage are conditional. They are given when they are received.*** Compatibility in marriage is simply the effective delivery of care and protection by both spouses to each other. But that mutual care and protection are very conditional in practice. A husband commits himself to meet his wife's emotional needs and to protect her from his Love Busters with the understanding that she will do the same for him. And vice versa.

When you are not receiving care and protection from your spouse, it is hard to continue giving care and protection. Most people feel justified in breaking their agreement when their spouse seems to have broken it first.

We saw this with Joan and Mike on their honeymoon. When Mike insisted on his agenda, belittling Joan's, he broke his agreement (made just two days earlier in the wedding ceremony!) to care for and protect her. Minor infringements happen all the time, so Joan gave Mike a little time to realize his error and set things right. But when he showed no signs of protecting her from his temper and judgments, Joan reneged on her side of the agreement. She stopped caring for his emotional needs.

I'm not saying that any little slipup wrecks a relationship. Spouses regularly allow a cushion, a margin of error. Sometimes the offending spouse recognizes the problem, apologizes, and makes up for it. Sometimes the offended spouse has to call attention to the problem, challenging the other spouse to keep up his or her end of the bargain (though this can backfire when it's interpreted as unjustified criticism). If that doesn't straighten things out, the offended spouse may stop mentioning the problem and simply show less care in return. *Why should I keep giving and giving,* the offended spouse thinks, *when my mate isn't putting the smallest effort into this marriage?* That can have a snowball effect, causing the other spouse to shut down or blow up, which further justifies the lack of care from the originally offended spouse, and so on. Eventually both spouses regard each other as undeserving of any care whatsoever.

That's reality.

But wouldn't unconditional love solve this problem? Not really. Sometimes it can defuse a crisis in the short term, but it often creates patterns of behavior that lead to long-term disaster.

You may have noticed that doing nice things for your spouse does not *necessarily* improve his or her behavior toward you. Oh, your kindness may be appreciated, but it's not always repaid.

Don't get me wrong: I encourage kindness. But if your spouse does not reciprocate, your kindness may actually be rewarding inconsiderate behavior.

Think about it. Say Bob is expected home from work at 6:00. His wife, Cathy, gets home at 5:00 and hurries to prepare dinner. One night, though, it gets to be 6:30, 7:00, and Bob still isn't home. Dinner's getting cold, and Cathy's worried about Bob. He stumbles in at 7:10, muttering something about working late.

Let's say Cathy tries the unconditional love approach. In spite of Bob's inconsiderate behavior, she reheats the dinner (for the fifth time) and tries to suppress her anger. "You poor dear, you must be tired," she says. Nothing is said about his failure to call and tell her he'd be late.

A few days later, it happens again. Bob's an hour late at the office, and he doesn't call. But Cathy still acts as if nothing's wrong. It happens twice more that month, and Cathy still clings to her unconditional love.

Cathy thinks that she's helping her marriage by putting up with his rudeness, but she's not. If he thinks he can mistreat her here, where will he stop? At some point her Taker will jump in and draw the line.

One evening Bob will find a note: "Got tired of waiting. Had dinner. Went shopping. Fend for yourself."

Negotiations are in order. Somehow Bob and Cathy must come to an agreement that if he wants Cathy's great home-cooked meals, he needs to get home on time or call home to say he'll be late.

This may seem like a trivial example, but the principle applies to much more serious issues, such as infidelity or abuse. Forgiveness is a great thing in a marriage but it must be accompanied by a mutual commitment to protect and care for each other in the future. A unilateral commitment does not resolve marital conflicts.

To be more realistic, we might rewrite the wedding vows so the answer is "I will if you will." It is foolish, even dangerous, to assume that happy marriages can be one-sided, with one spouse doing all the caring and protecting. A good marriage is bilateral and conditional. Both spouses protect and care for each other by mutual agreement and consent.

This is why a marital agreement to meet each other's emotional needs is so important. In the next chapter I will lead you into negotiations for mutual need meeting. This is a crucial step in the restoration of your marriage. It clearly defines the rights and responsibilities of your relationship. You are clearly defining the kind of care you need to give and receive. You are "getting real" about those marriage vows you made long ago, communicating what you really expect and what you're really offering in return.

The Second Illusion and Reality

The Illusion: ***A husband and wife should love and accept each other as they are and not try to change each other.*** Remember that Billy Joel song in the 1980s: "I Love You Just the Way You Are"? Its huge popularity at the time suggests that it struck a romantic chord with millions of listeners. "Don't go changing to try to please me," the song began—and people everywhere thought, *Yes, that's true love.*

But is it really?

I suppose all of us want that kind of love for ourselves, being loved for who we are, instead of what we do. (It's a lot less work for us!) But is that the kind of love that gets us into marriage in the first place? I don't think so.

We decide to marry someone on the basis of what he or she has done for us, is doing, and will continue to do (we hope). As of the time you were married, the one you picked as your life partner had done an incredibly good job of meeting your needs—and obviously you expected that need meeting to continue.

But our needs change as we grow. In most cases, we choose marriage partners who can meet our needs at the time. If we marry as happy, healthy young adults, we do not consider the needs of middle age, sickness, parenting, emotional distress, or the many other events that will fill our lifetime. Some become disillusioned when they discover that the person who was just perfect for them at age twenty is no longer compatible with their needs at age fifty (or age twenty-five, for that matter). Needs that were unknown when a couple began having a family can emerge when the grown-up children move away from home!

Even if you're savvy enough to anticipate your future needs, the *sense* of need does not arise until the change actually takes place. For example, most women have a need for their husband to take an interest in the development of their children, but until children arrive, a woman might find herself very satisfied with a husband who dislikes children. They may have several delightful years together before he has an opportunity to disappoint her by leaving this need unmet. Once children are on the scene, and he ignores them, a marital conflict of major proportions arises.

Here's another problem: A person's good intentions are not enough to satisfy ordinary needs. For example, a woman may agree at the time of marriage to meet her husband's sexual needs but she may find after marriage that she has almost no interest in doing so. She may even come to think that sex is disgusting and degrading. He married her with the expectation that she would meet his sexual needs (among others), as she fully intended to do. But if her intentions do not carry over into practice, he may remain sexually unfulfilled throughout life.

A man who is chronically unemployed poses the same sort of dilemma for his wife. During the first few years of marriage, his wife might see his unemployment as little more than a difficulty adjusting to the right job. But after a while, she comes to realize that he simply does not like to work as much as most other men. He wants to please her and will take jobs just to show her that he loves her. But eventually he quits or is fired because he hates the work so much. It's only then that she realizes that her need for financial support will be unfulfilled throughout marriage unless he takes radical measures to resolve his problem.

Problems such as these lead to very unpleasant situations. Couples show each other disrespect and outright abuse, both verbal and physical. Why? Because they're not committed to the marriage? In most cases, they are committed. They just don't make the changes necessary to meet each other's emotional needs.

"I want to be loved for who I am," one of these spouses might say. "Why do you keep trying to change me? Don't you love me just the way I am? If you really loved me, you would look beyond my behavior and accept me this way."

The spouse who says that desperately needs a dose of reality.

The Reality: ***A husband and wife's love and acceptance of each other depend on the changes they make to accommodate each other.*** Marital compatibility requires change; if people do not make changes in their abilities to care for and protect each other, incompatibility is the certain result. We are moving targets. Throughout life, no one stays in the same place emotionally and intellectually. Most of us are prepared for the needs of our spouse at the moment we are married. We prove it during courtship. But after marriage, almost immediately, marital needs begin to change. When we make a commitment to care for better or for worse, we sometimes assume that we'll be doing the same things in good and bad times. However, caring, particularly in bad times, may require that you learn new abilities to meet the new, sometimes unexpected, needs of your spouse.

Husbands and wives will change, whether they like it or not, so they must change in order to keep making each other happy.

It's easy for us to forget that whenever we show we care for someone, we're changing our behavior to meet their needs. A husband may change his normal route home from work to buy flowers for his wife. A wife may change her plans so she can cheer her husband on at his softball game. When your spouse asks you to change your behavior to accommodate him or her, your spouse is simply keeping you up-to-date on the latest emotional needs—he or she is asking for your care.

Illusions and Realities in Marriage

The First Illusion: Care and protection in marriage should be given unconditionally. They should be given even when they are not received.

The First Reality: Care and protection in marriage are *conditional.* They are given *when they are received.*

The Second Illusion: A husband and wife should love and accept each other as they are and shouldn't try to change each other.

The Second Reality: A husband and wife's love and acceptance of each other *depend on the changes they make* to accommodate each other.

Inability to meet needs can be changed to *ability* if couples recognize the necessity of change as an act of care and submit themselves to the training that it takes to make the change.

There is a certain predictability to the changes in marital needs. If you know what's coming, you can go with the flow. When there are no children in the home, the needs of affection, conversation, sexual fulfillment, recreational companionship, physical attraction, and admiration usually dominate. But after children are born, the emotional needs of family commitment, financial support, and domestic support become more important to a couple. Furthermore, children can make it much more difficult to meet the needs that had previously been easy to meet. Many marriages are ruined when men and women fail to make the changes necessary to accommodate new needs and keep meeting the old ones.

If you refuse to change your behavior, you're inviting disaster. And if you're honest, you probably expect your spouse to make some changes for you. The man who won't keep a steady job and still insists that his wife lose weight is a hypocrite. The woman who disdains sex with her husband but begs him to chat with her at breakfast is being grossly unfair. You can't expect your spouse to do all the changing!

It's the epitome of selfishness to assume that we should be loved and cared for regardless of the way we treat others. Do not be lulled into the unrealistic belief that your marital relationship is secure, regardless of your own behavior.

On the other hand, you have the right to receive love and care from your spouse as your needs change.

If you and your spouse identify and learn to eliminate Love Busters through mutual agreement and learn to meet each other's most important emotional needs through mutual agreement, you will have a marriage that's the envy of all who know you well. But more important, you will find each other absolutely irresistible. You will have the marriage you had always hoped for.

But it requires change. Your change. You must learn to become compatible with the feelings and needs of your spouse. Your spouse must also make changes to accommodate you, but you're the only one who can change you. Do your part the best you can and hope that your spouse keeps up his or her end of the agreement.

Chapter Thirteen

If You Scratch My Back . . .

How to Get Your Spouse to Meet Your Most Important Emotional Needs

Joan and Mike were emotionally ready to meet each other's needs. They had overcome their Love Busters and knew how to protect each other from their own hurtful behavior. If I had sent them away at this point, they might have done all right on their own. After all, they must have met each other's needs rather well before marriage—well enough to fall in love.

But I wanted to be on the safe side. It takes work to identify and meet each other's emotional needs, and I wanted to be sure Mike and Joan put their effort in the right places.

Remember that need meeting is the best way to build up your account in your spouse's Love Bank. But we all have minor needs and major needs. Why waste your time and effort on trivial needs, which may only deposit a few units in the Love Bank? Why not concentrate on your spouse's most important emotional needs, which have a much greater payoff? You can exert the same effort and get much more impact.

First you should know what those most important emotional needs are. Then you should commit yourself to do what it takes to meet them.

I recommend that you and your spouse negotiate an agreement to meet each other's most important emotional needs. There is some negotiation involved, which we'll discuss shortly, but at its heart the agreement says: *I will learn to meet your most important emotional needs if you learn to meet mine.*

You may be meeting some of these needs already. That's great, but the ones you're missing could make the difference between a ho-hum marriage and a sensational one.

I made this same recommendation to Joan and Mike. At first they weren't sure what they were getting into. It sounded like a blank check: I'll meet your needs if you meet mine. That's dangerous to say, if you don't know the other person's needs.

"Absolutely," I responded to their objections. "I don't sign blank checks either." Spouses need to know what their end of the agreement will cost before they agree to anything. But the Policy of Joint Agreement still applies. In the need-meeting agreement that I'm proposing, you will not be asked to do anything for your spouse that you cannot enthusiastically agree to.

Need-Meeting Agreement

I will learn to meet your most important emotional needs if you learn to meet mine.

Many of the women I've counseled look at the need-meeting agreement and say, "I know what this is. It's a way to force me to have sex with my husband whenever he wants!" Some women in my workshops have refused to sign the agreement because they think it's a license for their husband to rape them every night. But if they had listened to me more carefully, they would have known that this agreement puts them in no danger of pain or suffering.

When a couple agrees to meet any of each other's emotional needs, whether it's sex or family commitment, the way they go about it must be in the best interest of both spouses, not just one.

On the other hand, an agreement to meet a spouse's emotional needs is a serious commitment. It's a goal that takes priority over most other goals and should not be neglected.

Most couples agree that they need to change the way they treat each other, but they argue about what needs changing. They usually get so bogged down debating which changes to make, they don't change anything.

Change begins with knowing what to change and agreeing to those changes. If you want to improve the way you and your spouse meet each other's needs, you must first agree on what needs changing.

What follows are three steps that will show you how to get your spouse to meet your most important emotional needs. Of course, you will have to meet your spouse's most important emotional needs too.

Step 1: ***Identify the most important emotional needs.***

During their years of courtship, Joan and Mike didn't have to complete any questionnaires to discover what they needed from each other. They spent countless hours talking to each other about every subject imaginable, and those conversations included information about each other's emotional needs. They told each other what they needed and then learned to meet each other's needs. It was just that simple.

But it had been years since those deep and intimate conversations, and we couldn't instantly bring back those days when they spontaneously shared their deepest feelings. So I had to help them explain their emotional needs to each other simply and quickly.

Only you can identify your most important needs. And your spouse is the only one who can identify his or her needs. Though I may know the emotional needs that people *in general* have, I don't know the needs of anyone in particular until that person tells me. To help couples identify their needs for each other, I've designed the Emotional Needs Questionnaire. (One is printed in appendix B. Make two copies, one for you and one for your spouse.) Joan and Mike completed these questionnaires, and I went over the results with them individually.

Joan expressed some ambivalence about her answers. That didn't surprise me, since she had been in the state of Withdrawal for so long. In Withdrawal, people don't want their needs met by their spouses; they try to fend for themselves. Though Joan had moved out of that state, she still had some of its hesitancy.

We started with the last page of the questionnaire, where she ranked her five most important emotional needs:

Rank	*Emotional Need*
1	Conversation
2	Affection
3	Family commitment
4	Financial support
5	Admiration

The five emotional needs left unranked were sexual fulfillment, recreational companionship, physical attractiveness, honesty and openness, and domestic support. It wasn't that she didn't need any of these met. In fact, she wanted to include honesty and openness, but she could pick only five, and admiration was more important to her. (You'll notice that her list included only four of the five needs chosen most by women. I identified, in chapter 11, the five needs that women *in general* rank highest, but any one woman rarely picks all five. Joan came close, but she opted for the characteristically "male" need of admiration over the "female" need of honesty and openness.)

Though we would soon focus on the highest-ranked need—conversation—we reviewed all five, just to be certain Joan understood them all and was comfortable with the order she had chosen. "If I could wave a magic wand and give Mike a special talent to meet one of these needs to your fullest satisfaction—but only one, leaving the other nine completely unmet—which need would you want him to meet?" I asked.

"I wouldn't want to be married to someone that only met one of my needs," she replied.

"Suppose you had no choice," I persisted. "Suppose you had to marry a man who could only meet one of your needs. Which need would you want fulfilled?"

She looked at the list again. "I would pick conversation," she said, confirming her previous ranking. "What made our relationship click while we were dating was his eagerness to talk to me, and I have really missed that part of our relationship the most."

"Okay," I went on, "if Mike could meet only two of your needs, which would you pick second?"

After thinking about it for a minute, she confirmed her number 2 pick, affection.

The only one she had trouble with was the fifth need. "It's a toss-up between honesty and openness and admiration," she sighed. "I can't decide which is more important. They both are."

In such cases, I bend the rules and allow a list of six. "How would you feel if Mike added a sixth need to his list so you could include honesty and openness?" I asked. That sounded good to Joan.

Then it was Mike's turn. On the last page of his questionnaire, the needs were ranked as follows:

Rank	*Emotional Need*
1	Sexual fulfillment
2	Recreational companionship
3	Affection
4	Physical attractiveness
5	Domestic support

The five emotional needs he left unranked were conversation, financial support, family commitment, honesty and openness, and admiration. He admitted that he needed some of these too, but they were not as important.

I told him that he could pick one more, because Joan could not settle on five, so he chose family commitment as well. It was very important to him for Joan to play a role in the development of their children.

We discussed his answers to each of the questions in the questionnaire, and then I went over his ranking once more, using the same "magic wand" question I had used with Joan. Mike confirmed his ranking of all six needs.

It immediately occurred to me that the number 1 needs of Mike and Joan were not on the other spouse's list of needs at all. Joan had not included sexual fulfillment in her top six, and Mike had not included conversation in his. In other words, the most important needs they could meet for each other were not their own needs.

I have found this in many, many marriages. I have already explained that the five needs usually ranked most important by men are different from the five needs usually ranked highest by women. But it is particularly striking when you see that the number 1 needs of both spouses don't even appear on the other spouse's list. This makes the identification and fulfillment of these needs much more of a challenge than newly married couples anticipate.

Step 2: ***Agree to meet each other's most important emotional needs.*** When you and your spouse have identified each other's five (or six) most important emotional needs, make a trade. You agree to meet your spouse's five most important emotional needs, and in return, your spouse agrees to meet yours.

Your Givers will object to such a trade. After all, you should be doing these things for each other simply because you've committed yourselves to each other's care. Your Giver says, *Just give me the list, and I'll start learning how to meet your spouse's needs.* If you are in the state of Intimacy, this approach just might work. If both you and your spouse have Givers in charge and you learn to meet each other's needs at the same time, it's just as effective as a trade.

But if you are not in the state of Intimacy, but in the state of Conflict, your Takers will object to the trade. They will want to be certain that there's something in it for you before you do anything for your spouse. Your Taker will say, *Remember all those years when you were meeting your spouse's needs and he (or she) never met yours? You'll be a chump all over again unless your spouse meets your needs first.*

In spite of the fact that a trade makes no sense to either the Giver or the Taker, a trade is actually in the best interest of both. The Giver has a chance to do something significant for your spouse, and your Taker will find your spouse's efforts to make you happy effective. If you override both of their reservations and simply make the trade, you'll find that both of these characters will eventually settle down.

But it just doesn't seem right! (Is that what you're thinking now?) *Marriage isn't about trading; it's about love. This trade talk doesn't feel right.*

I understand. Intuitively, you find the whole negotiation process in rather bad taste. But much of what couples learn to do to create compatibility in marriage is not intuitive. That's why there are so many bad marriages, even among marriage counselors. The secret to a successful marriage is to do something that may not feel right at the time. When I suggest a trade for need fulfillment, many couples are uncomfortable with the idea, but they eventually agree, and it works out great in the end.

Joan joined Mike in my office, and I asked them if they were ready to agree to meet each other's most important emotional needs. I handed Joan's list to Mike and Mike's list to Joan, explaining that I would probably help them with only the first two needs they listed. Once they learned to fulfill those, they would be well on their way, and they could continue without my help.

They both agreed to learn to fulfill each other's emotional needs, and they were ready for the next step.

Step 3: ***Learn to meet each other's most important emotional needs.***

Begin where your effort will do you the most good. Take the number 1 need of your spouse and learn how to meet it. In exchange for your effort, your spouse is to learn to meet your number 1 need.

But what if you are already meeting your spouse's number 1 need? Then skip to number 2. Take the most important need that you have not been meeting. If you are already meeting your spouse's greatest need, your Taker may argue, *Wait a minute, you've already done your job. Now it's your spouse's turn. Shouldn't your spouse catch up to you by meeting your number 1 need first?*

I don't recommend it. If you are already doing a good job meeting an important need, great! But if you expect your spouse to meet a new need for you, you should learn to meet a new need for your spouse. It's the incentive your spouse's Taker will require to get him or her through the project.

So when you have learned to meet each other's number 1 need, then go on to number 2, then to number 3, and so forth. Each time, make sure that you have a new bargain—you will meet a new need for your spouse in return for your spouse meeting a new need for you.

If you have kept your end of the bargain, meeting a new need for your spouse, but your spouse has not yet learned to meet your new need, wait before you begin working on another need. Your Taker will not let you go on to meet another need until your spouse has fulfilled his or her end of the bargain.

How to Get What You Need

1. Identify your needs and the needs of your spouse.
2. Agree to meet your spouse's needs as your spouse agrees to meet yours.
3. Learn to meet each other's needs.

When you have learned to meet all five needs, if you want to learn to meet even more, go right ahead! There's nothing magic about five needs. You and your spouse could agree to meet four or six of each other's most important emotional needs. But my experience has shown me that by the time a couple learns to meet each other's five most important needs, they are depositing so many love units that it's not necessary to deposit any more. They're so crazy about each other that the state of Intimacy is secure.

I helped Mike and Joan meet four of each other's most important emotional needs, two for each of them. In the next four chapters, we'll get into the details. I'll explain how they learned to meet the needs of conversation, sexual fulfillment, affection, and recreational companionship.

Why Can't We Just Talk?

How to Meet the Emotional Need for Conversation

Chapter Fourteen

Joan had never dreamed she'd have trouble talking with Mike. They had met at school, where they attended the same science class. At first they talked about homework assignments, but soon they could make just about anything a conversation piece. Talking seemed effortless, and that's how they spent most of their time together. Before long, they were in love.

But after marriage, conversation took a decided turn for the worse. Instead of being effortless and enjoyable, it became argumentative and distasteful. Almost every subject was laced with land mines. No matter what was said, there was a way to take it wrong and be offended. Soon this put their marriage at serious risk.

George and Alice also had a problem, but it had nothing to do with fighting. In fact, they never argued with each other at all—they didn't talk enough to have anything to argue about.

Like Joan and Mike, this couple had had no difficulty talking while they were dating. But after marriage, their conversation didn't turn ugly—it just faded away. Their relationship was cordial and polite but emotionally distant. Marriage had become a prison sentence; both George and Alice were in solitary confinement.

Vicki had the opposite problem with Sam. He wouldn't stop talking. Whenever they were together, he talked, whether or not she was listening, and she could rarely get a word in edgewise. She found his topics of conversation totally boring, yet she made every effort to look interested. Eventually she couldn't take it any more.

These and countless other couples have come to my office with divorce in mind. Conversation, which had been the centerpiece of their relationship prior to marriage, had become intolerable—or imperceptible.

Conversation can make us feel wonderful or terrible. In most marriages, it has both effects. Wouldn't you like to use conversation to make your spouse feel wonderful? Wouldn't you like to avoid using it to hurt your spouse?

Care is what it's all about—caring for your spouse by meeting his or her emotional need for conversation. Your effort to meet this need is an act of care, and you communicate the quality of your care whenever you have a conversation.

The Emotional Need for Conversation

What do people mean when they say, "We need to talk?"

We talk to each other whenever we want to exchange ideas, opinions, observations, or emotions. Such conversation helps educate us and helps solve our problems. Without conversation, we are very limited in the way we can function as a society. With conversation, we draw on the resources of others.

But sometimes a person will talk with another person just for the sake of talking, because he or she enjoys it so much. There is a need that's met by the conversation itself, not necessarily the subject of conversation.

People who don't need conversation very much are often confused by those who give it a higher priority. "Why did you call? Haven't we exhausted that subject? Where is this conversation headed?" These people, these nonneeders, converse in order to give or receive information or to solve problems. They view conversation as a means to an end, not an end in itself.

But the needers know that conversation conveys far more information than the words themselves contain. In the passage of conversation, we reveal the very essence of ourselves, our personal history, our present activities, our future plans, and our emotional reactions to life as we see it. Through conversation we can become emotionally connected to others and emotionally vulnerable.

Marriage depends on conversation for its emotional survival, even when conversation itself is not a highly ranked need. That's because conversation is the gateway to most of the other emotional needs.

Showing affection, for example, is almost impossible without conversation that communicates love and concern. The need for sexual fulfillment cannot be met without the expression of sexual feelings. Recreational companionship also requires conversation regarding activities mutually enjoyed, as do family commitment, honesty and openness, and admiration. All of the most important emotional needs are at least partially met through conversation.

Your Conversational Habits Make You Irresistible or Repulsive

Almost all of our behavior is in the form of habits. Certain situations trigger our behavior so smoothly that we are able to go about our business efficiently and effectively. If we were required to think about everything we did, we'd spend most of our day immobilized, wondering what to do next. It's like trying to fly an airplane for the first time without an instructor: We'd crash.

But some of these smooth and well-rehearsed habits do us more harm than good. In marriage they may make our spouse unhappy or prevent us from meeting his or her emotional needs. Some habits make us repulsive.

All of us have conversational habits, ways of communicating (or not communicating) that we practice without thinking.

Some people routinely bully their spouses into agreeing with them, forcing their own opinions rather than respecting any other point of view.

Others regularly point out the mistakes their spouse makes or remind him or her of past mistakes.

Still others use conversation to punish their spouses, tossing insults right and left, inflicting pain with words. At some instinctive level, these people are trying to even the score, to exact revenge for some previous injury, but such punishment only awakens the spouse's desire to launch a return attack.

These three bad habits—(1) trying to force our way of thinking, (2) dwelling on mistakes, and (3) verbally punishing our spouse—

are enemies of good conversation. They build walls within a marriage and make us repulsive to our mate.

Why be repulsive when you can be irresistible?

You can become irresistible by developing positive conversational habits—habits of sensitivity that help you meet your partner's emotional needs and avoid causing unhappiness.

A sensitive conversation begins with understanding. You must understand how your spouse feels about things and why. Without that understanding, you run the risk of being a bull in a china closet, smashing your spouse's feelings at every turn—not because you want to, but because you don't know any better.

How do you get this understanding? You talk. Ask how your spouse feels about all sorts of things, and listen to his or her response. Then share your own feelings. This mutual understanding is a major step on the way to becoming irresistible.

Become interested in your spouse's favorite topics of conversation. This not only shows that you care, it also makes a conversation much more enjoyable, adding newly acquired information and creative perspectives. It also adds to a couple's feeling of marital compatibility. Genuine interest in your spouse's favorite topics will make you even more irresistible.

No one, not even the one doing all the talking, enjoys one-sided conversations. The best conversations are balanced, with both spouses contributing and listening to each other equally. Nor can anyone enjoy talking with someone who keeps being distracted. "Don't I deserve your full attention?" a person questions mentally when his or her partner cannot stick with the conversation.

When you give your spouse equal time to talk (and your fullest attention), you're showing respect for your spouse and what he or she has to say. This, too, makes you irresistible.

These four friends of good conversation—(1) understanding, (2) interest in favorite topics, (3) balance, and (4) undivided attention—can become second nature to you. In the past, you may have developed bad habits like bullying or punishing without even trying. (We are usually bystanders in the formation of our bad habits.) But you can control your habits if you want to. You can learn good conversational habits and eliminate bad ones.

I challenge you to think about the way you talk to your spouse. How do your conversational habits affect him or her emotionally?

What conversational habits do you need to change in order to stop hurting your spouse? What habits do you need to learn in order to bring you closer together?

Friends of Good Conversation

Try to imagine, for a moment, a conversation that you'd consider emotionally fulfilling. In fact let's make it the most fulfilling conversation you could possibly have. What would it be like?

Would the person having this conversation with you know you well and understand how you feel? Would the person be supportive and encouraging? Would you have his or her undivided attention? Would you find empathy for the conflicts you face? Would the person show interest in the events of your life and the topics you enjoy talking about?

How can you possibly find a conversation like this?

Maybe by having an affair.

Don't get me wrong. I am not suggesting that you have an affair. I think it's the most cruel and painful experience a person can put a spouse through. For the offended spouse it's often worse than a physical beating or rape.

But, ironically, some people find their ideal conversations while they're in the arms of the "other" man or woman. You might think that sex is the major ingredient of extramarital affairs, but in my counseling I've found that conversation is usually the key. Unfaithful spouses have often told me that their lover spoke to them with incredible kindness, giving their fullest attention. The lover seemed so thoughtful, supportive, and unconditionally accepting that the illicit relationship became addictive. Conversation led to sex, the cheaters have told me, and not the other way around.

Isn't it a pity that what people want the most in marriage is often achieved through infidelity?

I must say that the kindness and "unconditional support" some people find in affairs is difficult to sustain. As soon as one of them doesn't like what the other is doing, the conditionality of the relationship is exposed. They can't handle the hard work of negotiation—that makes the relationship seem no different than their marriages. Most people who have affairs eventually return to their spouses convinced that an affair is not the answer.

I hope you and your spouse never go through the pain of an affair. But I'd like you to learn to be able to talk to your spouse the same way people having an affair talk to each other. If you're at all interested in saving (or just improving) your marriage, you simply must talk to your spouse with kindness, consideration, and empathy. You cannot be judgmental, critical, or argumentative. You cannot make threats or do anything else that will make your spouse feel bad. You must educate yourself in making your spouse feel good whenever he or she talks to you.

If you can learn to do this, you'll be meeting one of your spouse's most important emotional needs, and you'll be irresistible.

The First Friend of Good Conversation: ***Using conversation to investigate, inform, and understand your spouse.***

Before we can engage in intimate conversation, we must understand the person with whom we're talking. That includes learning about the person's sensitivities, likes, dislikes, background, and interests—all sorts of personal details. If we don't tune in to these sensitivities, we will stumble all over them, and the person will toss us out of his or her innermost self at the first opportunity.

But understanding doesn't just happen. We arrive at an understanding of another person through investigation—we ask questions to get to know someone better.

People don't give out this personal information to just anyone. You have to prove you can be trusted. One way to do that is to share information of your own. Intimate conversation works both ways. You need to investigate and inform, eventually arriving at a mutual understanding.

Counselors have a tremendous advantage in the collection of intimate details. Clients expect to share their most personal thoughts with a counselor, because they want help and know that the counselor needs these facts to help them. Because of this trust, a counselor can get to know someone very well within a very short period of time.

I find it ironic that some of my clients will tell me things about themselves that their spouses don't know. Why? Because I'm investigating. That's my job.

When a couple comes to my office to learn how to improve their marriage, I try to teach them to do what I do, in a way. If they can investigate each other's inner thoughts and feelings, they can begin to know each other more intimately. It's a simple process, really: investigate, inform, understand.

Investigate the facts of each other's personal histories, present activities, and plans for the future. Also investigate each other's attitudes and emotional reactions to those facts. You are bound to each other, through marriage, in a partnership that requires you to navigate through life with skill and coordination. It's important for you to see each other's mental control panels so you can keep your crafts flying together without crashing into each other.

Why is investigation so important? Why can't you just inform each other? Well, this is the sort of information most people don't give out unless they know the other person is genuinely interested. Your curiosity about your spouse's life is essential.

But once personal information is requested, *inform* each other of the facts of your personal histories, present activities, plans for the future, and your attitudes and emotional reactions to those facts. To withhold accurate information about your inner self prevents intimacy and leaves the need for meaningful conversation unmet.

Keep calendars of your activities for the day and plans for your future and share them with each other. Don't keep secrets from your spouse.

Once you have investigated and informed each other of personal activities and feelings, you're in a position to *understand* each other. What motivates you and your spouse to do what you both do? What are your rewards, and what do you find punishing? What are your beliefs, and how are they put into practice? What are your most common positive and negative emotional reactions? What are your strengths and weaknesses? The list goes on and on. There is so much to know about each other.

This process meets the need for conversation in two ways. Obviously, there is lots of conversation involved as you investigate and inform each other. But you also come out with an understanding that enables you to reach a new level of sensitive and meaningful conversations.

And investigating-informing-understanding is not a one-time event. It's something you should continue throughout your marriage, as you maintain and build intimacy.

The Second Friend of Good Conversation: ***Developing interest in each other's favorite topics of conversation.***

Topics drive most conversations. We usually talk about *something*, and these topics keep our conversations going. But we all like some topics better than others.

What happened when you were dating? You probably tried to find topics of conversation that interested your date. If you found, on a first date, that there wasn't much to talk about—well, you probably didn't have a second date. *Unless,* of course, you were *very* attracted to the person. In that case, you probably *developed* an interest in topics that your date enjoyed. You quickly tried to gain a working knowledge of, say, ice hockey or Indian cuisine. After all, you wouldn't want this gorgeous doll or hunk to think you two were incompatible. In other words, you *created* compatibility by developing mutual interests.

Then what happened during your courtship? Presumably, you and your spouse-to-be *perfected* your compatibility as you became comfortable talking about these new topics.

But interests change over time. Topics that may have interested your spouse when you both were younger may have lost their attraction. And topics that once were completely boring, you may now find fascinating. Besides, you're encountering brand-new topics all the time.

Maybe you and your spouse had compatible interests when you married but have you kept up with each other's changing interests? Once you and your spouse could talk for hours about mutual interests but now do you find yourselves struggling to find *anything* you have in common?

If that's the case, you need to get back to the mind-set you had when you were dating. If you keep talking about *your* interests when your spouse is bored by them, you'll withdraw love units and hurt your marriage. But if you want to deposit love units, you need to talk about topics that your spouse finds interesting. That may require some education on your part.

But what if you try and you're simply not interested in your spouse's favorite topics? Say your spouse has discovered quantum physics and you failed Algebra I. What then?

Well, there's really no point in faking an interest in something that's totally boring to you. You need to discover those interests that both you and your spouse will enjoy together. The Policy of Joint

Agreement can help immeasurably in your development of mutual interests. If one of you is not enthusiastic about a topic (after giving it a chance), switch to one of the thousands of other topics you could be discussing.

The Third Friend of Good Conversation: ***Balancing the conversation.*** Conversation is a two-way street. When someone tries to turn it into a one-lane street, it becomes a speech. Some people are so fascinating that we don't mind listening to them go on and on, but you must not assume you're one of them. And you probably know your spouse isn't.

Conversation is enjoyable for most of us only when we participate interactively, when the different talkers contribute equally. But a problem that often arises in marriage counseling is that couples violate rules of conversational etiquette. They interrupt each other or try to talk over each other. One or the other tries to dominate the conversation. Those who do this may be enjoying themselves, but it isn't very pleasant to the one who can't get a word in edgewise.

In many marriages, one spouse is less talkative than the other one. Unless he or she is given time to start sentences and finish thoughts, uninterrupted, conversation tends to be dominated by the more talkative partner.

If this has been a problem in your conversations, learn how to balance your conversation so both of you have opportunities to express your thoughts and feelings.

The Fourth Friend of Good Conversation: ***Giving each other undivided attention.***

Intimate conversation requires undivided attention. Some people may be able to do several things at once, but even these nimble folk will fail to deposit love units if they try to carry on a conversation with their spouse while watching television.

One of my more curious experiences occurred while I was completing a marriage counseling internship. My supervisor would meet with me each week to discuss my cases and, in the middle of one of my explanations, I found he was asleep! I took it personally, of course, and promised myself that I would never again be so boring.

What made his slumber even more outrageous was that I was paying him one hundred dollars an hour to pay attention to me, and he still couldn't do it!

Yet I knew what he was up against. I also had difficulty paying attention to my clients. Coffee helped, but eventually I learned to schedule my most uninspiring clients in the time of day when I was the most alert.

Marriage partners don't usually consider each other boring but they do try to talk to each other when they're exhausted. Their most creative, ambitious, interesting, and alert time of the day is spent at work. But they tend to talk to each other either in the morning, as they are trying to build up steam, or in the evening, as they're falling apart. In either case, undivided attention is hard to find.

Friends of Good Conversation

1. Investigate, inform, and understand.
2. Show interest in favorite topics.
3. Create balance.
4. Give undivided attention.

My solution to this problem is this: I recommend that couples set aside a *quality* fifteen hours a week for undivided attention. Whether or not you set aside that much time, you won't be depositing love units unless your spouse has your *undivided* attention. And you won't be able to give undivided attention unless you schedule it during some of your most creative and alert time of the day.

The friends of conversation that we've been discussing will help you meet your spouse's need for conversation (and may help meet other needs as well). But there are also *enemies* of good conversation. These bad habits *withdraw* love units from the Love Bank and should be avoided at all costs. Your spouse may need to talk with you, but if you bring the enemies of conversation along, the pain will be too great, and he or she will try to avoid conversation with you entirely.

Enemies of Good Conversation

Have you ever been talking with your spouse, going on and on about some obscure matter, when you suddenly realized he or she had left the room a few minutes earlier? Maybe your spouse thought you were finished and innocently walked away, but you never noticed. You had something to say, and it didn't matter that no one was listening.

We sometimes forget that conversations include someone other than ourselves. It can be so important to make our points that we ignore the needs and sensitivities of the person we're talking with.

This is the way our Takers run conversations. Not only do such tactics ruin conversations, but they damage relationships as well. When you let your Taker talk for you, you say things that ignore your spouse's feelings, and that brings out your spouse's Taker. Unless you're a masochist, that's a big mistake.

We have previously discussed Love Busters and the problems involved in failing to protect your spouse from your own Taker. But when you hurt your spouse *in conversation*, there's a double whammy. Not only do you make your mate unhappy, but you also poison the process of conversation. When you attack, he or she gets defensive. When you say things that are offensive to your spouse, he or she is almost certain to keep you at a safe distance emotionally.

So your hurtful habits of conversation—these "enemies"—mark off *all* conversation as dangerous territory, a "no-man's land." If you have used words to attack your spouse, your spouse will shy away from using intimate words with you. Suddenly you're talking about the weather, the car, the schedule—facts, not feelings. Because you have used conversation as a weapon, it's hard to use conversation to repair the damage.

If you want to meet your spouse's need for conversation, the enemies must be defeated. They add nothing of value and take away what you want the most: a mutually safe and emotionally supportive relationship.

The First Enemy of Good Conversation: ***Using conversation to force agreement to your way of thinking.***

The telephone rings. It's a salesman hawking magazine subscriptions. You want to be polite, right? You say, "Thank you, but no, I'm not interested."

"I can understand that," the voice replies, "but have you ever considered the advantages—"

"No, really," you insist, "I'm not interested."

"But surely you won't want to pass up a chance to save money on—"

Eventually you realize that politeness is not an option. You have the right, and actually the responsibility, to hang up on the tenacious brute. And you do.

But when the salesperson is your spouse, it's not so easy to end the conversation. Instead of selling you a product, he or she is trying to sell an idea, belief, or plan. The conversation may begin on a pleasant note, but as soon as you express any reservation, the pressure rises. Your right to disagree is not acknowledged.

Or maybe *you're* the obnoxious salesperson. Do you ever force your opinions on your spouse?

You may convince yourself that your spouse is about to make a serious mistake, and unless you force a change in opinion, he or she will self-destruct. But if you look at your motives a little more closely, you'll find that they're not quite so pure. Underlying your comments is the assumption that you know what's right and your spouse doesn't. That lack of respect is sure to withdraw love units, and under those conditions, your spouse is likely to reject your opinion, regardless of its merit.

On the other hand, when you enter a discussion with respect for your spouse's opinion, you strengthen your relationship and increase your chances of getting a fair hearing for your opinions. Everyone wins when there's mutual respect, and everyone loses when there's not.

The Second Enemy of Good Conversation: ***Dwelling on mistakes, past or present.***

We all need criticism. As an author, in order to keep improving my work, I ask for helpful criticism. Whenever I write a book or article, someone I respect must give me negative feedback so I can correct my errors. I often ask my wife to be my critic.

But when she criticizes my work (and she is usually right), I react with pain. While I want to improve, her criticism hurts me terribly.

When others criticize me, however, it doesn't bother me much at all, particularly when I ask for it. I *encourage* some people to criticize me because it helps me improve myself. If I don't agree with them, I can easily ignore their comments. If I agree, I make a change.

Joyce has a music ministry and she sings in church concerts throughout the area. Like me, she wants to keep improving what she does, so she often asks me to critique her concerts. But whenever I point to her failures, she becomes very upset.

Years ago, when she was recording a gospel album in Nashville, I sat in the recording studio, providing her with critical feedback. If she made a mistake, I'd bring it to her attention, and she'd do the song over again. Soon she sent me home.

Why is criticism from a spouse so painful?

In an intimate relationship you give someone the keys to your inner self so that your emotional needs will be met. That makes you vulnerable. Once inside your life, your spouse can wound you with the slightest indiscretion. You are like a china closet, with your fragile wares displayed to those you allow inside. Sometimes your spouse can be like the proverbial "bull in a china closet," but he or she is not always so brutish. Spouses are more like children in a china closet, picking up this or that delicate item, not realizing how precious it is or how easily they could break it.

You let your lover into the most intimate places of your heart because that person can make you very, very happy. Intimacy magnifies your pleasure. But it can also magnify your pain. As a result, criticism in marriage is far more emotionally destructive than criticism in any other area of life.

You can inflict many different types of criticism on your spouse. You can carp about past mistakes or present mistakes, mistakes that affect you and mistakes that don't. There's criticism based on your moral convictions and criticism that has little or no moral basis.

In any form, criticism has the same result: It makes your spouse feel terrible and usually causes him or her to become emotionally distant.

Criticism itself is bad enough, but all too often you do something that makes it even worse—you *dwell* on your spouse's mistakes. And that's usually the way criticism works. You don't mention a mistake once and then drop it. You mention it over and over. You want to be certain your spouse understands and will do something to correct it.

As I've said, most behavior is habitual. You don't do things once, you do them over and over again. Criticism is a habit, too, a destructive one. With each offense, you are withdrawing love units from your spouse's Love Bank. And if you're in the habit of being critical of your spouse, frequently mentioning his or her mistakes, you are crippling your ability to carry on good conversations. This keeps you from building your Love Bank account back up.

In order to restore compatibility and good conversation, you must face up to this harmful habit and overcome it.

The Third Enemy of Good Conversation: ***Using conversation to punish each other.***

Gang warfare operates according to a rather simple psychology. Peace is not an option. "You killed my brother, so I'll kill you, and your brother will kill me." The only option is for one gang to completely humiliate or decimate the other. As more gangs form, the violence will escalate until everyone involved is dead or in prison. How many young people will die having lived totally unproductive lives—all because a basic instinct was triggered and, once triggered, could not be stopped?

Marriage can resemble gang warfare. That same instinct—hurt the one who hurts you—can easily be turned against a spouse. Once it starts, it can escalate to a point where couples actually kill each other. Domestic abuse is common, and law enforcement officers know how dangerous it is—not only to the couples involved, but to those who try to intervene. As a counselor, I've had my life threatened several times when I've tried to keep couples from killing each other.

Of course couples don't enter marriage with murder on their minds. It starts with minor pain inflicted and minor retaliation. I may use threatening words to prevent you from hurting me again, and that threat may seem to stop the pain, for a while. But if you do hurt me again, I have to deliver on my threat. My punishing words or actions cause you pain and humiliation, so you counter by punishing me with pain and humiliation. Round and round it goes, as we punish each other for punishing each other.

When you verbally punish your spouse, you're *trying* to withdraw love units. You *want* your spouse to feel bad. In an intimate relationship where we give each other opportunity to magnify emotional effects, punishment is especially devastating. We not only feel the intense pain of the attack, but we know that the person we've let into our innermost being is doing as much damage as he or she can. We feel betrayed.

While it's an instinct common to all of us, any effort you make to punish your spouse verbally will backfire. Not only do you destroy the trust you've built, but your spouse will very likely pay you back. First, your spouse will toss you out of his or her innermost self. Second, your spouse will build a strong emotional defense. And third, he or she will let you have it with both barrels.

When that happens, you can forget about meeting each other's emotional needs. You're in a state of war.

> **Enemies of Good Conversation**
> 1. Try to force your way of thinking.
> 2. Dwell on mistakes.
> 3. Use conversation to punish.

Why do we insist on punishing each other in marriage? To even the score. We somehow feel that to leave our spouse unpunished is unfair, and punishment is fair.

But punishment does not work! It does not even the score; it just tears up the scorecard. It undermines everything you hope to accomplish emotionally. In the end it will leave you and your spouse bitter enemies.

"But what if my spouse has really hurt me?" you may ask. "Don't I have a right to get revenge?"

Well, I'm not talking about rights, I'm talking about wise choices that will take you where you want to go.

What if your spouse had an affair? Infidelity is one of the most painful mistakes in marriage, and you might want to keep reminding your spouse of the offense. This is a form of punishment. You would still be nursing the pain, and you'd want your spouse to feel some humiliation—it's only fair.

But your constant reminders would do nothing to prevent future indiscretions. In fact, it might just encourage your spouse to put up emotional defenses to block your repeated criticism. This would prevent intimacy from redeveloping between you, and it might lead your spouse into another affair—partly to meet emotional needs your nonintimate marriage is leaving unmet and partly to repay you for your punishment.

Infidelity is terribly wrong—but once it is discussed, drop the subject. If you want to restore your relationship, continued punishment is counterproductive.

In your marriage it may not be infidelity; many lesser mistakes made in marriage may also tempt you to verbally punish your spouse. Such punishment should be avoided at all costs—it will only make matters worse.

I've described three enemies of good conversation, but there are many others. If you habitually say something that makes your spouse feel bad, it's an enemy. To have good conversations, you need to overcome these habits.

A Plan to Meet the Need for Conversation

Since Joan had identified conversation as her most important emotional need, I encouraged Mike to become an expert at meeting that need. He said he'd try to become the conversationalist that Joan remembered from their dating years.

There are two fundamental considerations in meeting any emotional need: quality and quantity. Quality is the way a need is met and quantity is how often it's met. Unless both of these considerations are up to your spouse's standards, you will not succeed in meeting his or her need.

If you bring the quality of your effort up to standard, but don't do it very often, your spouse will be left frustrated. And if your quality is substandard, it won't matter how often you make the effort, because each time it won't be what your spouse wants.

Obviously, Mike had to learn to make his conversation with Joan mutually enjoyable (quality) and he had to set aside enough time each week for conversation to meet her need (quantity).

Step 1: ***Determine whether improvement is needed in quality, quantity, or both.***

Before planning our strategy, Mike and I took another look at Joan's Emotional Needs Questionnaire (turn to page 258 in appendix B to review the questions she answered).

Joan had said she was "very unhappy" when Mike was unwilling to talk with her, and she was "somewhat happy" when he did talk to her. The reason she was only somewhat happy was that his conversation included many enemies, making it unpleasant much of the time.

Evaluating Mike's conversation, she rated her satisfaction a minus 3 (extremely dissatisfied). Both quantity and quality came up short (she answered no to the statements "My spouse talks to me as often as I need" and "I like the way my spouse talks to me").

How much conversation would meet her need? Joan estimated that fifteen times a day and five hours a week would suffice. Of course she really couldn't know for sure, since they had not talked nicely to each other for such a long time.

Joan also indicated that her need for conversation could be better met if Mike would stop criticizing her and lecturing her on what he considered her personal failures.

She acknowledged that these problems had become a thing of the past since he had overcome his two major Love Busters, angry outbursts and disrespectful judgments. But she was afraid they would return.

Step 2: ***Identify the friends and enemies of good conversation.***

To create an effective plan, we needed more detailed information. So I gave Joan a new questionnaire to complete, the Friends and Enemies of Good Conversation Inventory (printed for you in appendix C.)

The questionnaire gave Joan an opportunity to describe what she liked and disliked most about her conversations with Mike. She could identify friends and enemies that I had described to her (and to you, earlier in this chapter), and she could add some of her own.

As it turned out, Joan wanted Mike to develop all four of the friends we had discussed earlier. She wanted him to be more understanding, develop more of an interest in her favorite topics, balance the conversation so that she would be able to share her feelings equally with him, and give her more of his undivided attention.

The enemies that had dogged them for so many years had been essentially eliminated when we overcame Love Busters in the first phase of their counseling. When he learned to overcome angry outbursts, Mike stopped using conversation to punish her. And when he learned to overcome disrespectful judgments, he stopped trying to force his way of thinking on her and stopped dwelling on her mistakes.

So, with regard to eliminating any enemies of good conversation, our work was done. All that remained was to create some new friends.

Step 3: ***Create a strategy to meet the need for conversation.***

I gave Mike a form to help him think through a strategy that would help him meet Joan's need for conversation. (A copy of Strategy to Meet the Need of Conversation is in appendix D for your use.)

First, he had to review Joan's answers to *her* questionnaire, Friends and Enemies of Good Conversation Inventory, listing the conversational behavior Joan wanted him to learn. Then he described his plan for creating those friends of conversation.

To help him create understanding, he decided to buy a version of the Ungame, a deck of cards that asks personal questions of your game partner. Joan, of course, would also ask him questions from the cards they selected. If a question inspired him to ask others, he could ask whatever he wanted. Following the Policy of Joint Agreement, she could avoid answering any questions that made her uncomfortable. He suggested playing the game two hours each week, Saturdays from 2:00 to 4:00 P.M.

A strategy for developing interest in Joan's favorite topics of conversation was a little more complicated. First Mike needed to know what her favorite topics were. He thought he knew a few of them, but to be certain, he asked her to make a list of topics she would enjoy discussing. Then he would pick topics from her list that he also thought were interesting. He also planned to do a little reading on some of those topics where they shared an interest.

His strategy to balance the conversation was more mundane. He simply said he would be more careful to be sure he did not interrupt and would give her equal time to talk. He thought he could do it without an elaborate plan.

Undivided attention was also something he thought he could do without a plan, but when he told me his nonstrategy, I cautioned him. Men often think they're giving their wives undivided attention when they're not. It's harder than it seems. A man must maintain perfect eye contact and keep his mind focused on what his wife is saying. She feels unattractive and uninteresting when his attention strays.

But what if she is uninteresting, how does a man keep his attention focused then? The Policy of Joint Agreement races to the rescue. She isn't uninteresting: It's the subject. Conversation should always be mutually enjoyable, and if she is off on a subject that he finds boring, he should not suffer through it, pretending to be interested. It is up to him to change the subject to something they both find enjoyable.

With my help, Mike created a workable strategy. If he found his mind wandering, he would change the subject to a topic of mutual interest.

Since he had already overcome the enemies of good conversation, he didn't need to complete the remaining part of the strategy form. But for those who find enemies creeping into their conversation, the plan Mike used to overcome Love Busters is similar to those used to overcome the enemies of good conversation.

Finally, we needed to set a goal for the total amount of time he would spend each week talking with Joan. She had suggested fifteen times a day, five hours a week, and Mike accepted that as a goal. He would be keeping track of the number and duration of their talks.

Step 4: ***Measure your effectiveness in meeting the need for conversation.***

Finally, we put the strategies into action. But we needed a measure of success and failure, so that Mike would know whether he was on the right track. I gave Joan the Friends and Enemies of Good Conversation Worksheet (appendix E) to complete each week to give Mike feedback.

To be honest, this worksheet is a lot of trouble to complete, and Joan did not follow the instructions precisely. Rather than logging in every conversation immediately afterward, she took some time at the end of the day to remember the talks they'd had, noting some of the friends and enemies he had used. That gave him a good enough idea of how their conversations were going.

Joan's reports were very complimentary. Mike's effort to try to understand her, develop interest in her favorite topics, balance the conversation, and give her undivided attention paid huge dividends, and few enemies intruded. Almost from the beginning, she let him know how much she appreciated the way he talked to her, and he was depositing love units in unprecedented numbers.

Whenever I see the kind of accolades that Joan wrote in her worksheet, I am skeptical. "Are you writing these compliments just to encourage him?" I asked, "Or do you really feel good about the way he is talking to you?"

She assured me that she was genuinely thrilled with the way their conversation had improved. "I have my Mike back again," she said.

Meeting the Need for Conversation

1. Determine whether improvement is needed in quality, quantity, or both.
2. Identify the friends and enemies of good conversation.
3. Create a strategy.
4. Measure your effectiveness.

While Joan was evaluating their conversation each day, Mike was completing his own worksheet, counting how often he talked with his wife, giving her undivided attention, and for how long. He discovered that the conversations grew longer and more frequent as they got better. At first they met Joan's goal of fifteen conversations a day, totaling five hours a week. But after about a month, he was counting more than twenty-five conversations a day, and many weeks they talked together for more than fifteen hours.

That's the way it had been before they were married. They talked to each other every day, several times a day. And if they could not get together for a date, they would talk on the telephone for hours at a time. That's what had convinced Joan that Mike was the right man for her, because she just loved the way he talked with her.

This gave Mike an advantage over other men I've counseled: He had met her need for conversation before they were married. He knew how to do it. He had just stopped the conversation after they married.

It's more difficult for a man to meet his wife's need for conversation if he has never done so. But even in these cases, the vast majority of them end up receiving the same kind of good report that Joan gave Mike in her worksheets.

Of course, not all the couples I counsel do as well as Mike and Joan. The worksheets do not always show a successful resolution of the problem, at least not right away. But if they don't, we simply go back to the drawing board and plan a different strategy. Don't be discouraged if your initial efforts are ineffective. This is a crucial need, this need for conversation, and I strongly recommend that you make whatever effort is necessary to meet it.

Take pride in this effort. Become a professional at being the kind of conversationalist who meets your spouse's need in a far better way than anyone else could. You need to be the one who deposits the most love units in your spouse's Love Bank, and you can do that by meeting your spouse's need for conversation, if it's one of the most important needs.

Chapter Fifteen

Is It "Nobody Does It Better" or Is It "Never Gonna Get It"?

How to Meet the Emotional Need for Sexual Fulfillment

Many of the most important emotional needs can be met outside of marriage. You don't expect your spouse to avoid *conversation* with others—not unless you're one of those crazy talk-show guests who appear on shows with titles like "Domineering Spouses Who Lock Up Their Mates."

Nor do you discourage *recreational companionship*—she can still go shopping with her friends, and he can shoot hoops with his. *Honesty and openness* are good qualities we should all practice with everyone, and *financial support* is provided to the entire family and perhaps to other relatives and charities.

But if your spouse wants *sexual fulfillment* from someone else, you've got a serious problem. This is, without a doubt, the most exclusive emotional need. *Affection* comes in a distant second, but it's still acceptable to give and receive affection among family members and some close friends as long as it does not become sexual. But if you turn to anyone other than your spouse to meet your sexual need, you will cause unbearable pain and resentment.

With exclusivity comes responsibility. If you fail to meet your spouse's need for, say, recreational companionship, he or she can find that elsewhere. But if you expect your spouse to be your exclusive sex partner, you have a special responsibility to meet your spouse's sexual need.

Ideally a husband and wife should meet all of each other's most important emotional needs—better than anyone else does. When they don't, there is some danger that one or the other will fall in love with someone else, whoever succeeds in meeting the needs left unmet. For this reason, and a host of others, I encourage couples to make the meeting of all their most important emotional needs as exclusive as possible.

That means, if your most important emotional need is conversation, your best conversations should be with your spouse. If your most important emotional need is recreational companionship, your favorite recreational companion should also be your spouse. Why waste the deposit of so many love units on someone to whom you're not married?

If this is true of those other needs, it is *especially* true of sex. Since you cannot (and should not) tolerate a spouse who engages in sex outside of marriage, there is no other option. You have a special responsibility to meet that need in marriage.

How Sex Is like Water

Over the years, I have helped thousands of couples learn to experience sexual fulfillment. The men in particular have been eternally grateful. While there are some women with a strong need for sex, this is overwhelmingly a male need. Most husbands *need* to have sex more than their wives *want* to. As you might guess, this causes problems—misunderstanding, resentment, and frustration.

A man will do almost anything to motivate his wife to fulfill his sexual need. Granted, not all men are sensitive or caring about this, but women have a great deal of power here. Veto power.

Most men know what it feels like to need sex only to find their exclusive sex partner "not in the mood." I know of very few men who understand why a headache should prevent anyone from enjoying sex.

If a husband presses the issue and his wife reluctantly meets his sexual need, they both feel resentful. He feels cheated and she feels used.

The best way I can describe the feeling is to associate it with our need for water. Suppose your spouse is sitting beside a pitcher of water, and you are immobilized, completely dependent on him or her for a drink. You ask your spouse to give you a glass of water, but you're told to wait a while. You patiently wait, and ask again a few hours later. Your spouse still seems unwilling to help you quench your thirst. As you become more and more thirsty, you become angry and demand water, whereupon your spouse gets up and leaves the room, telling you that you will never get water by acting that way. Only after much begging does your spouse reluctantly bring you a glass of water.

Are you grateful? Are you satisfied? No! You are angry and resentful because you felt your spouse should have been kind enough to bring you the water the first time you asked. In spite of your resentment, however, you know that in a while you'll be thirsty again. So you have to be careful what you say—you don't want to wait even longer next time. You simply simmer in your anger, wondering how you ever could have put yourself in such a position.

I've had conversations with many women who challenged my analogy. No one has ever died from having had too little sex, they say. That's true, but *marriages* have died for lack of sex. When sex is one partner's most important need and the other fails to meet it, their love cannot grow.

Being male, I'm not in a good position to argue my case, because most women don't believe I can be objective. Maybe not, but I know that if someone has a need that should not be met outside marriage, it must be met within marriage. If that person—man or woman—needs sexual fulfillment and cannot get it from the spouse, that person is in a vulnerable and frustrating position.

Occasionally a woman is given a prescription for the male hormone testosterone to correct a hormonal imbalance. When that happens, she usually experiences a sexual desire that seems to come from nowhere. Some women go into a panic when this feeling comes over them because they feel so vulnerable—they suddenly have a strong sense of need they didn't have before. But most men have that feeling most of their lives, and it's particularly strong when they're young.

Some women have argued that sexual aggression is motivated by a need for power, claiming that men don't seem to honor a woman's "no" because they want to show their dominance. But I don't agree. Such an argument doesn't take the strength of the sex drive into account.

Using my water example again, suppose you have been without water for two days and someone offers you a glass of water. Then, just as you are about to drink, the water is taken away. How do you think you'd react? Aggressively, perhaps. But where would that aggression come from? Your need for power? Hardly. *From your thirst!*

This is by no means an excuse for rapists and molesters. But I do feel that the sex drive of many people, especially men, is one of the strongest drives there is. And in marriage, the unmet need for sex can be the cause of enormous resentment and frustration, because of the exclusive commitment involved.

Sexual Habits Make You Irresistible or Repulsive

Mike and Joan never did have a very fulfilling sexual relationship. They decided not to make love before marriage, anticipating the great satisfaction they'd find on their honeymoon. Of course you already know how their honeymoon turned out. It was a big disappointment for both of them, but especially for Joan. She had saved herself for what she expected to be heaven on earth with Mike, but it turned out to be a glimpse of hell. Mike felt cheated and Joan felt used. Those general feelings had continued throughout their life together.

In our counseling sessions they had managed to learn conversational fulfillment fairly easily, because they had conversed well in the past and merely had to rediscover this lost art. But sexual fulfillment would be much more difficult, since they had never experienced it.

Ralph and Diane also had sexual problems, but both of them had known sexual fulfillment earlier in their marriage. Over a number of years, they had grown apart, becoming incompatible. Sex was one of many victims of their withdrawal from each other. For years they had slept in different bedrooms with no sexual contact at all. However, in spite of their years of sexual isolation, it was much easier for them to restore sexual fulfillment than it was for Mike and Joan, because they had experienced it at one time.

Like the need for conversation, the need for sexual fulfillment can be met if you develop good habits. There is a right way and there is a wrong way to make love. The right way takes the feelings of your spouse into account, and the wrong way doesn't. We could talk about the friends and enemies of good sex, but let's just call them good and bad sexual habits.

Men find themselves sexually frustrated for many reasons. (Some women get frustrated, too, but for now I'll focus on husbands, since they're usually the ones who need sex more.) Sometimes sexual ignorance keeps couples from enjoying all the pleasure that sex has to offer. Or Love Busters ruin the bond of intimacy between husband and wife. Biological factors can also affect sex, such as infection or medicine that lowers sex drive.

But the main cause of sexual frustration is this: Many men have developed sexual habits that are repulsive to their wives. Not only is this the most prominent reason, but it's the one thing men can do something about right away. The Policy of Joint Agreement can guide these men out of the mess they've created for themselves.

To rephrase the policy in sexual terms: *Never make love in a way that does not have the enthusiastic agreement of both you and your spouse.* Getting rid of the double negatives, we might say: *Only make love in a way that has the enthusiastic agreement of both you and your spouse.*

When you're making love and you fail to take your spouse's feelings into account, you're repulsive. Your spouse doesn't want to be near you. But if you follow the Policy of Joint Agreement whenever you make love, I guarantee you, you won't be repulsive but irresistible.

> Only make love in a way that has the enthusiastic agreement of both you and your spouse.

Granted, your sex drive tends to put your Taker in charge of the sex act. It knows what makes you happy and encourages you to get it regardless of how anyone else feels. But even your Taker can understand the wisdom of planning for the future. The best way to have frequent and fulfilling sex is to learn to accommodate your spouse's feelings.

The Stages of Sexual Experience

The sexual experience has five very important stages. In each of these stages, there are good habits that lead to sexual fulfillment and bad habits that lead to sexual disaster. These habits make you either irresistible or repulsive in each of these stages, and for the sake of your marriage (and your emotional need) you must learn the good habits and avoid the bad ones.

1. Where It All Begins: ***The stage of sexual desire.***

Do you feel like making love right now? If you are like most women, you will say no. If you are like most men, you will say yes (or, "I could be, if you'd give me a minute").

You're in the stage of sexual desire when you *want* to make love but are not feeling sexually aroused at the time. Most men want to make love most of the time, particularly when they are young. Testosterone is the culprit. The level of testosterone drops as we age, and sexual desire is usually reduced along with it.

Most men report a feeling that accompanies sexual desire, but it is not the same as sexual arousal. The feeling is sometimes similar to butterflies in the stomach, but it is not unpleasant to most men. On the other hand, when women experience this feeling, many find it unpleasant, particularly those who have been raised in a tradition where sexual feelings are repressed.

For most women, this initial stage seems to be more sexual willingness than sexual desire. They are receptive to lovemaking, but not necessarily desiring it.

But even without desire, willingness is of critical importance to women in lovemaking, and it determines whether or not the rest of the experience will be pleasant or unpleasant. I believe that sexual willingness depends on emotional bonding, and most women experience sexual willingness only when they have bonded with their partner.

That's why Joan and Mike had so much trouble making love after their honeymoon fight. Joan felt disconnected from Mike, so she was incapable of entering the stage of sexual desire. And without that desire, or willingness, the rest of the sexual experience was disgusting to her.

Mike, on the other hand, had no such qualms. He was in the stage of sexual desire in spite of the fight. His need for sex overcame his need for emotional bonding. In other words, he could enjoy making love to a person from whom he was emotionally disconnected because his need for sex was so great.

Granted, men enjoy sex immeasurably more when they are in the state of Intimacy. But they don't exactly suffer when not in that state. Most women do not know what that's like.

If sexual desire requires emotional bonding for most women, then it's extremely important for men to appreciate the importance of emotional bonding. And what helps create emotional bonding? Affection, attentiveness, warmth of personality, kindness, and thoughtfulness. All the things that deposit the most love units. Those are some of the good habits that help create this first stage of the sexual experience.

And what destroys emotional bonding? Anger, disrespect, demands, annoying habits, and dishonesty. All the Love Busters that withdraw love units. Those bad habits prevent couples from entering that first stage.

If you expect to make love to your spouse very often, get rid of every Love Buster in sight. Each one of them represents a good reason for your spouse not to meet your need.

For most women, the sexual attractiveness of their husbands is in direct proportion to their Love Bank balances. *How effective is her husband in meeting her emotional needs?* That's what turns her on. As a rule, the more "in love" a woman is, the more willing she is to make love.

So if your wife is having trouble getting through the stage of sexual desire, I suggest you first eliminate the Love Busters in your marriage and then get to work meeting her most important emotional needs. The rest should be a piece of cake.

I have counseled hundreds, if not thousands, of women who thought they would never have sexual feelings toward their husbands again, only to discover these feelings returning with greater strength than they'd ever known. What changed? Did they have to develop a new attitude about sex? No. In most cases the only change was in the husband, who learned how to stop hurting the wife and started meeting her emotional needs.

2. Sexual Feelings Are Born: ***The stage of sexual arousal.***

The stage of sexual arousal is marked by some distinctive physiological changes in men and women. The penis becomes erect, and the vagina secretes a lubricating fluid. Distinctly sexual feelings accompany these physical changes, and when they occur, most people consider it a sexual experience.

Most men view this sexual arousal, particularly in women, as a signal to cut loose sexually, throwing caution to the wind. Women do not necessarily see it the same way.

For most women, feelings of arousal are very fragile. Insensitivity by their husbands can turn them off quickly and make arousal very difficult to restore.

Almost every woman reading this book can think of times where her husband did something in the stage of arousal that completely turned her off. And once turned off, it's hard to get turned on again.

Most women want their husbands to follow a particular procedure that makes it easy for them to become sexually aroused and prevents them from losing that feeling. This procedure defines good sexual habits. It usually follows a sequence of steps that begins with affection and nonsexual touching. Blatantly sexual acts, such as touching a woman's genital area, are usually regarded as a major turnoff and not at all helpful in the early stages of arousal. In the later stages, such touching is not only encouraged by most women, but often necessary to help them reach heightened sexual feelings.

Something as innocent as a small deviation from her preferred procedure can be enough to break the spell. But most men are much more blatant in their insensitivity, doing things to their wives in a state of sexual passion that they know their wives don't like. It's their Takers forgetting about the Policy of Joint Agreement again. It's shortsighted. Next time, their wives won't be as willing to go through the ordeal again.

Joan had not had sex with anyone before she married Mike. Her first experience, on the night of their wedding, was enjoyable (they had not had their disagreement yet), but she did not experience sexual arousal. She was simply willing to have intercourse with the man she loved.

In fact, in all the years she had been married, she had not experienced sexual arousal more than a few times, and even then she didn't know why she was aroused. The truth was, she did not know how to create those feelings. She saw lovemaking as affection, where she and Mike would hug and kiss each other while having intercourse. Most of the time, because she was not sexually aroused, her vagina was not lubricated, and they had to use lubricating jelly whenever they made love.

But Mike wanted Joan to be sexually aroused—that was his definition of quality sex. I explained this to her: "For Mike to be sexually fulfilled, you have to share sexual feelings with him whenever you make love. Besides, once you learn how to become sexually aroused, it will be much more enjoyable for you to meet his needs."

She didn't believe me at first. For her, sexual arousal was completely unnecessary. She enjoyed affection during sex, and she was willing to let him have intercourse with her to meet his sexual need. But why did she have to be aroused herself?

"Have you ever tried to be affectionate with Mike when he didn't feel like being affectionate?" I asked.

"Many times," she sighed.

"If Mike tried to meet your need for affection without feeling affection for you, how would you feel about it?" I asked.

"I'd hate it." Then she paused. "I see your point."

One of the most important insights about need fulfillment is that it must be mutual and enthusiastic. Affection only works when both spouses feel affection for each other. Conversation only works when both spouses enjoy talking to each other. And sex only works when both spouses are sexually aroused by each other.

There are many books on how women can learn to become sexually aroused and learn to climax. At the end of this chapter I will list a few of them. Joan came up with a method all by herself and then taught Mike how to help her become aroused. It took about two weeks for them to achieve a level of sexual experience that they had never had before in their marriage.

In most of the couples I counsel, the women are sexually experienced and know how to teach their husbands to arouse them sexually. In these cases, I don't need to discuss this issue with them. After we have swept out the Love Busters and their husbands have learned to meet their most important needs, they have sex as often as their husbands want. And each time, these women are sexually aroused.

Stages of Sexual Experience

1. Desire
2. Arousal
3. Plateau
4. Climax
5. Recovery

Of course women aren't the only ones who have difficulty being sexually aroused. Men sometimes have the same problem. In older men, this is often due to lower levels of testosterone. But I have counseled a number of men who are turned off for the same reason many women are: They feel emotionally disconnected.

I tried to help Frank overcome impotence a few years ago. He claimed to have a wonderfully fulfilling relationship with his wife, Karen, but he simply could not perform sexually. Then I discovered that he was having an affair.

In Frank's other relationship, his sexual performance was superb. It turned out that his emotional distance from his wife prevented him from being sexually aroused by her. After the affair ended and his sexual relationship with his wife was restored, his impotence with her was cured.

3. Sexual Feelings Intensify: ***The stage of sexual plateau.***

The plateau stage differs from arousal both physiologically and emotionally. The erect penis becomes hard and the lubricated vagina contracts. And the sexual feelings born in arousal now intensify. Many couples find this stage to be the most sexually satisfying and try to maintain it as long as possible.

While most women need very special and increased stimulation to reach a plateau, men need much less stimulation. Intercourse itself is almost always sufficient stimulation for men, but there are relatively few women who can predictably reach this stage with intercourse alone unless they use a quick thrusting motion with a voluntary tightening of the vagina. Many women exercise their pubococcygeus (PCG) muscle each day so that, when they make love, they can tighten the vagina enough to reach the plateau stage.

The thrusting position is also critical for most women. Women usually prefer being on top with a supporting pillow under their husbands to create greater stimulation to the clitoris. Rapid thrusting, tightened vagina, and correct position are all good habits that help create this stage of sex. If a man does not give his wife freedom to create those good habits, he loses out on sexual fulfillment because he prevents her from enjoying the experience with him.

Unfortunately, rapid thrusting coupled with a tightened vagina sometimes creates a sexual problem for a man, premature ejaculation, brought on by too much sexual stimulation. He sometimes experiences a climax too soon and loses his erection before she can reach a plateau or climax. Because of these inherent differences in timing, many couples have trouble with this sexual stage, even if they're emotionally bonded and both enthusiastically willing to get the most out of their sexual relationship. Most of the couples I've counseled eventually solved the problem through tried and proven procedures that are explained in popular books on sex. (It usually involves bringing a woman to a heightened state of arousal prior to intercourse, along with teaching a man to remain in the plateau stage without a climax for about ten minutes. This is usually time enough for a woman to reach the plateau and climax at least once.)

Joan and Mike were very naive sexually, and making the most of this stage of sex required quite a bit of sexual practice and sophistication. But before I stopped seeing them—for a total of six months of counseling—she had reached the plateau stage during intercourse on a fairly regular basis. As long as they had a loving and caring relationship, they didn't mind practicing, and it was only a matter of time before their practice paid off. Once they learned a technique that worked for them (good sexual habits), it brought out their best sexual feelings. The practice involved no pressure, no guilt, no frustration, simply a wonderful adventure into coming to understand each other's physical and emotional reactions.

4. Ecstasy or Anxiety? ***The stage of sexual climax.***

A climax (or orgasm) is the most intense sexual feeling men or women experience. Physiologically, a man's penis ejaculates semen in bursts and a woman's vagina repeatedly tightens and relaxes involuntarily. Men and women who reach the plateau stage are only one small step from reaching a climax; it only takes a little more time and stimulation.

One interesting difference between men and women is that women can climax repeatedly, while most men can climax only once when they make love. Almost any woman who can climax can also learn to climax several times with relatively little additional effort.

I counseled one woman who said she could climax more than two hundred times during a time of lovemaking. Granted, it took some training on the part of her husband and more time than most couples care to devote to lovemaking, but sex was definitely the high point of her day.

However, I have counseled many more women who know how to climax but often prefer not to. Most men find this puzzling. *Why have sex without an orgasm?* Often a man feels personally responsible for his wife's orgasm and sees it as his own failure when she does not climax. The husband needs to put aside this attitude and let his wife have a free choice whether or not to climax.

For many, the peak sexual experience is one where both spouses climax together. So they try to time things for that outcome. But sometimes this emphasis on a simultaneous orgasm distorts the entire lovemaking experience. It puts too much pressure on a woman to experience something that, in perspective, is not that important.

When either spouse feels pressure to perform, it takes the joy out of lovemaking. Instead of feeling immersed in love for each other, couples become preoccupied with technique and specific sexual outcomes. Couples who do not climax together, or fail to climax at all, have not failed. It should not be a cause for disappointment or dissatisfaction.

On the other hand, women should know how to climax. If you do not climax because you have never learned to do so, then you should practice until you have learned how. But I believe it is a skill that women should bring to their lovemaking. Once the skill is there, then it's up to the woman when she wants to implement it.

Ignorance is a great and unnecessary barrier to sexual fulfillment in both men and women. That's why I encourage women to learn to experience sexual climax, much the way I encourage people to attend college. It's a skill that you should not go without. Once you have it, it's for life, and no one I know wishes they had not learned it.

Joan had never experienced a climax, so I gave her a book to read that showed her how. (Kline-Graber and Graber, *Woman's Orgasm.* See resource list at end of chapter). She followed the assignments and was able to experience her first climax within two weeks of her first assignment. The book also showed her how to have an orgasm during intercourse. While she did not achieve that objective while I was counseling with them, she continued to pursue it after they stopped seeing me.

5. Afterglow or Resentment? ***The stage of sexual recovery.***

Recovery is an important last stage of the sexual experience. Physiologically, the penis relaxes and is no longer erect. The vagina stops secreting lubricating fluids and also relaxes. Emotionally, men and women experience a warm feeling of contentment.

For many couples, the effect is very relaxing, and many women find it prepares them for a very restful sleep. At the same time, it usually gives a woman a feeling of unprecedented closeness to the man with whom she has shared her most intimate experience. Some women react with a desire to share their deepest feelings; they want to talk to their husbands after they make love. Others just want to embrace for the time that it takes for recovery to be complete.

Unfortunately, many men, who recover much more quickly than women, do not see recovery as a necessary part of lovemaking. As soon as they climax, they roll over and go to sleep or are out of bed and on to their next project. When that happens, they risk leaving their wives feeling very abandoned at a moment of intense vulnerability. That, in turn, can lead to resentment that carries to the next time he wants to make love.

I encourage couples to discuss the recovery stage with each other to be certain that they end their lovemaking with consideration for each other's feelings. Sometimes all it takes is a little communication to resolve the problem once and for all.

Joan noticed that, in the stage of recovery, she felt like telling Mike about all the times he had hurt her feelings. That's a common instinct in women who have experienced years of Love Busters. While the Love Busters were gone, the memories were still there, and they seemed to pop up after they made love. I reminded her of the enemies of good conversation and explained how destructive it can be to dwell on past mistakes, particularly when sharing an intimate moment.

"But why can't I express my deepest and most honest feelings?" she asked. "Why should I keep that part of me away from Mike? Shouldn't he know how I feel?"

Good question! What about honesty and openness? Why shouldn't couples feel free to say whatever they feel?

Joan wouldn't be telling Mike anything he didn't already know. Dwelling on his past mistakes would only make him feel bad without offering any new information that might help the marriage.

Joan felt a need to say these things to get them off her chest, which would make her feel good at his expense. But where would the conversation go? He would apologize for acts he'd apologized for many times already. She would expect him to explain to her how a man who promised to care for her would treat her with such disregard. The whole conversation would have nowhere to go but downhill.

Men often complain that, after they make love, their wives "punish" them by bringing up their feelings of resentment. But women don't really intend this as punishment for making love, they just want to be open and candid at a time of emotional bonding. Still, I urge women to avoid this enemy of good conversation, even though it seems instinctive at the time.

A Plan to Meet the Need for Sexual Fulfillment

If I had told Joan when she first set foot in my office that within two months she would be making an effort to meet Mike's need for sexual fulfillment, she probably would have walked out. Sex had been a nightmare for her from the second day of their honeymoon right up to the day she agreed to learn to meet his need.

What appealed to her was the Policy of Joint Agreement. In the process of trying to meet his need, she would never be required to do anything that did not meet with her enthusiastic agreement. While she agreed to work on the problem, she would not be forced to do anything unpleasant.

As with conversation, meeting the need for sexual fulfillment involves *quality* and *quantity*. So we used a plan that targeted each of these considerations for review and, if necessary, improvement.

Step 1: ***Determine whether improvement is needed in quality, quantity, or both.***

Joan and I spent about fifteen minutes reading Mike's Emotional Needs Questionnaire as it related to sexual fulfillment (see appendix B).

Mike said he was "very unhappy" when Joan refused to make love to him, and only "somewhat happy" when she agreed. They had not made love for over a year because he simply did not enjoy forcing her to have sex with him. And she was certainly not going to volunteer.

He reported being "extremely dissatisfied" with their sexual relationship, expressing unhappiness with both its quality and quantity. He wanted to make love at least three times a week, and he wanted her to respond sexually whenever they made love. They certainly had a long way to go!

Joan could not imagine ever meeting his standards for quality or quantity. "Even if I loved him again, I wouldn't want to have sex that often!" she said. "And I can't just turn it on and off. He'll have to be satisfied just to have sex again."

Although it feels awkward to me to explain the predicament of most men when it comes to sex, I charged ahead anyway. This was when I used the comparison with conversation.

"For you to be happy," I explained, "Mike needs to talk with you often and with enthusiasm. You wouldn't enjoy it at all if he was obviously bored or resentful when he talked with you."

"I see your point," she finally said. "But I can't imagine ever being enthusiastic about having sex."

Not only did she lack any positive memories of sex to think back on, but her experiences with Mike had been quite negative. She had never understood her own sexual responses, and Love Busters had ruined any pleasure she might have had when they made love. From her perspective, sex was associated with the worst experiences of her life. How could she hope to overcome such an aversion?

Though Joan was sure it would never happen, we completed this first step by defining what Mike considered sexual fulfillment: (1) Sex three times a week; and (2) Joan responding sexually whenever they made love.

Step 2: ***Determine your understanding of the five stages of sex and your ability to experience them.***

Before Joan left my office, I gave her a new questionnaire to complete for our next session, the Sexual Experience Inventory (appendix F).

The questions simply ask about the sexual responses of the person in each of the five stages of sex (desire, arousal, plateau, climax, and recovery) and his or her ability to create those responses. With this information, we could identify the stages that needed work.

Joan answered the questions very defensively. In several blanks she wrote that she would discuss the answer with me but not put it in writing. Her reaction reflected the years she had been in emotional withdrawal and had not let Mike get close enough to hurt her. By the end of our session, however, she agreed to write down her answers so Mike could read them later.

Each section asks the same four questions:

1. How often do you experience [the stage in question]?
2. Describe the conditions that tend to create [that stage]?
3. Are you more likely to experience it with or without your spouse?
4. If you are having difficulty with [this stage], are you willing to create a plan with your spouse to overcome the difficulty?

Since she never masturbated and was not having sex with Mike regularly, Joan's sexual experience was very limited. She reported having a sexual desire occasionally but not usually with Mike. She would fantasize about some make-believe person with whom she would have a wonderfully romantic relationship. When she did that, it would usually arouse her sexually, but that's as far as it would ever get.

However, in response to the fourth question for each stage she expressed willingness to create a strategy to help her overcome the difficulties she had.

Most of the clients I counsel are not nearly as naive as Joan. They have a rather complete understanding of each stage and know how to experience each of them, with or without their spouse. But some have an incomplete understanding—one stage or another needs work. (The stages of plateau and climax seem to be the most poorly understood.)

But Joan needed to start at the beginning, with the stage of desire, and work completely through to the stage of recovery. She was willing to try.

Step 3: ***Create a strategy to meet the need for sexual fulfillment.*** I gave Joan five copies of another form, Strategy to Discover a Stage of Sexual Experience (appendix G), one for each of the stages. We took the stages one at a time and in sequence.

First we worked on sexual desire, her willingness to have sex with Mike. She knew enough about herself to suggest that conversation and affection would help. During their dating years, she had been sexually motivated whenever they spent an evening talking and being affectionate with each other. Maybe it could happen again. We would see whether Mike's renewed ability to converse and be affectionate with her would create a sexual desire.

Not much of a plan. It's easy to make up strategies for other people. When Mike read this, he playfully suggested that they first try making love three times a week, and *then* he might be a better conversationalist. And he would certainly be more affectionate!

But he was already trying to meet her need for conversation and he understood (that is, his *Taker* understood) that showing affection would make Joan more responsive. She had such an aversion to sex that we had to approach the problem with great sensitivity. Fortunately Mike understood this.

As it turned out, Joan responded to him much more quickly than either of them anticipated. The very next week she reported feeling some sexual desire for him.

It's not always this easy. I worked with one couple for six months before the wife felt any sexual desire at all. Each time I saw them, the husband seemed ready to come apart emotionally because his wife never wanted him to even touch her. Then one day, she not only felt sexual desire for the first time in years but was able to be sexually aroused. She climaxed during intercourse, and they both reported that it was the best sexual experience they had ever had. His patience throughout those six months was the deciding factor in the sudden recovery of their sexual relationship.

I cannot emphasize enough the importance of the Policy of Joint Agreement, especially when it comes to sex. Never engage in any sexual experience that does not meet with your spouse's enthusiastic agreement. This policy pays gigantic dividends.

As we turned to the next stage, arousal, Joan was way ahead of us. She had already been thinking about what would sexually arouse her, and she had tried a few techniques without Mike knowing what she was doing.

Joan knew she'd be turned off if Mike made any overt sexual advances. So she had to teach him a whole new way of being affectionate, a way that was not just a stepping-stone toward sex. Specifically, he was not to touch her breasts or genital area.

That gave her the courage to try to kiss him in ways that she found sexually arousing. She also took note of where she liked being touched and what mood she needed to be in.

I encouraged Mike to let Joan teach him what she learned about herself, and he was never to take advantage of her vulnerability. He could go no further than she wanted, and was to stop whenever she wanted to stop.

At this point in the therapeutic process I sometimes run into serious trouble. I was afraid Mike's Taker would take matters into his own hands.

Look at it from his side. He is talking to Joan more than he has talked to her in years, and he's being more affectionate than he's been in years. Some of this is hard work for Mike; he's still on the tough end of the learning curve. And now, even though he listed sex as his number 1 need, he is supposed to avoid being sexually aggressive. Joan and I are telling him to try to ignore his sexual drive for the time being and just be affectionate for affection's sake. Easier said than done!

Many men stumble at this point. *Where is the fairness*? yells the Taker. *Here I am meeting her needs. When will she meet mine?*

Meeting the Need for Sexual Fulfillment

1. Determine whether improvement is needed in quality, quantity, or both.
2. Determine your understanding of the five stages of sexual experience and your ability to experience them.
3. Create a strategy.
4. Measure your effectiveness in meeting the need.

It's natural for strong emotions to surface here. The stakes are high and the wounds deep. One of my jobs as a counselor is to keep the emotional lid on the situation long enough for the solution to start working.

But some men are not encouraged by the fact that we are working on getting *all* the high-ranked needs met. In the most sensitive part of the process, they blow it. *We've made enough progress*, they contend. *My wife owes me this!* And just when their wife is beginning to respond sexually to them, they force sex on her. This does not always ruin the process we've started, but it certainly sets us back.

Fortunately Mike showed self-control, making no sexual advances until Joan gave him the go-ahead. As with her feeling of sexual desire, Joan was a quick learner in the area of sexual arousal, too. As Mike gently rubbed her back, legs, and arms, she freed up her sexual responses.

Once Joan was able to be sexually aroused by Mike, she was ready to plan strategies for the stages of plateau, climax, and recovery. I gave her the book I mentioned earlier *(Woman's Orgasm)* to help her learn to reach a sexual plateau and climax, even during intercourse. So her strategy was to follow the plan outlined in that book.

When Mike had first said he wanted to make love at least three times a week and wanted her to be sexually aroused each time, Joan considered it ridiculous. But it wasn't long before she met and exceeded his expectations, as long as he kept up his end of the bargain, offering conversation and affection. Soon she was regularly experiencing the plateau and climax stages with Mike.

Finally Joan wrote a simple plan for the stage of recovery. After making love, she wanted Mike to be affectionate with her for at least fifteen minutes. He was more than happy to oblige.

Step 4: ***Measure your effectiveness in meeting the need for sexual fulfillment.***

Joan completed a Sexual Experience Worksheet (appendix H) for each of the five stages of sex and discussed her answers in her sessions with me. I gave Mike the Sexual Fulfillment Worksheet (appendix I) to measure Joan's effectiveness in meeting his need. He was to complete it each time they made love and then discuss it with Joan.

That may sound as if he was "grading" her "performance"—but it was actually a way to keep them talking about this very personal issue. Still, some couples are so emotionally vulnerable with regard to sex that it's a bad idea to "keep score" of sexual fulfillment. If you find it difficult to measure your progress, keep it simple. Just count the times you make love and give a rough idea of how you feel about it.

In Mike's case, the worksheets were full of appreciative comments about Joan. And three times a week? By the time I stopped seeing them, they were making love almost every day. As you might guess, Mike was delighted with Joan's sexual enthusiasm—he thought a miracle had taken place.

I'm sure it seemed miraculous, but the reason for Joan's newfound enthusiasm was that she had learned to enjoy making love. And Mike had learned to make it an enjoyable experience for her. She had resisted it earlier in their marriage, partly because of Love Busters unrelated to sex, but also because Mike had made sex unpleasant for her. Now it was something she looked forward to as much as he did.

In fact if they had made a new list of emotional needs, Joan might have included sexual fulfillment among her most important needs. As with many of the couples I've counseled, once they became sexually compatible, they lost sight of exactly whose need was being met.

Suggested Reading

Books written from a Christian perspective include:

Wheat, Ed, M.D., and Gaye Wheat. *Intended for Pleasure.* Grand Rapids, Mich.: Fleming H. Revell Co., 1977. Dr. Wheat combines his vast knowledge from a long medical practice with his strong Christian convictions and understanding of the needs and God-given design of men and women to produce an excellent discussion of new approaches to sexual intimacy in marriage. See especially chapter 5, "One Flesh: The Techniques of Lovemaking," which discusses the four phases of sexual intercourse. Other good chapters include chapter 6, "Solutions to Common Problems," and chapter 7, "For the Impotent Husband: Fulfillment Again."

Penner, Clifford, and Joyce Penner. *The Gift of Sex.* Waco, Tex.: Word Inc., 1981. This book grows out of a widely popular counseling and seminar ministry conducted by Dr. Penner and his wife. Clifford Penner is a clinical psychologist and his wife is a registered nurse. Together they make an excellent sexual therapy team, and they have reported their observations, advice, and practical suggestions to produce a very helpful manual for married couples. See especially chapter 8, "Sexual Response—Four Phases"; chapter 20, "Enhancing the Sexual Response"; and chapter 31, "No Arousal or No Release—Some Women's Frustrations."

Books written from a secular perspective:

Kaplan, Helen Singer, M.D., Ph.D. *The New Sex Therapy.* New York: *New York Times* Book Co., 1974. While this book is more than twenty years old, it's still a valuable guide to help married couples discover the nature and causes of sexual dysfunction and develop new techniques for solving their problems. The best chapters are 15–20, which cover the three most common sexual problems of men and women. The rest is probably too technical for most readers. Call 1-800-733-3000 (Random House order department) to order the book.

Kline-Graber, Georgia, R.N., and Benjamin Graber, M.D. *Woman's Orgasm: A Guide to Sexual Satisfaction.* New York: Warner Books,

1975. This book is particularly useful to women who do not know how to climax because of the way it takes the reader through the process, clearly and step by step. The chapter entitled "A Ten-Step Program for Achieving Orgasm with Intercourse" is excellent, especially for women who know how to climax, but not during intercourse. I found that not all of the recommended steps are necessary to achieve a successful outcome. You may modify them to accommodate your values and sensitivities. Call 1-800-343-9204 (Little, Brown order department) to order the book.

Chapter Sixteen

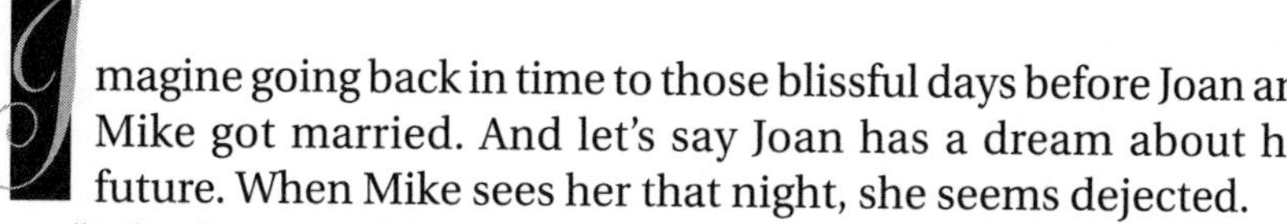

When You Need Me, I'll Be There

How to Meet the Emotional Need for Affection

Imagine going back in time to those blissful days before Joan and Mike got married. And let's say Joan has a dream about her future. When Mike sees her that night, she seems dejected.

"What's wrong?" he asks.

"I dreamed that we were married, but we never talked anymore."

Putting a reassuring arm around her shoulders, Mike says, "That would never happen. You know that. We'll always talk to each other."

But let's say Mike has also had a disturbing dream—that he and Joan would rarely make love after getting married and that it would never be much fun. Of course, he wouldn't tell Joan about this dream, but it would trouble him deeply—if he thought it could ever happen.

"But there was even more to my dream," Joan says. "You stopped showing me affection. You were cold and distant. You never touched me."

Now Mike takes Joan fully in his arms. "That's crazy, honey. We will always be affectionate. See, we can't keep our hands off each other."

"And you're always doing nice things for me," Joan adds. "Like these flowers you brought tonight and that little necklace you gave me last week."

"Why would we ever stop being affectionate, huh? Relax. It was just a silly dream."

As we return from our little Twilight Zone episode, we realize the truth of the matter. Conversation and sex did stop soon after the wedding, and by the time they came to see me, affectionate behavior was long gone. If *before* the wedding they had been able to glimpse what life would be like just a year or two *after* the wedding, they surely would have called the whole thing off. Then again, if they had had that glimpse, they probably would have considered it "just a silly dream." Who could imagine that these two talkative, passionate, crazy-about-each-other kids would become strangers in their own home?

Affection was probably the most surprising casualty of their marriage. Conversation changes as people's interests change, and sex was uncharted territory for both of them, but affection? They were always touching and hugging, continually showering each other with expressions of their love. They loved each other more than they had ever loved anyone before and they freely described those feelings to each other whenever they could. How do you lose that?

The Emotional Need for Affection

Affection is the cement of a relationship. Without it, virtually everything else falls apart. Like many other couples, Mike and Joan became bitterly disappointed as they saw their mutual affection fade. If they had maintained their affection, they might have held together other aspects of their marriage. But as affection slipped away, so did the rest.

Because of this cementlike quality, the emotional need for affection is often ranked high, especially by women. It is perhaps the most strategically significant need a couple can meet.

Remember, an emotional need is something that, when met, makes you feel terrific. When it's not met, you feel frustrated and unfulfilled. When someone has a need for affection, what exactly do they need?

To put it simply, they need to know they are loved. This can be expressed in words, cards, gifts, hugs, kisses, and common courtesies.

Earlier I described two forms of love: romantic love and caring love. Romantic love is an intense feeling of attraction toward someone, while caring love is a decision to help make someone happy by meeting his or her needs.

In marriage, affection is the expression of both kinds of love, but especially caring love. When a spouse is affectionate, he or she is communicating concern for problems faced and a willingness to help solve those problems.

Affection, by definition, is expressive and symbolic. Take, for instance, a hug. What is it?

In purely physical terms, a hug gives you a warm feeling, a feeling of being surrounded (or squeezed). To a minor extent, a hug can meet a need for warmth or physical contact. But hugs are effective primarily because of what they mean. A hug is a symbol of intent to care for the person being hugged. "I am here for you. I will protect you. I care for you." When you are hugged, you feel surrounded by the person's love.

Of course, if that's all it is, a symbol with no substance, the hug doesn't mean much. Perhaps we have all experienced insincere hugs at dinner parties or in church lobbies. But if the hug is accompanied by acts of thoughtfulness and concern, then with each hug the recipient is reminded of the security there is in being loved.

It's hard for most women to imagine, but a great many people (especially men) fail to see the importance of affection. These people apparently don't need much affection themselves, so they don't see what all the fuss is about.

Such people are not necessarily uncaring. They may actually feel a great amount of care for their spouses; they just don't see a need to express it very often. When they do express their love, it's often with concrete actions rather than simple symbols such as words and touches. For instance, a nonaffectionate husband may work extra hours to afford a vacation trip his wife has been wanting, but never say, "I love you." He prefers the "real" expression of love (his work), to the symbolic expression (mere words).

Habits of Affection Can Make You Irresistible or Repulsive

Since affection is a symbol of care, it's very important to be certain that the symbol is being interpreted correctly. Misunderstood, your act of affection can send a noncaring message. When the person you hug interprets it as your way of saying, "I care about you and want to meet your needs," your affection makes the person feel good. It deposits love units.

But you've probably had some hugs you'd rather not have. Sometimes a hugger gets too close, holds you too tight, or doesn't know you well enough to hug you that way. In those cases, the message is: "I'm doing this for my own satisfaction and don't care whether or not you like it." It makes you feel bad and withdraws love units from the hugger's account.

In other words, the interpretation of your affection can make you either irresistible or repulsive. That's why your habits of affection must clearly convey the message of care and protection.

When the person being hugged has a need for sexual fulfillment, the hug can have sexual overtones without reducing the impact of the message. In that case the hug would communicate sexual care for someone who appreciates it. But what if the person hugged, let's say it's the wife, does not rank sexual fulfillment as an important need? Then the sexual implications of her husband's hug may be resented. The hug is communicating his selfish desire to meet one of his own needs, not his desire to meet her needs.

That's why, in most cases, a woman can express affection to a man in sexually arousing ways without any fear of resentment—because most men have a strong need for sexual fulfillment. But a man must be careful to avoid expressing affection sexually, if he wants the affection to communicate his sincere desire to meet her needs. Many men don't see much of a difference between these two needs, affection and sexual fulfillment. To them, a hug is foreplay. But women know the difference very well. Unless a woman has a strong need for sexual fulfillment, she'll feel used when her husband zooms past affection and into sex.

Mike tried to be affectionate with Joan only when he wanted sex. Since Joan did not have much need for sex, she never interpreted his hugs as his way of showing care, but as his own self-serving sexual acts. She felt that he did it for himself, not for her—and so his acts of affection were repulsive.

Some men have tried to bargain with their wives to exchange acts of affection with acts of sex. When their wives have wanted more affection, these men agree to be affectionate whenever they make love. The more sex, the more affection: It seems like a fair bargain to most men.

But most women would agree with me that such a bargain does not work. Affectionate behavior given only during sex is not affection at all. It is sex. "What's wrong?" a man might protest. "We're kissing, we're touching—that's affection." But true affection is not in the physical acts themselves, but in what they mean. If a husband wants to go to a football game and his wife wants to go on a picnic, it is not a fair solution to take a picnic basket to the football game—they wouldn't really be picnicking. In the same way, affectionate behavior during sex is not the same as affection—it is meeting a whole different need.

So Mike had to learn to be affectionate in nonsexual ways. Then his message of care would be correctly interpreted. I wanted him to create an environment of affection so that Joan could be reminded repeatedly that Mike cared for her and was willing to meet her needs. That way, he'd be depositing love units every day, throughout the day. If he could communicate his care through these habits of affection, they would help make him irresistible, not repulsive, to Joan.

Roadblocks to Restoring Affection

Since acts of affection are so easily misinterpreted, sometimes it's difficult to develop good habits of affection. In fact Joan felt that if a hug ever became a habit, it was no longer affection. For her, affection had to be spontaneous and from the heart. It was not something anyone could learn to do.

She had a point. During their courtship, neither Mike nor Joan decided to learn habits of affection. Their affection seemed spontaneous. That's because they were in the stage of Intimacy, where their Givers were in charge. The Giver is, by nature, affectionate; its goal is to care for others. So whenever Mike and Joan were with each other, their Givers made every effort to show care for each other. Both were solidly convinced that they were loved.

That was then. Affection "just happened"; they didn't have to work at it. Joan wistfully remembered that time but she had just about given up hope of ever returning to it. Her desire for spontaneous affection was certainly understandable, but it actually prevented her from receiving the affection that she needed so much. It was a roadblock to restoring affection.

Now affection wouldn't "just happen"—at least for a while. Now they would have to work at it. It might make things a bit awkward, but it would still be genuine affection.

Another roadblock was that the old symbols of affection had lost their meaning. For Joan, a hug used to mean that Mike loved her. That was when his Giver was influencing him to do the hugging. But now, with his Taker in charge, it meant he wanted sex. In fact all the symbols of care that Mike had used prior to marriage had become symbols of his selfishness. Whether or not he intended them selfishly (and often he did), she saw them that way.

In order to restore affection in their marriage, they would both need to learn new symbols or come to a new understanding about the old ones. Joan would have to trust Mike to hug her without sexual motives—and of course Mike would have to learn to do that.

A third roadblock was that Joan clung to the idea of unconditional love. Remembering the way Mike's Giver had treated her and how self-sacrificing it had been, she regarded affection itself as acts of self-sacrifice, where you do something that may be quite painful and yet expect nothing in return. She yearned for the days when she and Mike could care for each other with no thought of themselves whatsoever.

But those days never really existed. Even in those idyllic months of Mike and Joan's courtship, their Takers were allowing their Givers to give freely because of all that they were receiving. The affection that Joan had felt back then was never really unconditional. So it would be totally unrealistic to insist that it be unconditional now.

Affection and the Policy of Joint Agreement

When they were dating, Mike enthusiastically dropped whatever he was doing to help Joan. His Taker was behind his caring acts 100 percent because of what Joan did for him. He never resented doing what he did, because his relationship with her was so rewarding to him.

But Joan misread his willingness to be there for her whenever she needed him. She saw it as unconditional love, something she deeply wanted to believe in. Truth is, there were conditions. As they cared for each other, they were both getting something back from each other in exchange for their efforts, so their Takers were satisfied. But there was no formal agreement, so it all seemed genuinely spontaneous and from the heart.

If Mike and Joan had both continued to care for each other consistently, they might have gone through their entire lives happily living in their illusion. But I've never known any couple that has pulled that off for any length of time. Sooner or later, one of them becomes frustrated or hurt, waking the sleeping Taker, which instantly deposits them into the state of Conflict. And that is, of course, what happened to Mike and Joan on their honeymoon. When one of them failed to meet the other's need, their illusion evaporated. They saw the relationship for what it was: conditional.

It was a shock. Joan expected that Mike would always sacrifice his own desires for her, and Mike expected the same from Joan. When selfish behavior surfaced—in both of them—they didn't know what to do. Both felt betrayed, cheated.

But that didn't mean they cared any less for each other. If, in the days and weeks after their disastrous honeymoon, they had recommitted themselves to care for each other, they could have spared themselves the nightmare that the next few years would bring. But that would have required negotiation: *What do I have to do to get you to do what I want you to do?* Since each expected unconditional love from the other, neither Mike nor Joan saw the need for give and take. They wallowed in their hurt feelings and let their marriage deteriorate.

I tried to help Joan understand that the best form of care was mutual care. If she expected Mike to sacrifice for her, she would not be caring about his feelings. And if he expected unconditional care from her, he would not be caring about her feelings.

If you do something that benefits you at someone else's expense, that would be wrong, wouldn't it? Most of us would agree about that. But when you require unconditional love in a marriage, you are asking your spouse to do something that benefits you at his or her expense. Wouldn't that be just as wrong?

The most caring relationship is one with mutual care, where sacrifice is not expected or even tolerated by either spouse because neither wants the other to suffer.

The Policy of Joint Agreement *(never do anything without an enthusiastic agreement between you and your spouse)* clearly directs couples toward mutual care, showing affection for each other in ways that make them both happy. Expecting a spouse to sacrifice to prove that he or she cares would violate this policy.

"But shouldn't Mike care enough about me to be willing to make sacrifices?" Joan wondered.

"Mike's Giver is willing to make sacrifices for you," I answered. "But it's not in the interest of your marriage to accept that sacrifice."

"But what if his Giver is enthusiastic about sacrificing? How would I know that it's a sacrifice?" Joan asked.

Good question! But the Taker is the only part of us that's enthusiastic. If we're truly enthusiastic, it's not a sacrifice. What makes us enthusiastic is knowing that there's something in it for us. Just because it's hard work does not make it a sacrifice. It's only a sacrifice when hard work produces no reward. That's when our Takers scream foul.

Fortunately, as I explained this to her, Joan saw the wisdom of the Policy of Joint Agreement. Care did not need to be unilateral, where one cares for the other unconditionally; it could (and should) be bilateral, mutual.

That insight was a crucial step for Joan in helping Mike meet her need for affection. Without a change in her interpretation of affection, nothing Mike did would have convinced her that he cared.

A Plan to Meet the Need for Affection

In meeting the need for affection, once again we have two fundamental considerations: quality and quantity. Mike had to show his affection in an appropriate manner, and it had to be often enough to satisfy Joan.

As we have already discussed, affection is essentially symbolic. So while one spouse can offer an act of affection that he or she considers high quality, the other one can miss the point entirely. Interpretation is everything. So Mike had to be sure that his affection would be appropriately interpreted.

At the same time, according to the Policy of Joint Agreement, whatever he did had to be enjoyable for him too.

Step 1: ***Determine whether improvement is needed in quality, quantity, or both.***

Reviewing Joan's Emotional Needs Questionnaire (see appendix B), we saw that she was "very unhappy" when Mike was not willing to be affectionate. But even when he tried to show affection, she was still "unhappy." She explained in the margin: "I don't like the way he tries to be affectionate."

She was "extremely dissatisfied" with the way Mike met this need (or failed to), and flunked him in both quality ("No" to "I like the way my spouse gives me affection") and quantity ("No" to "My spouse gives me all the affection I need").

How could he improve the quality of his affection? "He shouldn't molest me," she had written. How could he improve the quantity? She just put a question mark. Until he learned how to show affection, it wouldn't help to increase the frequency of his attempts.

At the time she completed this questionnaire, Joan's definition of affection made it impossible for Mike to meet her need. Whenever he tried to be tender, she was convinced he was out to get something, usually sex (which is why she thought he was "molesting" her). She simply did not believe that he genuinely cared about her, so nothing he did would be interpreted as true affection.

According to the Policy of Joint Agreement, of course he's out to get something! We usually are. But that doesn't mean we don't care. After we talked, Joan decided to redefine her idea of affection, giving Mike a break. He would still have to learn to satisfy her, but at least she was giving him a chance to do so.

Thinking back to the days when they were dating, she felt that if he could be as affectionate as he was then, she would probably be very satisfied. During that time, whenever they had been together, Mike would do and say things that thoroughly convinced her that he loved her. He had done it almost continually and very convincingly. She wanted him to try doing what he once did, and perhaps she would be convinced again.

Step 2: ***Identify habits that meet the need for affection.***

Using the Affection Inventory (appendix J) we began to identify habits Mike should (a) develop and (b) avoid as he tried to meet her need for affection. We came up with these suggestions:

Habits to Create

1. He hugs and kisses her and tells her he loves her every morning while still in bed.
2. He brings her orange juice before she gets out of bed.

3. He tells her he loves her and gives her undivided attention while they have breakfast together.
4. He calls her at least three times a day to ask her how her day is going and to tell her he loves her.
5. He buys her flowers at least once a week, attaching a handwritten note expressing his love for her.
6. He calls her before he leaves for home in the afternoon, so she can know when to expect him and he tells her he loves her.
7. When he arrives home, he gives her a big hug and kiss, tells her he loves her, and spends a few minutes talking to her about how her day went.
8. He tells her he loves her and gives her undivided attention while they have dinner together.
9. He helps her clear off the table and wash the dishes after dinner, gives her a hug and kiss at least once, and tells her that he loves her.
10. After the children are in bed, he gives her his undivided attention as he talks with her for at least thirty minutes.
11. He hugs and kisses her in bed before they go to sleep and reminds her that he loves her.

Habits to Avoid

1. When they are not making love and he hugs her, he should avoid trying to touch her breasts or genital area.
2. When he is telling her he loves her and cares for her, he should avoid making reference to his sexual attraction to her.
3. When he compliments her, he should avoid reference to her sexual attractiveness.

Joan wanted Mike to understand that, for her, sex and affection were not the same. So when he wanted to express affection to Joan, he had to learn to do it in nonsexual ways.

Not all wives would come up with Joan's list of habits to avoid. I know of many women who want their husbands to tell them they are sexually attractive. They want to be sexually caressed whenever they are hugged. But the majority of women I've counseled regard affection as a nonsexual demonstration of care and want their husband's habits of affection to reflect it.

Many women complain that the only way they can get any affection from their husbands is to have sex. During lovemaking their husbands seem to be caring and thoughtful, truly concerned about their wife's feelings. But as soon as the lovemaking ends, they ignore their wife until their next sexual encounter.

That's not affection. Affection is an environment of love, where a man's care for his wife is expressed continually throughout the day. It's expressed when they make love and it's expressed when they are not making love.

Step 3: ***Create a strategy to meet the need for affection.***

With Joan's list of habits to create and avoid, Mike's next task was to create a strategy to meet her need of affection. I gave him a form to complete, Strategy to Meet the Need of Affection, to help him think it through (appendix K).

After reading Joan's Affection Inventory, Mike added a few items of his own that he thought she would appreciate. He knew that she wanted assurance that he cared about her, so in his conversation with her he made a special point of respectfully listening to problems that she had and expressing his willingness to help her with them. The Policy of Joint Agreement guided his care in a way that prevented him from sacrificing his own happiness for hers yet at the same time communicated his care for her.

For example, if she asked him to help her wash the windows, and he really didn't want to, what should he do? Choice 1 is to wash them, showing his affection for Joan but making his own Taker angry. Choice 2 is to refuse, keeping his Taker tame but making Joan feel as if he doesn't care about her. But there is a choice 3—helping Joan solve the problem, perhaps by suggesting that they hire a teenage neighbor to do the job. That way, he shows affection for his wife without riling his own Taker. Everybody's happy.

As Joan and I had discussed earlier, affection should not be a reflection of unconditional care, but rather a willingness to show care under the conditions of the Policy of Joint Agreement. Marital affection is mutual care, leading to win-win outcomes where the whole couple, not just one spouse or the other, benefits.

Mike made a list of affectionate habits that he wanted to learn and he checked them off each day as they were accomplished. The list was essentially the same as the one Joan made up in her "habits to create." Orange juice every morning. Three calls or more a day. Flowers, dishes, undivided attention. He did it all. And Joan loved every minute of it.

She proved to herself something that I've known for years. Acts of affection are valuable in their own right. People with a need for affection like to be hugged. They like to be told they are loved. They like flowers. Once Mike got into the habit of being affectionate, Joan just ate it up, and Mike deposited love units by the truckload.

Step 4: ***Measure your effectiveness in meeting the need for affection.***

To provide feedback, Joan used the Affection Worksheet (appendix L). She filled it with glowing reports of his progress.

But a funny thing happened. Mike was making a special effort to avoid mixing sex and affection. But meanwhile, Joan had been learning to meet his need for sexual fulfillment. As soon as Joan developed the ability to experience sexual arousal with Mike, her resentment about his sexual references during affection seemed to disappear. In fact she began to encourage him to tell her about his sexual attraction to her.

Meeting the Need of Affection

1. Determine whether improvement is needed in quality, quantity, or both.
2. Identify habits that meet the need.
3. Create a strategy.
4. Measure your effectiveness.

In spite of her change of attitude, I advised Mike to modify his original plan only slightly. I suggested that at least 75 percent of his affection to Joan should have no sexual references at all. And he should mix sex with affection only when he was reasonably sure she would not be annoyed by it.

The Affection Worksheet that Joan completed each week gave Mike good insight into her changing attitude. The more affectionate he was, the more he convinced her that he truly cared and was committed to her happiness.

As their relationship improved, they rose from the state of Conflict (where their Takers prevailed) to the state of Intimacy (where their Givers prevailed). In the state of Conflict, Mike had regularly confirmed Joan's conviction that he did not care for her—every time he did a thoughtless act (which he did often, inspired by his Taker). But as soon as they were in the state of Intimacy, Mike's Giver went overboard to show Joan that he really did care, and it took very little time for her to be convinced.

Affection and the state of Intimacy go hand in hand. Once a couple is in the state of Intimacy, affection is automatic and effortless. No one needs to make lists or learn habits; it all seems to come instinctively. That's what had happened to Mike and Joan when they were dating, and it convinced Joan of his deep and lasting care. Why? Because Mike really did care about her, and he proved it over and over again. His Giver saw to it that he did.

But once in a while our Takers encourage us to act in thoughtless and uncaring ways, temporarily taking us from the state of Intimacy to the state of Conflict. At those times, we need to be reminded that acts of affection are important, because affection is not instinctive in the state of Conflict. And it doesn't hurt to have a plan handy, a list of thoughtful things we should be doing to show we care. In those times our Takers need to be reminded of what's really in our best interest: caring for each other.

Chapter Seventeen

You'll Love the One You're With

How to Meet the Emotional Need for Recreational Companionship

I'm not sure if I'm just lazy or what, but I always look for the easiest way to get something done. And one of the easiest ways to deposit love units in other people's Love Banks is to be around them when they're having fun. You don't have to do anything—you simply stand there as they're enjoying their favorite activity and let love units pour into your account.

Remember, you only have to be associated with enjoyment to deposit love units. You're not required to actually make the person happy. So recreational companionship is one of the easiest ways for married couples to build good feelings about each other. All they need to do is be with each other when they're having a good time.

Unfortunately most married couples do not recognize the obvious. Instead of being with each other for their favorite recreational activities, they limit their time together to taking care of cranky children, cleaning their messy house, and other unpleasant but necessary chores of life.

Then, when a husband or wife does manage to grab a moment of fun, it's usually by "getting away"—spending time with outsiders who have little if anything to do with the happiness of their marriage or the strengthening of the family. All those love units are wasted on people who are essentially irrelevant to their ultimate happiness.

"Wait a second," you might say. "Can't I spend time with my friends? There's nothing wrong with going out with the gang once in a while, is there?"

Once in a while, sure. Marriage is no prison. But think this through for a minute. Who is the most important person in your life? Your spouse. Whoever's second doesn't even come close! So when you are enjoying yourself the most, shouldn't you be with your spouse? If you really want to restore your marriage, how can you pass up this easy way of depositing love units?

"Yes, but you don't know my spouse," you might continue. "I could never have as much fun with my spouse as I'd have with my friends—especially lately. My spouse would be a huge wet blanket, keeping me from enjoying myself. It would never work. It's a nice idea, but my spouse can never be a good recreational companion for me."

I hear you. But let me remind you that, even if others are more fun to be with, you'd be wise to invest these recreationally created love units in your spouse's Love Bank—if you want to save your marriage, that is.

But there's another reason. Your spouse is potentially the best recreational companion you could ever have. Better than "the gang." Better than the friends you shop or shoot hoops with. Oh, it may not seem that way now, especially if you're deep in the state of Conflict (or Withdrawal). It may take some investment, but the investment will pay off.

Think about it. When you and your spouse were in the state of Intimacy and you were crazy about each other, you'd love just about any activity as long as you were together. You'd have more fun just sitting on a bench together than you could ever have being apart from each other.

Prior to marriage, couples have great fun together. They (a) tend to choose activities that both find enjoyable, (b) try to entertain each other on dates with style and humor, and (c) they're in love. Being in love, they're constantly meeting each other's emotional needs when they're together. They can't help but enjoy being together.

After they get married, however, the changes take place. When Love Busters ruin romantic love and the state of Conflict replaces Intimacy, recreational time spent together is not nearly as much fun anymore. Spouses are no longer each other's best recreational companions because their relationship is ravaged by conflict. Who wants to spend an evening with someone who argues all the time?

Joan and Mike sure didn't. Interestingly enough, their honeymoon fiasco arose from a disagreement over recreational activities. Joan wanted to go to the beach, and Mike wanted to tour the Mayan ruins. He lost his entire perspective when he thought his need for recreational companionship would not be met. His honeymoon was destroyed by his desperate reaction.

The truth was, if Mike had gone to the beach with Joan, he would have had a good time with her, because they were still in love with each other. But after their fight over a recreational activity, neither of them would have had much fun doing anything.

In the course of one morning, they changed from great recreational companions to lousy ones. And what caused the change? The sudden withdrawal of love units from their Love Bank accounts. They were less in love.

If they could restore their feelings of love for each other, they could become great recreational companions again. That became a goal for us as I counseled them.

But notice the two points I've made in this chapter. They fit together.

1. Recreational companionship deposits love units in great amounts, helping you to fall more deeply in love.
2. If you're in love with your spouse, he or she is the best recreational companion you could ever have.

In other words, when you're in love, you love to play together; when you play together, you grow more deeply in love. Round and round it goes.

But what if you're not in love?

Joan and Mike were not in love when we started working on recreational companionship. We had to find activities that were so much fun that they would enjoy them in spite of each other's presence. That may sound odd, but it's where you have to start if you're in the state of Conflict. Eventually you'll get credit for your spouse's enjoyment of the activities, and your spouse's love for you will grow. As that happens, the range of acceptable activities expands tremendously. But until then, we needed to focus attention on their very favorite activities and hope that they were conflict proof.

Spheres of Interest

The best way to develop recreational compatibility involves your "spheres of interest." Figure 1 shows your present sphere of interests in one circle and your spouse's present sphere of interests in another. Inside these circles are your favorite recreational activities.

Each sphere has two parts: mutual interests and exclusive interests. The area where your two spheres intersect is labeled "mutual interests," representing interests that you both share. Other interests, not shared between you and your spouse, are labeled "exclusive interests."

If you've been married recently, your two circles will have a large intersecting area, just like the circles of figure 1.

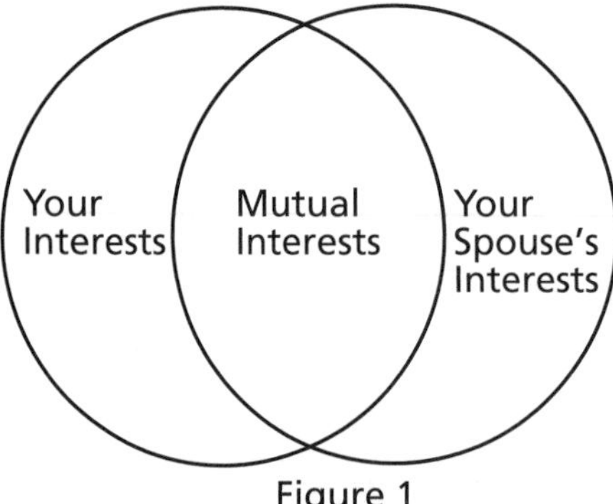

Figure 1

By the time most couples get married, they have already spent considerable time and effort discovering recreational activities of mutual interest. Even if these interests were not shared when they started dating, chances are that each partner has tried to develop knowledge and skill in the other's area of interest. Because of these efforts to get to know each other, that intersecting area of mutual interests has probably grown during courtship. In fact the decision to marry is often based on the assumption that the partners have enough interests in common to be compatible.

But after marriage, they have much less incentive to develop common recreational interests. My wife, Joyce, explained it succinctly to me when I asked her why she wouldn't play tennis with me more often. "Before we were married, I played tennis with you so we could be together. But now that we're married, we can be together without playing tennis. Why bother?"

She had a point. Her incentive to play tennis was gone, and an area of common interest disappeared along with it. And it wasn't just tennis. Many of my interests held her attention before we were married simply because they were her ticket to be with me. In the same way, I was far more willing to shop with her before we were married than I was after marriage. It was an excuse to be with her.

Figure 2 shows what can happen after marriage. The circles representing our spheres of interest start to separate from each other, leaving a smaller area of common interests. In some marriages the circles seem to separate entirely, leaving no mutual interests at all.

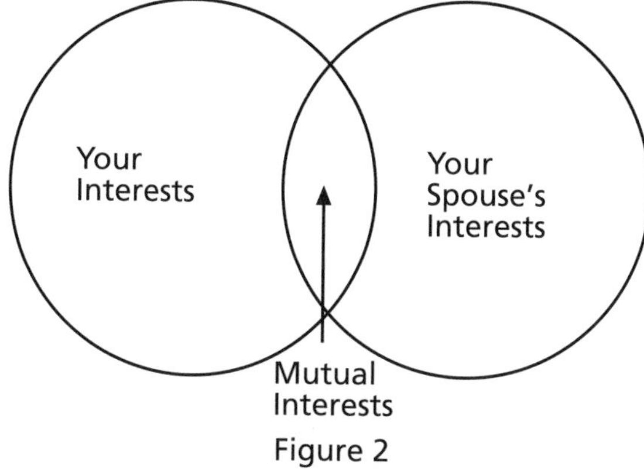

Figure 2

Joyce and I grew apart after marriage because we had no incentive to maintain or create mutual interests. I was in graduate school, trying very hard to complete my degree. As soon as our first child arrived, Joyce quit work to devote her full attention to raising Jennifer. My mind was filled with psychology. Her mind was filled with Jennifer. I was either working or studying fourteen hours a day, seven days a week. She spent the same amount of time caring for our new daughter. Joyce wanted me to be home more, helping her with the family. I wanted her to join me whenever I could take a break, to go out and have some fun. Neither of us did either.

When our son, Steve, arrived, the situation became even worse. I finally completed my degree and began teaching graduate-level psychology courses at a university, spending eight hours preparing each hour of lecture and more time grading papers. Joyce wanted me to be more interested in her and the children, and I was just trying to keep my head above water. Halfway through the year I developed stomach ulcers that left me sick every day for more than two years. Joyce was not getting what she'd bargained for, and I thought I was going to die.

Many marriages like ours end in divorce. Joyce still has trouble talking about those and subsequent years when I was so wrapped up in my work that I spent little time with her and the children. (By the way, my children have no unpleasant memories because Joyce protected me. She never complained to them about my shortcomings or argued with me in front of them. Whenever I *was* home, I spent much of my time playing with Steve and Jennifer, so all they remember is how much fun they had with me.)

Figure 2 accurately illustrates our spheres of recreational interest during this time. I was absorbed in my own world, and Joyce was focused on hers. We drifted apart, and our recreational compatibility was close to zero. When we were together, we dealt with logistical problems—how to pay the bills, not how to meet each other's emotional needs (let alone recreational companionship). Were we incompatible? Yes. Was it because we no longer shared any common interests? Certainly. Could we regain those interests? Absolutely.

Figure 3 illustrates the solution to our problem, adding an important dimension: spheres of potential interest. These are the larger circles that describe the areas of interest we *could* have if we wanted them. It takes some investigation to find these, but it's well worth the effort.

Note: The smaller circles show the interests that presently capture our attention. The larger circles depict our potential interests, those we could develop in an effort to find common ground.

Joyce and I had grown apart. We recognized this dangerous situation and decided to do something about it. Neither of us wanted to hurt the other, and we valued our marriage above anything else. I thought

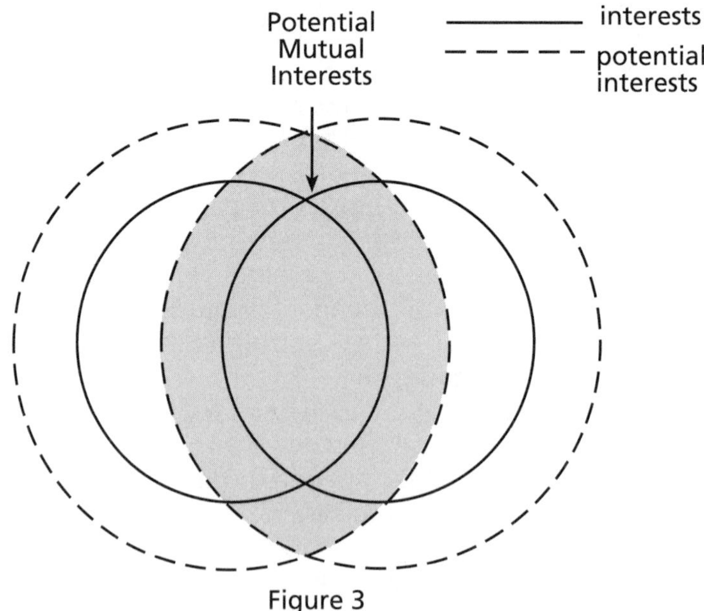

Figure 3

my career was necessary to support the family. But if my career was causing us to drift apart, it was hurting more than helping. We both made an effort to become more involved and interested in each other's spheres of potential interests.

Figure 4 shows what happened to us after we made a deliberate effort to create compatibility. Our spheres of interest became reunited, just as they were when we were first married (figure 1).

If you develop a recreational interest that is not shared by your spouse, and you come to enjoy it a great deal, it may eventually come between you two. It will cause you to take more and more precious time from your spouse; he or she will consider it competition and come to resent it. It may destroy your marriage.

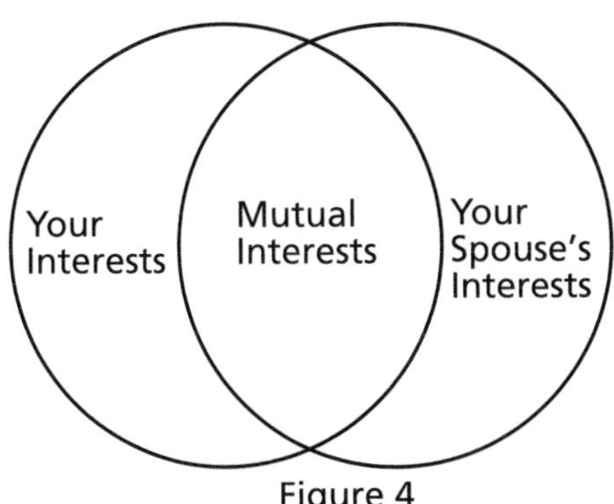

Figure 4

Since there's such a huge sphere of potential interests that you and your spouse *could* share, why focus any of your attention on interests that you *don't* share? You may find activities that are far more interesting than what you're presently engaged in—and they would be interesting to your spouse as well. You don't *lose* personal opportunities when you concentrate on interests you can share, you *gain* personal opportunities. Even more important, these mutual interests will greatly improve your time together.

"But why can't my spouse just join me in the things I already like to do?" you might ask. "To be fair, I'll even bite the bullet and join in one of my spouse's activities."

If you do not truly share your spouse's interests, you will be a lousy recreational companion. If you "bite the bullet" and participate anyway, you'll end up withdrawing love units from both of your Love Banks. Neither of you will be having any fun. Soon you'll give up, saying, "I tried. It didn't work. Let's just go our separate ways."

You cannot meet your spouse's need for recreational companionship unless *you* are also engaged in *your* favorite activities. You will be a good recreational companion only if the activities are mutually enjoyable. That's the only way to fulfill your spouse's need.

If you find that you and your spouse have drifted apart, and your present spheres of interest are far apart, I'd like you to consider a plan that will help you discover recreational interests that you and your spouse can share.

A Plan to Meet the Need for Recreational Companionship

There are literally millions of recreational activities to choose from. Of those there are hundreds of thousands that you could begin pursuing *next week*. There are tens of thousands that you would thoroughly enjoy the first time you tried them, and there are thousands that you would enjoy as much or more than anything you're doing now.

Why, then, should you be wasting your time on those few activities in which you have no common interest? Why do anything apart when there are so many activities that you could enjoy together? It's simply a matter of discovering what they are and then doing them together.

To help Joan meet Mike's need for recreational companionship, we started with an analysis of Mike's need:

Step 1: ***Determine whether improvement is needed in quality, quantity, or both.***

Joan and I began with research. What had Mike told us about his emotional need for recreational companionship? The Emotional Needs Questionnaire he completed gave us a good start (appendix B).

Mike said he was "very unhappy" when Joan would not join him in recreational activities, and "very happy" when she did. But he was somewhat dissatisfied (–2 out of a possible –3) with the recreational companionship Joan offered. He wanted her to engage in at least three recreational activities with him each week, spending a total of about ten hours. When asked how the quality of their recreational activities could be improved, he suggested that she learn the rules of football and watch it on TV with him.

As I met with Mike, I encouraged him to consider recreational activities that Joan would enjoy just as much as he enjoyed them. He didn't think that would be possible, and it certainly would rule out football! Still, he was open to the possibility—and that made it possible to take the next step.

Step 2: ***Identify your mutual recreational interests.***

Several years ago I designed the Recreational Enjoyment Inventory (appendix M), listing 122 activities that couples might find mutually interesting (and there's space to add other favorites). Joan and Mike completed this form.

First, they had to add their favorite activities not already listed. I recommended that they take a few days to think about this, taking time to stretch their imaginations, remembering activities that they enjoyed in the past and imagining activities they might enjoy in the future.

In this first step, each of them identified his or her individual spheres of interest. Each would certainly be including things the other didn't enjoy, but that was all right here. Besides, you can never be sure what your spouse might enjoy doing in the future.

At first, Mike and Joan just listed movies, various sports and games, and dining out. But I encouraged them to consider *anything* they enjoyed, focusing on how much they enjoyed it, not whether or not it is a traditional "activity." For Mike, geology was recreational and so was cooking.

But I wanted them to be as specific as possible when they made their lists. For example, geology is too broad. Although Mike enjoyed doing many things that involve geology, the truth is, he couldn't possibly enjoy them all. He needed to limit it to the activities within geology that he knew he enjoyed, such as visiting the Grand Canyon and observing its geological formations.

Again Mike needed to be more specific with cooking. What type of cooking interested him? How would he like to do it? Did he like to share recipes? Did he like to cook with someone else or by himself?

I also asked them to indicate *when* they liked to engage in recreational activities. After work? On weekends?

Joan and Mike worked on this list at least fifteen minutes each day for about three days, and when they were finished, they entered their lists in the blank spaces at the end of the Recreational Enjoyment Inventory.

They were then ready to rate each activity according to how much they'd enjoy it, circling numbers from minus 3 (very unpleasant) to plus 3 (very enjoyable).

What I'm after, of course, is a rough idea of which activities are likely to deposit the most love units. Other things being equal, why waste your time on activities that are not depositing love units into both of your Love Banks at the same time?

So, after they completed the rating of each activity, they were to consider only those with positive ratings for both of them. In other words, if either found an activity "unpleasant," it was ruled outside of their mutual sphere of interest and therefore eliminated from consideration.

Then they were to add each of their ratings together, coming up with ratings from 0 to 6 (all negative numbers had been eliminated).

Evaluating the list, they would first consider all the 6s. Joan and Mike found four of these. (Some couples can only manage 4s or 5s, but I encourage them to think of new activities until they can identify at least two that are "Very enjoyable" for both.)

Step 3: ***Create a strategy to meet the need for recreational companionship.***

When Joan finally had a list of activities that both she and Mike could enjoy together, she was ready to map out a strategy to meet his need. I gave her another form, the Strategy to Meet the Need of Recreational Companionship (appendix N), to help her organize her plan.

First, she listed the recreational activities that had combined ratings of 4, 5, or 6. These included downhill skiing, sailing, and swimming (all rated 6); gardening, movies, and dining out (all rated 5); and aerobic exercise, ballroom dancing, tennis, and volleyball (all rated 4).

Then Joan scheduled three of those activities to engage in each week, covering a total of ten hours (the quantity Mike had requested). I usually recommend scheduling the same time each week for recreational activities. That way, you can fix it in your datebook from week to week and you won't let other priorities crowd out this important need.

I also suggest that almost all of a couple's recreational time should be spent together. The myth that men and women simply cannot enjoy the same activities is rubbish. Joan and Mike discovered that they had a lot more in common than they first thought.

Step 4: ***Measure how effectively you're meeting the need for recreational companionship.***

To help Joan measure her effectiveness, I gave Mike the Recreational Companionship Worksheet (appendix O) to complete. Each time they engaged in an activity, he described his reaction to their time together.

You must remember that, while Joan was trying to meet Mike's need for recreational companionship, she was also working on sexual fulfillment. And Mike was making progress meeting Joan's needs for conversation and affection. In other words, there were plenty of love units being deposited. I'm sure that this combination of things contributed to the high marks Mike gave Joan on the worksheets he completed.

Still, for the first time since their honeymoon, they were consistently engaging in recreational activities together, with neither one sacrificing for the other. They had chosen activities that they both enjoyed, so why shouldn't they have a good time with each other? But with all the other improvements in their relationship, it turned out that they had a sensational time with each other.

When they came to see me after they had started their recreational plan, they both reported that they couldn't remember when they enjoyed being with each other as much.

I attribute most of the plan's success to the fact that they were moving from the state of Conflict to the state of Intimacy just as the plan was unfolding. But what if you're still in the state of Conflict? Can you expect this strategy to succeed?

Meeting the Need for Recreational Companionship

1. Determine whether improvement is needed in quality, quantity, or both.
2. Identify mutual interests.
3. Create a strategy.
4. Measure your effectiveness.

It's true that, in the state of Conflict, recreational activities just aren't as much fun as they are in the state of Intimacy. Couples often become discouraged when their time together is not as much fun as they hoped.

But stay with it! This recreational plan will move you in the right direction. Love units will be deposited regularly, ultimately leading you back into Intimacy, where you can enjoy each other's company all the more.

Sometimes, when spouses hate each other so much that all of the common recreational activities don't help their situation, I introduce a new plan that's drastic but highly effective. I send them on three consecutive vacations, each lasting about four days, with three days in between. During these three in-between days, I meet with them at least once and sometimes on all three days. The vacations are designed to make them feel good when they are together, in spite of the negative balances in their Love Banks. And it definitely works!

On the first trip, in spite of beautiful and enjoyable surroundings, most couples come back still upset with each other and still considering divorce. If they were in the state of Conflict or Withdrawal when they left on this mini-vacation, they're in the same state when they return. But love units are still deposited during this trip because they make a valiant effort to avoid Love Busters, and the vacation takes care of the rest.

On the second trip, they make some progress toward breaking the emotional barriers that have been keeping them isolated from each other. They begin to make an effort to meet each other's needs, and they express willingness to have their own needs met. Most of the couples return from the second trip still in the state of Conflict, but no longer considering divorce.

On the third trip, they tend to break through to the state of Intimacy and return in love with each other. In three weeks, they have traveled from the icy world of a marriage on the rocks to the tropical climes of passion.

How can a couple on the verge of divorce make that journey? And in such record time? Divorce is inspired by pain, and anything you can do to relieve the pain and replace it with pleasure greatly improves the chances of marital recovery. If a couple can enjoy themselves when they're together—even under these artificial circumstances—they can break the stranglehold of their Takers and take a chance on pleasing each other.

But I only use this technique when a situation is desperate. For one thing, it's a very expensive way to resolve marital conflict. More important, the vacations do not teach couples how to treat each other in their normal home environment. After the third getaway, they still need to try the plan I used with Joan and Mike, engaging in normal recreational activities, learning to enjoy each other's company in everyday life. Otherwise, even the vacations wouldn't make much difference in their marriage—except they might have better tans.

You can try the "home version" of my plan and spend a lot less money. After identifying activities of mutual interest, try them out over a three-week period and see what happens. Your results will probably be similar to those of my vacationers: Not much improvement the first week but steady progress thereafter. As couples continue to spend time together doing things they enjoy, the relationship starts to improve. Within several weeks, you too can break through to Intimacy.

As Joan and Mike learned to meet their four most important emotional needs, they saw a decided difference in their marriage. I stopped counseling them six months after they first arrived, and they were both in love with each other.

Before I let them go, however, I helped them with a little marital housekeeping. Most couples have a slew of minor conflicts, odds and ends that have very little to do with emotional needs. Before I finish this book, I would like to share with you some of the advice I gave them as they finished their counseling with me.

Chapter Eighteen

Give and Take Your Way to Compatibility

How to Resolve Everyday Conflicts with the Policy of Joint Agreement

If you haven't already figured it out by now, I think the Policy of Joint Agreement is the best thing since sliced bread. In one simple rule you have the solution to almost every conceivable marital problem.

Just before I sent Joan and Mike on their way, I gave them a few problems to solve—case studies from my files illustrating problems that can drag most marriages down, if they're not handled correctly. I wanted to be certain they knew how to use my policy to deal with issues they'd be facing in the future.

In this final chapter, I will present these problems to you one at a time, showing how to use the Policy of Joint Agreement to solve them. Then, like Joan and Mike, you'll be well on your way toward creating what I hope will be a terrific marriage.

Resolving Conflicts over Friends and Relatives

Judy's Giver worked overtime. Whenever someone was in need, Judy rushed to the rescue. It was a trait that attracted Bill to her when they were dating, especially when he was on the receiving end of her generosity. But after marriage, it became a source of conflict when her sister, Barbara, and Barbara's husband, Jack, had moved in with them while Jack was "looking for work."

Bill didn't have any say in the matter. He came home one day to find his in-laws' possessions filling his house. That alone upset him, but it got worse as the weeks dragged on. Barbara and Jack seemed to be permanent fixtures.

"We cannot continue to support your sister and brother-in-law," Bill finally told Judy. "He'll just have to find a job like everyone else."

"But he's tried," Judy pleaded, "and if we don't help, who will? I can't just put my sister out on the street."

Our Givers can get us into a lot of trouble because they are willing to see us suffer for the sake of others. And when we're married, it's not just our own Giver that we have to watch out for. Our spouse's Giver can also give us fits when it's generous at our expense. That's what Bill was up against. Judy's Giver wanted Bill to sacrifice along with Judy.

When is it wrong to be generous? When your generosity takes advantage of someone else. Granted, Judy suffered to help her sister survive. But she also made her husband suffer.

Even if Bill's Giver had persuaded him to be generous, too, I'm not sure it would have been good for their marriage to have had Jack and Barbara living with them. Neither Judy nor Bill would have been enthusiastic about supporting them, so they would not have been following the Policy of Joint Agreement.

But Bill was not going along with this. His Taker convinced him that Judy cared more for her sister than for him. She was willing to let him suffer so that her sister would not suffer. So Bill was furious. Besides losing their privacy, they had trouble paying their own bills, and their support of Jack and Barbara put them under needless financial pressure. Ironically, her generosity had become a Love Buster.

Again and again Bill tried to get Judy to ask them to leave, but she insisted on letting them stay until Jack found a job. "I just can't turn my sister away. You'll have to understand."

He understood all right! Love units were drained from Judy's account in his Love Bank until there were none left to withdraw. When that happened, he could no longer tolerate the situation and he left his wife and daughter, Kim, whom he loved dearly.

Bill's decision brought them to my office for counseling, where I introduced them to the Policy of Joint Agreement—neither Bill nor Judy should do anything without the enthusiastic agreement of them both.

Technically, the decision about Jack and Barbara had already been made. They were already living there. To follow the policy, Bill and Judy had to agree on any change in the situation. Since Judy did not want her sister to leave, how would the policy help them in this situation?

That's the question I posed to Joan and Mike. They both agreed that Judy's sister should not have been invited without Bill's enthusiastic agreement to begin with. But what should they do after they violated the Policy of Joint Agreement?

"If the policy has already been violated," Joan suggested, "you should try to restore the situation that existed before the violation, shouldn't you? Then you can make the decision again, but use the policy this time."

She was right.

In this case, they had to go back to the time when Judy invited her sister to live with them. That was when the policy was violated. To restore the original situation, Judy had to ask Barbara and Jack to find another place to live. It was a tough decision for Judy, but that's what she did. And once Jack and Barbara were out, Bill came back.

Now they could start over, applying the Policy of Joint Agreement to their care of Judy's sister. Remarkably, Bill was willing to help them, but not in a way that would ruin his privacy and marriage. He suggested that they loan Jack and Barbara enough money to pay rent for a few months, and Bill even let them use some extra furniture that was stored in the basement. Judy enthusiastically agreed to his generous plan.

From that time forward, they learned to apply the Policy of Joint Agreement to all of their decisions, and as far as I know, Judy's generosity never again got them into such serious marital trouble.

Friends and relatives are a common problem in marriage because the interests of your spouse are often in conflict with the interests of your friends and relatives. In many situations, you cannot please your family and friends and please your spouse at the same time. The Policy of Joint Agreement shows that, whatever solution you choose, it must please both you and your spouse, even if it does not please your friends and relatives. It's the only answer with longlasting benefits. And it's the answer that proves your care for each other.

Resolving Conflicts over Child Discipline

Alex had a short fuse. His friends and family all knew it. But when he fell in love with Christine, he cared so much for her that he managed to keep his temper under control whenever he was with her. Christine became his bride because of his victory over this ugly Love Buster.

Their marriage went well because he kept his vow never to subject her to his angry outbursts. He never punished her either verbally or physically.

However, he had been reared in a tradition where heavy-handed discipline was considered a parent's duty. As a child, he had been beaten by his father on many occasions—if he disobeyed, he could expect disastrous consequences. And since no one's perfect, he knew all about disastrous consequences.

When Alex and Christine had their first child, Alex expected the same unwavering obedience that his parents had expected of him. Whenever little David misbehaved, Alex disciplined him the way *he* had been disciplined as a child.

The first time this happened, Christine became very upset and begged Alex to stop. When his violent methods continued, she went to her pastor for help. Recommending that she leave the discipline up to her husband, the pastor gave her examples of children who grew up to be criminals because women raised them without a father's punishment.

But the pastor didn't realize everything that was going on here. Alex had been holding back his temper with Christine but now he was releasing all that pent-up fury on young David. Whenever he felt irritated about something, he punished his son more severely. The boy grew up in considerable fear of his dad.

All the while, Alex was careful never to treat Christine abusively. In fact he went out of his way to be sure she understood that his punishment of David was merely a father's responsibility, something that had to be done. But still she suffered every time he punished the child, crying as if he were punishing her. Even though Alex had shown her exceptional care in other ways, this punishment caused a huge withdrawal from her Love Bank.

I asked Joan and Mike to solve the problem. *What should Alex do?*

The answer was obvious by now. Following the Policy of Joint Agreement, he would never beat David again. Every act of discipline had to meet with Christine's enthusiastic agreement, and Alex had to change his approach to discipline in order to obtain that agreement.

In my experience counseling families, I have found that every couple's *joint* methods of discipline are superior to their *individual* methods. In other words, couples are wiser in the way they train their children when they agree on a training method. By discussing options and agreeing on a particular approach, they eliminate many of the foolish and impulsive acts of discipline that either one of them might try individually. Furthermore, children take parents more seriously when they both agree on an objective.

Christine wanted Alex to focus more attention on David's good behavior than on his bad behavior. She wanted him to reward his son far more often than he punished him. And she wanted the punishment to be nonviolent—taking away privileges rather than physical beatings or verbal assaults.

When Alex was not angry (and that was most of the time), he knew she was right, so he enthusiastically agreed to her plan. It took some effort on his part to break his abusive habits, but in the end he broke the chain of violence that had been following his family for generations. Under the Policy of Joint Agreement, not only was David spared a traumatic childhood, but Christine's love for Alex was restored.

Resolving Conflicts over Financial Planning

It seems almost instinctive to spend more than we earn. We all seem to be descendants of the same spendthrift ancestor, and we've inherited his undisciplined ways. But Shirley seemed to have inherited the trait in its purest form.

From early childhood, she could not resist buying things she wanted. Her father had tried to help her control her spending, but she would become so upset that he'd usually give in and hand her the money to buy what she wanted.

While Joe dated her, he'd buy her gifts just to see her reaction. She seemed to live for her next gift from him. Joe's generosity brought out the best in her, and within six months they were head over heels in love with each other.

As an executive in a growing company, Joe earned a very good wage. But it never occurred to him that it was not nearly enough to support Shirley's buying habits.

In the first few years of marriage, he justified many of her acquisitions as necessary for their new home. But she wasn't satisfied with her initial purchases—she'd be off buying replacement items before some were even delivered. The closets in their home were soon so filled with her clothes that she had to give many of them away to make room for new wardrobes.

Joe became alarmed. "Shirley, I think it's time we discuss something. You're spending more than we can afford."

She was genuinely concerned. "Oh, Joe, are you having financial problems?"

"We are having financial problems! My income is better than ever, but I can't keep up with your spending," he complained. "We need to be on a budget. If I give you an allowance, will you stick to it?"

"Sure," she responded cheerfully. "That's okay with me."

Joe worked out a budget for Shirley, but she didn't stick to it. When Joe brought up the subject, she shrugged it off as a bad month and promised to do better in the next month. But the next month was no better.

Joe decided to take matters into his own hands. "Shirley, I must put a stop to your irresponsible spending. I'm taking your name off our checking account and canceling your credit cards. I'm sorry, but it's the only way to solve the problem."

Shirley was terribly hurt. She knew she had a problem, but he was treating her like a child. Even though he gave her a generous cash allowance each week, she resented him for taking control of their finances without her agreement. It wasn't long before her cheerful outlook turned into bitterness and anger.

Joe was experiencing the state of Conflict with both barrels. Within a month, they came to see me.

"What should they do?" I tested Joan and Mike. "Apply the Policy of Joint Agreement to this case."

They tossed around the issues.

"Shirley had been spending money wildly, without Joe's enthusiastic agreement," Mike noted. "That's what got them in trouble to begin with."

"But they did negotiate an agreement," Joan added. "That fits the policy, doesn't it?"

"Joe worked out the agreement," Mike corrected, "but Shirley didn't keep her end of the deal."

"But Joe violated the policy when he canceled the credit cards," Joan said. "Shirley certainly wasn't enthusiastic about that."

"But he had to protect himself!"

"He was treating her like a child."

"What was he supposed to do?" Mike wondered. "Sit by quietly while she dragged them both into bankruptcy?"

"He should have continued to negotiate with Shirley until the problem was resolved," Joan suggested. "His mistake was taking matters into his own hands."

Mike wasn't so sure. "But what if she never changed? She could have destroyed them both!"

The problem was a little too close to home for Mike. Before they had seen me, Mike would have responded to this problem exactly the same way that Joe did—by taking control of the situation. But that's a pattern of behavior that had caused him some trouble with Joan. It was very important for him to see the wisdom of Joan's reaction.

The problem that Shirley and Joe faced is very common in marriage. One spouse violates the Policy of Joint Agreement, so the other feels justified in violating it, too. This tit-for-tat approach to marital conflict sends most marriages into the tank, though it might seem fair at the time. After all, why should one spouse be mature when the other is being childish? Why shouldn't they both be childish?

But let's rewind this story a bit. When Joe suggested that they follow a budget, Shirley agreed, but not enthusiastically. It was his budget. She felt that he imposed it on her. Her Giver said yes, but her Taker harbored doubts—doubts which led her to overspend the budget. The first time this happened, it should have been clear that her Taker had not been part of the bargain. They should have gone back to the bargaining table, this time with her Taker present.

In my counseling office, I asked Shirley how she felt about budgets. "I hate them!" she shot back.

"Then why did you agree to go on a budget?"

"To get Joe off my back. He had no right telling me what to do, and I knew at the time I wouldn't follow his little rules." She suddenly looked a bit guilty. "You won't tell Joe what I've just said, will you?"

Shirley's Taker had slipped out just long enough for me to get a glimpse of it, and it made everything crystal clear.

To make a long story short, I showed Joe how to bargain with Shirley instead of imposing his will on her. In order to reach an agreement that she would honor, he had to appeal to her self-centered side. He was not accustomed to this approach, nor was she used to expressing her self-centeredness openly. It took a while for them to learn how to compromise, but within a few months they had reached an agreement that Shirley followed.

Amazingly enough, it was very close to Joe's original plan. Shirley actually decided that the best way for her to control her spending was to get rid of credit cards and their checking account. She shopped with the cash that she and Joe agreed they could afford.

You see, Joe's plan wasn't so bad. That was never the issue. The problem occurred when Joe didn't give Shirley a choice. Once they started to bargain with each other using the Policy of Joint Agreement, she regained control of the process and eventually came to the same conclusion as Joe did. But now it was also her conclusion, and she agreed to it enthusiastically.

To help Shirley learn new spending habits, I used a behavioral plan that monitored her spending over a period of three months. Prior to her agreement, she would never have followed through with that or any other plan, but this time she followed it perfectly and made changes that amazed everyone who knew her, particularly Joe.

Because financial planning is such an important marital issue, marriage counselors spend quite a bit of time helping couples manage their money. They don't give financial or investment advice, because that's not where their training lies, but they do help couples agree on how they will spend their limited resources in ways that take the interests of both spouses into account.

So the Policy of Joint Agreement is especially important in financial decisions: Financial planning should take the interests of both spouses into account. Such crucial decisions should never be left to one spouse alone. Both spouses should learn to review their finances regularly and come to enthusiastic agreement as to how their income is spent.

Which brings us to another common problem in marriage: How the money is earned. The Policy of Joint Agreement is a big help in showing couples how to spend the money they earn. But sometimes it's an even bigger help in making career decisions.

Resolving Conflicts over Career-Related Choices

Like many other women, Renee admired ambitious men, and Jim was one of the most ambitious she had ever known. Though he had worked his way through college by taking two jobs, he had outstanding grades. And he was so well organized that, in spite of his busy schedule, he made a point of seeing her almost every day.

After their marriage, his career took off, but Renee was squeezed out of his schedule. When she would complain to him about how little time they had together, he would explain how important this phase of his career was and how he would have more time for her and his family in a few years.

Ten years and three children later, nothing had changed. Jim was an absentee husband and father. At a point of desperation, Renee made an appointment, without Jim, for advice. During the session, she confided that she'd fallen in love with another man and wouldn't be all that disappointed if their marriage ended in divorce.

I asked Joan and Mike to suggest a solution to Renee's problem.

By now, Mike had a handle on the Policy of Joint Agreement. "Jim did not discuss his work schedule with Renee. And if he had, he would not have had her enthusiastic agreement," he observed.

"Do you think a wife has a right to overrule her husband's work schedule?" I asked Mike.

"I didn't think so a few weeks ago, but I do now," he replied. "I see how each decision made in marriage affects both husband and wife, so they need to consider each other's feelings when they make any decision, including his work schedule."

"And her work schedule?" I asked Joan.

"I guess so," she responded. "But what should a couple do with an existing schedule that has not been agreed to?" There was an underlying reason for Joan's question. She was working part-time as a waitress and Mike did not like her job. It kept her from doing housework that he felt should be done, and he was jealous of some of the men she knew from the restaurant.

"What would you have suggested to Renee?" I asked. "She had never agreed to Jim's schedule. What should she do about that?"

"She was in love with another man," Joan noted. "If Jim knew about that, I think he'd want to be home more often."

The truth was, by the time Renee got to me, she didn't want Jim home any more than he was. The time when she wanted his companionship had passed, and unless he included her in his schedule soon, he might lose her entirely.

In spite of her reservations, however, Renee was willing to give her marriage one more chance. And she agreed to inform her husband about her new relationship and how it was threatening their marriage.

Three days later, Jim came to see me in a panic. "What can I do to save my marriage?" I described a new way of life to him that included Renee's feelings in every decision he made, including those that involved his career. By the end of the session, he had agreed to the Policy of Joint Agreement, especially regarding career-related choices.

Renee was surprised and impressed by his reaction to the problem. She had been afraid to confront him about her growing feelings for another man, for fear he would divorce her on the spot and humiliate her in front of their children and her family. But he did the opposite. He never discussed with anyone else what she had told him, and from that day forward avoided unilateral decisions. Her relationship with the "other man" had never progressed beyond her feelings—the man didn't even know she was interested—so it was easy for her to put an end to it.

From then on, Renee was in Jim's schedule. In fact Renee helped write his schedule. Honesty and the Policy of Joint Agreement had helped them dodge a bullet.

"How do you feel about Joan's job?" I asked Mike.

Joan squirmed, because it was an issue she had successfully avoided in the weeks I had counseled them. She liked the job because it gave her a chance to get out of the house each day, and it also gave her extra discretionary money.

"To be honest," Mike confessed, "when we weren't getting along, I was very jealous. But now I feel more secure. It doesn't bother me that she's working."

Joan heaved a sigh of relief. Though she liked her job, she would have been willing to give it up if it bothered Mike.

But she certainly wouldn't be enthusiastic about quitting her job, so wouldn't this personal sacrifice violate the Policy of Joint Agreement?

No, it would just be a way of getting things back to square one. Mike had never been happy about Joan's job, and whenever you're in a situation that was never mutually agreed to, you probably need to undo it and start over.

Bill and Judy discovered this with their in-laws, since Bill had never agreed to bring them into the house in the first place. To set things right, they had to ask their guests to leave. Only then could Bill and Judy negotiate a mutually satisfying response to their in-laws' need.

Joe and Shirley had to throw out the budget that Joe had imposed without Shirley's enthusiastic agreement. Only then could they hammer out a new plan that both would feel good about.

And Renee, crowded out of Jim's schedule, did not ask Jim to quit his job (because she *was* enthusiastic about the benefits it offered). But he did need to toss out a number of time commitments he had made on his own without consulting Renee. Then they could work together in planning a new schedule they could both enjoy.

So, even though Joan enjoyed her job, she had to be willing to quit it and start over, negotiating a new decision that both she and Mike would be happy about.

Fortunately the problems Mike had with her employment had evaporated. Feeling more secure in their marriage, he decided he could trust her in her friendships with coworkers. Renegotiation was not necessary. He was offering his enthusiastic support of her job.

Mike and Joan were now reaping the rewards of the state of Intimacy, where each spouse automatically and effortlessly wants to please the other. Jealousy and resentment had disappeared, replaced by trust and enthusiasm for what made each other happy.

All they had to do to preserve that magical stage was to continue to meet each other's most important emotional needs and solve their conflicts with the Policy of Joint Agreement.

Two years ago, I happened to see them shopping together, though they didn't see me. Even from a distance, I could see they were still in love. It even seemed that Mike enjoyed shopping! Or was it that he enjoyed being with Joan?

APPENDIXES

On the following pages, you will find the questionnaires I used with Mike and Joan. I believe these will be helpful as you evaluate and improve your own marriage.

I recommend that you photocopy the questionnaires at 125 percent. You'll need plenty of room to write in your responses. Though photocopying from copyrighted material is generally illegal, the publisher hereby gives you permission to copy the following pages for use within your own marriage.

Appendix A

Love Busters Questionnaire

Name________________________________ Date____________________

This questionnaire is designed to help identify your spouse's Love Busters. Your spouse engages in a Love Buster whenever one of his or her habits causes you to be unhappy. By causing your unhappiness, he or she withdraws love units from his or her account in your Love Bank, and that, in turn, threatens your romantic love.

There are five categories of Love Busters. Each category has its own set of questions in this questionnaire. Answer all the questions as candidly as possible. Do not try to minimize your unhappiness with your spouse's behavior. If your answers require more space, use and attach a separate sheet of paper.

Your spouse should also complete a Love Busters Questionnaire so that you can discover your own Love Busters.

When you have completed this questionnaire, go through it a second time to be certain your answers accurately reflect your feelings. Do not erase your original answers, but cross them out lightly so that your spouse can see the corrections and discuss them with you.

The final page of this questionnaire asks you to rank the five Love Busters in order of their importance to you. When you complete the ranking of the Love Busters, you may find that your answers to the questions regarding each Love Buster are inconsistent with your final ranking. This inconsistency is common. It often reflects a less than perfect understanding of your feelings. If you notice inconsistencies, discuss them with your spouse to help clarify your feelings.

I. **Angry Outbursts.** Deliberate attempts by your spouse to hurt you because of anger toward you. They are usually in the form of verbal or physical attacks.

1. **Angry outbursts as a cause of unhappiness:** Indicate how much unhappiness you tend to experience when your spouse attacks you with an angry outburst.

0	1	2	3	4	5	6
I experience no unhappiness			I experience moderate unhappiness			I experience extreme unhappiness

2. **Frequency of spouse's angry outbursts:** Indicate how often your spouse tends to engage in angry outbursts toward you.

__________(write number) angry outbursts each day/week/month/year (circle one).

3. **Form(s) angry outbursts take:** When your spouse engages in angry outbursts toward you, what does he/she typically do?______________

____

____

4. **Form(s) of angry outbursts that cause the greatest unhappiness:** Which of the above forms of angry outbursts causes you the greatest unhappiness?______________________________________

____

____

5. **Onset of angry outbursts:** When did your spouse first engage in angry outbursts toward you?_________________________________

____

____

____

____

6. **Development of angry outbursts:** Have your spouse's angry outbursts increased or decreased in intensity and/or frequency since they first began? How do recent angry outbursts compare with those of the past?

____

____

____

____

____

____

____

____

II. Disrespectful Judgments. Attempts by your spouse to change your attitudes, beliefs, and behavior by trying to force you into his/her way of thinking. If (1) he/she lectures you instead of respectfully discussing issues, (2) feels that his/her opinion is superior to yours, (3) talks over you or prevents you from having a chance to explain your position, or (4) ridicules your point of view, he/she is engaging in disrespectful judgments.

1. **Disrespectful judgments as a cause of unhappiness:** Indicate how much unhappiness you tend to experience when your spouse engages in disrespectful judgments toward you.

   0 — 1 — 2 — 3 — 4 — 5 — 6

   I experience no unhappiness (0) · I experience moderate unhappiness (3) · I experience extreme unhappiness (6)

2. **Frequency of spouse's disrespectful judgments:** Indicate how often your spouse tends to engage in disrespectful judgments toward you.

   ________ (write number) disrespectful judgments each day/week/month/year (circle one).

3. **Form(s) disrespectful judgments take:** When your spouse engages in disrespectful judgments toward you, what does he/she typically do?

   ____
   ____
   ____

4. **Form(s) of disrespectful judgments that cause the greatest unhappiness:** Which of the above forms of disrespectful judgments cause you the greatest unhappiness? ______________________________

   ____
   ____

5. **Onset of disrespectful judgments:** When did your spouse first engage in disrespectful judgments toward you? ______________________________

   ____
   ____
   ____

6. **Development of disrespectful judgments:** Have your spouse's disrespectful judgments increased or decreased in intensity and/or frequency since they first began? How do recent disrespectful judgments compare with those of the past? ______________________________

   ____
   ____
   ____
   ____

III. **Annoying Behavior.** The two basic types of annoying behavior are habits and activities. Habits are repeated without much thought, such as the way your spouse eats or sits in a chair. Activities are usually scheduled and require thought to complete, such as attending sporting events or a personal exercise program. Habits and activities are "annoying behavior" if they cause you to feel unhappy. They can be as innocent as snoring or as destructive as infidelity or alcohol addiction.

1. **Annoying behavior as a cause of unhappiness:** Indicate how much unhappiness you tend to experience when your spouse engages in annoying behavior.

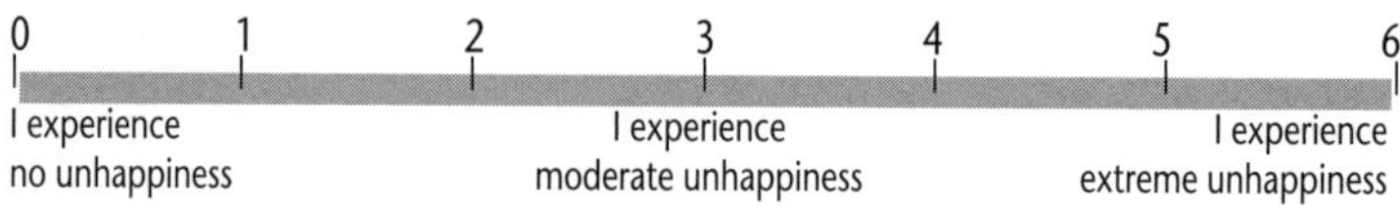

2. **Frequency of spouse's annoying behavior:** Indicate how often your spouse tends to engage in annoying behavior.

   ________ (write number) annoying behaviors each day/week/month/year (circle one).

3. **Form(s) annoying behavior takes:** When your spouse engages in annoying behavior, what does he/she typically do? ________________

   ____

   ____

4. **Form(s) of annoying behavior that cause the greatest unhappiness:** Which of the above forms of annoying behavior cause you the greatest unhappiness? ________________________________

   ____

   ____

   ____

5. **Onset of annoying behavior:** When did your spouse first engage in annoying behavior? ________________________________

   ____

   ____

   ____

6. **Development of annoying behavior:** Has your spouse's annoying behavior increased or decreased in intensity and/or frequency since it first began? How does recent annoying behavior compare with that of the past? ________________________________

   ____

   ____

   ____

IV. Selfish Demands. Attempts by your spouse to force you to do something for him/her, usually with implied threat of punishment if you refuse.

1. **Selfish demands as a cause of unhappiness:** Indicate how much unhappiness you tend to experience when your spouse makes selfish demands of you.

0	1	2	3	4	5	6
I experience no unhappiness			I experience moderate unhappiness			I experience extreme unhappiness

2. **Frequency of spouse's selfish demands:** Indicate how often your spouse tends to make selfish demands of you.

_______ (write number) selfish demands each day/week/month/year (circle one).

3. **Form(s) selfish demands take:** When your spouse makes selfish demands of you, what does he/she typically do? _______________

4. **Form(s) of selfish demands that cause the greatest unhappiness:** Which of the above forms of selfish demands cause you the greatest unhappiness? _______________

5. **Onset of selfish demands:** When did your spouse first make selfish demands of you? _______________

6. **Development of selfish demands:** Have your spouse's selfish demands increased or decreased in intensity and/or frequency since they first began? How do recent selfish demands compare with those of the past?

V. Dishonesty. Failure of your spouse to reveal his/her thoughts, feelings, habits, likes, dislikes, personal history, daily activities, and plans for the future. Dishonesty is not only providing false information about any of the above topics, but it is also leaving you with what he/she knows is a false impression.

1. **Dishonesty as a cause of unhappiness:** Indicate how much unhappiness you tend to experience when your spouse is dishonest with you.

   0 — 1 — 2 — 3 — 4 — 5 — 6

   I experience no unhappiness (0) · I experience moderate unhappiness (3) · I experience extreme unhappiness (6)

2. **Frequency of spouse's dishonesty:** Indicate how often your spouse tends to be dishonest with you.

   _______ (write number) instances of dishonesty each day/week/month/year (circle one).

3. **Form(s) dishonesty takes:** When your spouse is dishonest with you, what does he/she typically do? ______________________

   ____

   ____

   ____

4. **Form(s) of dishonesty that cause the greatest unhappiness:** Which of the above forms of dishonesty cause you the greatest unhappiness?

   ____

   ____

   ____

   ____

   ____

5. **Onset of dishonesty:** When was your spouse first dishonest with you?

   ____

   ____

   ____

   ____

   ____

6. **Development of dishonesty:** Has your spouse's dishonesty increased or decreased in intensity and/or frequency since it first began? How do recent instances of dishonesty compare with those of the past? _____

   ____

   ____

   ____

   ____

Ranking Your Spouse's Love Busters

The five basic categories of Love Busters are listed below. There is also space for you to add other categories of Love Busters not included in the list that you feel contribute to your marital unhappiness. In the space provided in front of each Love Buster, write a number from 1 to 5 that ranks its relative contribution to your unhappiness. Write a 1 before the Love Buster that causes you the greatest unhappiness, a 2 before the one causing the next greatest unhappiness, and so on until you have ranked all five.

______ Angry outbursts

______ Disrespectful judgments

______ Annoying behavior

______ Selfish demands

______ Dishonesty

______ ______________________________

______ ______________________________

APPENDIX B

EMOTIONAL NEEDS QUESTIONNAIRE

Name______________________________ Date____________________

This questionnaire is designed to help you determine your most important emotional needs and evaluate your spouse's effectiveness in meeting those needs. Answer all the questions as candidly as possible. Do not try to minimize any needs that you feel have been unmet. If your answers require more space, use and attach a separate sheet of paper.

Your spouse should complete an Emotional Needs Questionnaire so that you can discover his or her needs and evaluate your effectiveness in meeting those needs.

When you have completed this questionnaire, go through it a second time to be certain your answers accurately reflect your feelings. Do not erase your original answers, but cross them out lightly so that your spouse can see the corrections and discuss them with you.

The final page of this questionnaire asks you to identify and rank five of the ten needs in order of their importance to you. The most important emotional needs are those that give you the most pleasure when met and frustrate you the most when unmet. Resist the temptation to identify as most important only those needs that your spouse is not presently meeting. Include *all* your emotional needs in your consideration of those that are most important.

1. **Affection.** Showing love through words, cards, gifts, hugs, kisses, and courtesies; creating an environment that clearly and repeatedly expresses love.

   A. **Need for affection:** Indicate how much you need affection by circling the appropriate number.

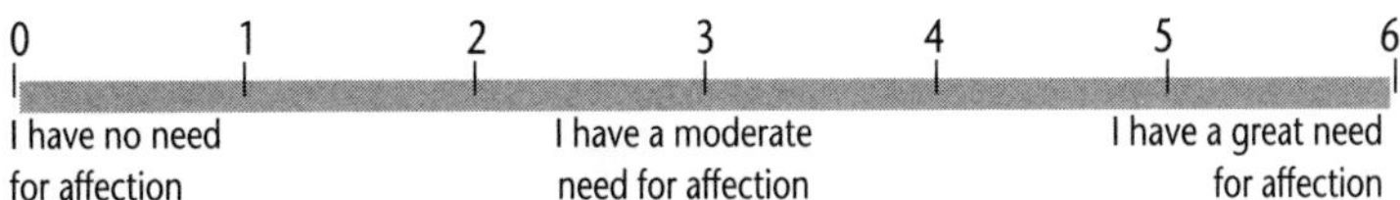

If or when your spouse is *not* affectionate with you, how do you feel? (Circle the appropriate letter.)

a. Very unhappy
b. Somewhat unhappy
c. Neither happy nor unhappy
d. Happy not to be shown affection

If or when your spouse is affectionate to you, how do you feel? (Circle the appropriate letter.)

a. Very happy
b. Somewhat happy
c. Neither happy nor unhappy
d. Unhappy to be shown affection

   B. **Evaluation of spouse's affection:** Indicate your satisfaction with your spouse's affection toward you by circling the appropriate number.

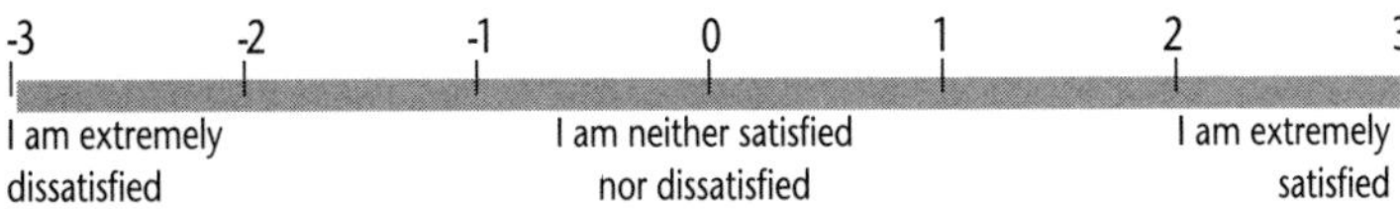

My spouse gives me all the affection I need. Yes No

If your answer is no, how often would you like your spouse to be affectionate with you?

_______ (write number) times each day/week/month (circle one).

I like the way my spouse gives me affection. Yes No

If your answer is no, explain how your need for affection could be better satisfied in your marriage. ____________________

____

____

____

____

____

____

____

2. **Sexual Fulfillment.** A sexual relationship that brings out a predictably enjoyable sexual response in both of you that is frequent enough for both of you.

   A. **Need for sexual fulfillment:** Indicate how much you need sexual fulfillment by circling the appropriate number.

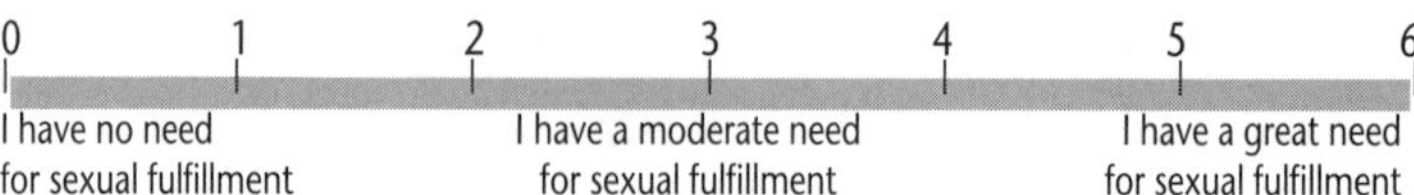

If or when your spouse *is not* willing to engage in sexual relations with you, how do you feel? (Circle the appropriate letter.)

a. Very unhappy
b. Somewhat unhappy
c. Neither happy nor unhappy
d. Happy not to engage in sexual relations

If or when your spouse engages in sexual relations with you, how do you feel? (Circle the appropriate letter.)

a. Very happy
b. Somewhat happy
c. Neither happy nor unhappy
d. Unhappy to engage in sexual relations

   B. **Evaluation of sexual relations with your spouse:** Indicate your satisfaction with your spouse's sexual relations with you by circling the appropriate number.

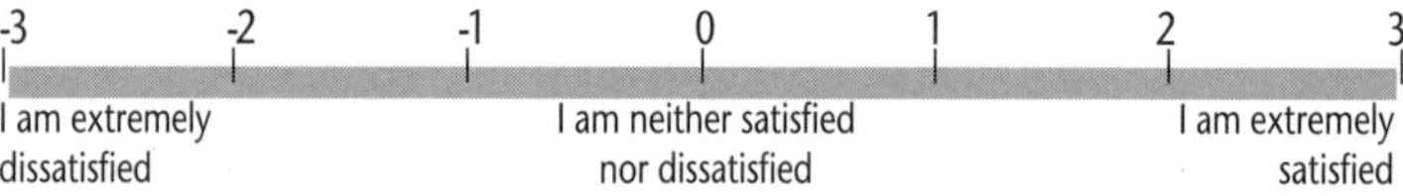

My spouse has sexual relations with me as often as I need. Yes No

If your answer is no, how often would you like your spouse to have sex with you?

________ (write number) times each day/week/month (circle one).

I like the way my spouse has sexual relations with me. Yes No

If your answer is no, explain how your need for sexual fulfillment could be better satisfied in your marriage. ______________________________

____

____

____

____

____

3. **Conversation.** Talking about events of the day, feelings, and plans; avoiding angry or judgmental statements or dwelling on past mistakes; showing interest in your favorite topics of conversation; balancing conversation; using it to inform, investigate, and understand you; and giving you undivided attention.

   A. **Need for conversation:** Indicate how much you need conversation by circling the appropriate number.

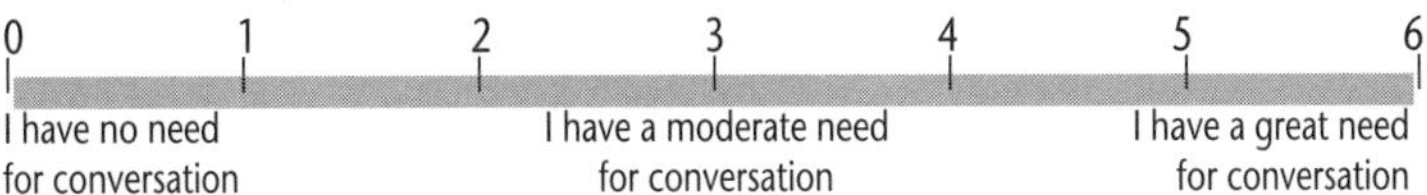

   If or when your spouse *is not* willing to talk with you, how do you feel? (Circle the appropriate letter.)

   a. Very unhappy
   b. Somewhat unhappy
   c. Neither happy nor unhappy
   d. Happy not to talk

   If or when your spouse talks to you, how do you feel? (Circle the appropriate letter.)

   a. Very happy
   b. Somewhat happy
   c. Neither happy nor unhappy
   d. Unhappy to talk

   B. **Evaluation of conversation with your spouse:** Indicate your satisfaction with your spouse's conversation with you by circling the appropriate number.

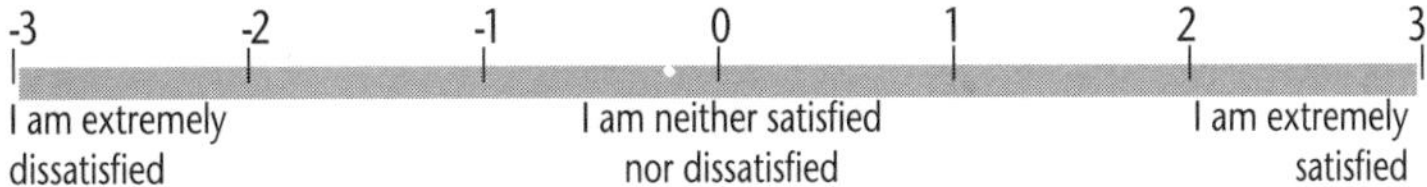

   My spouse talks to me as often as I need. Yes No

   If your answer is no, how often would you like your spouse to talk to you?

   ________ (write number) times each day/week/month (circle one).

   ________ (write number) hours each day/week/month (circle one).

   I like the way my spouse talks to me. Yes No

   If your answer is no, explain how your need for conversation could be better satisfied in your marriage. ____________________________

   ____

   ____

   ____

4. **Recreational Companionship.** Developing interest in your favorite recreational activities, learning to be proficient in them, and joining you in those activities. If any prove to be unpleasant to your spouse after an effort has been made, negotiating new activities that are mutually enjoyable.

   A. **Need for recreational companionship:** Indicate how much you need recreational companionship by circling the appropriate number.

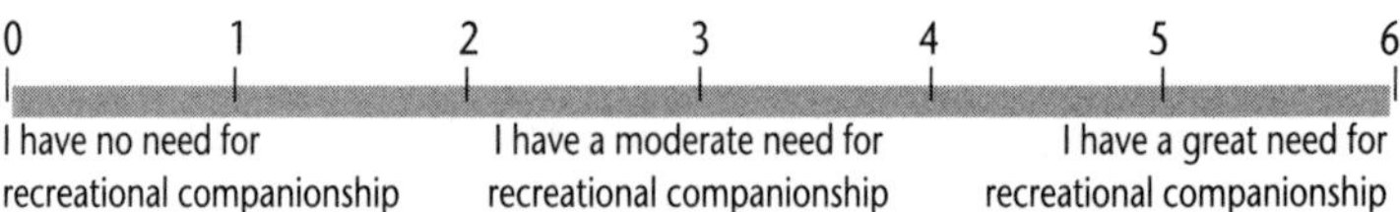

   If or when your spouse *is not* willing to join you in recreational activities, how do you feel? (Circle the appropriate letter.)

   a. Very unhappy
   b. Somewhat unhappy
   c. Neither happy nor unhappy
   d. Happy not to include my spouse

   If or when your spouse joins you in recreational activities, how do you feel? (Circle the appropriate letter.)

   a. Very happy
   b. Somewhat happy
   c. Neither happy nor unhappy
   d. Unhappy to join in recreational activities

   B. **Evaluation of recreational companionship with your spouse:** Indicate your satisfaction with your spouse's recreational companionship by circling the appropriate number.

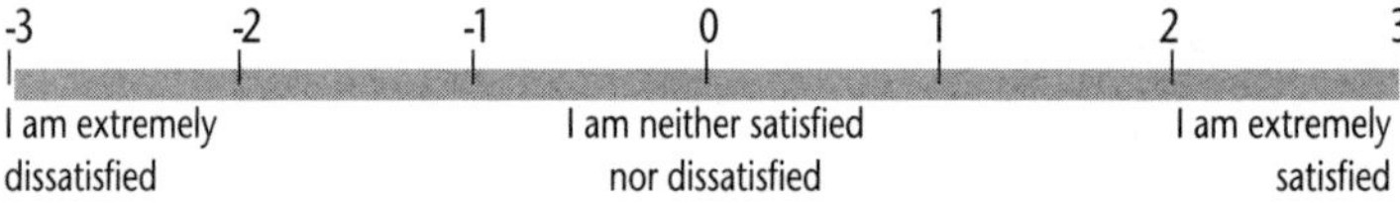

   My spouse joins me in recreational activities as often as I need. Y N

   If your answer is no, how often would you like your spouse to join you in recreational activities?

   ________ (write number) times each day/week/month (circle one).

   ________ (write number) hours each day/week/month (circle one).

   I like the way my spouse joins me in recreational activities. Yes No

   If your answer is no, explain how your need for recreational companionship could be better satisfied in your marriage. ________________

   ____

   ____

5. **Honesty and Openness.** Revealing positive and negative feelings, events of the past, daily events and schedule, plans for the future; not leaving you with a false impression; answering your questions truthfully.

   A. **Need for honesty and openness:** Indicate how much you need honesty and openness by circling the appropriate number.

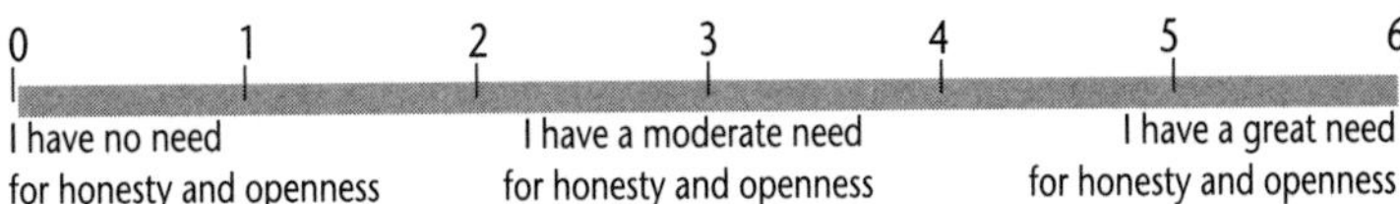

If or when your spouse *is not* open and honest with you, how do you feel? (Circle the appropriate letter.)

a. Very unhappy
b. Somewhat unhappy
c. Neither happy nor unhappy
d. Happy not to be honest and open

If or when your spouse is open and honest with you, how do you feel? (Circle the appropriate letter.)

a. Very happy
b. Somewhat happy
c. Neither happy nor unhappy
d. Unhappy to be honest and open

   B. **Evaluation of spouse's honesty and openness:** Indicate your satisfaction with your spouse's honesty and openness by circling the appropriate number.

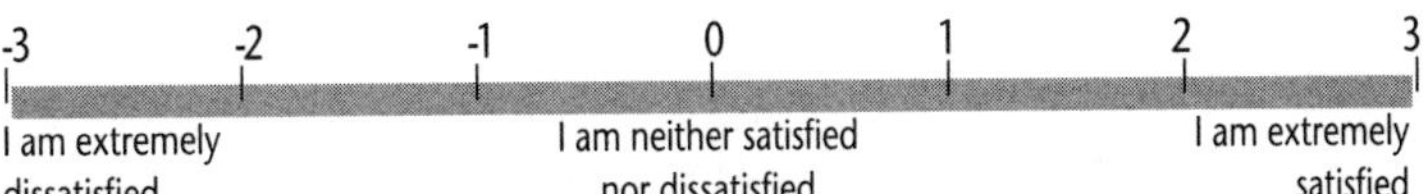

In which of the following areas of honesty and openness would you like to see improvement from your spouse? (Circle the letters that apply to you.)

a. Sharing positive and negative emotional reactions to significant aspects of life
b. Sharing information regarding his/her personal history
c. Sharing information about his/her daily activities
d. Sharing information about his/her future schedule and plans

If you circled any of the above, explain how your need for honesty and openness could be better satisfied in your marriage. ____________

____

____

____

____

____

____

6. **Attractiveness of Spouse.** Keeping physically fit with diet and exercise; wearing hair, clothing, and (if female) makeup in a way that you find attractive and tasteful.

   A. **Need for an attractive spouse:** Indicate how much you need an attractive spouse by circling the appropriate number.

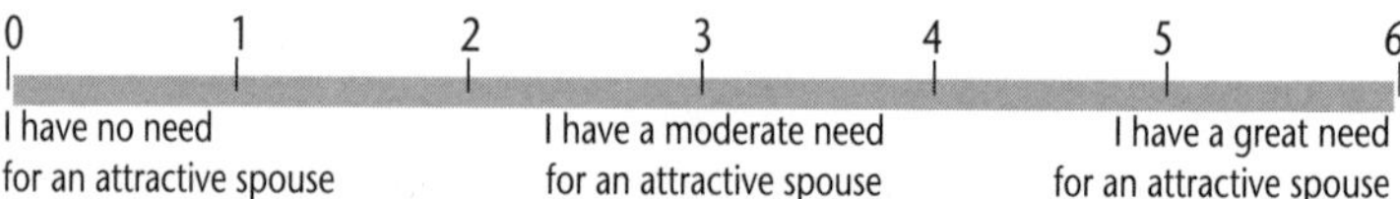

If or when your spouse *is not* willing to make the most of his or her physical attractiveness, how do you feel? (Circle the appropriate letter.)

a. Very unhappy
b. Somewhat unhappy
c. Neither happy nor unhappy
d. Happy he or she does not make an effort

When your spouse makes the most of his or her physical attractiveness, how do you feel? (Circle the appropriate letter.)

a. Very happy
b. Somewhat happy
c. Neither happy nor unhappy
d. Unhappy to see him or her make an effort

   B. **Evaluation of spouse's attractiveness:** Indicate your satisfaction with your spouse's attractiveness by circling the appropriate number.

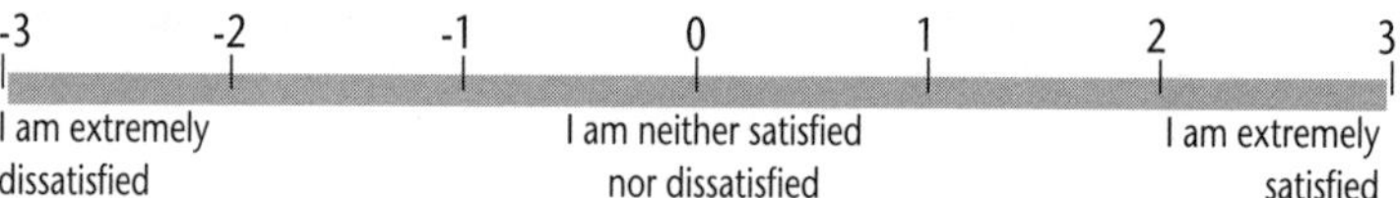

In which of the following characteristics of attractiveness would you like to see improvement from your spouse? (Circle the letters that apply.)

a. Physical fitness and normal weight
b. Attractive choice of clothes
c. Attractive hairstyle
d. Good physical hygiene
e. Attractive facial makeup
f. Other ____________________

If you circled any of the above, explain how your need for an attractive spouse could be better satisfied in your marriage. ____________

____
____
____
____
____
____

7. **Financial Support.** Provision of the financial resources to house, feed, and clothe your family at a standard of living acceptable to you, but avoiding travel and working hours that are unacceptable to you.

A. **Need for financial support:** Indicate how much you need financial support by circling the appropriate number.

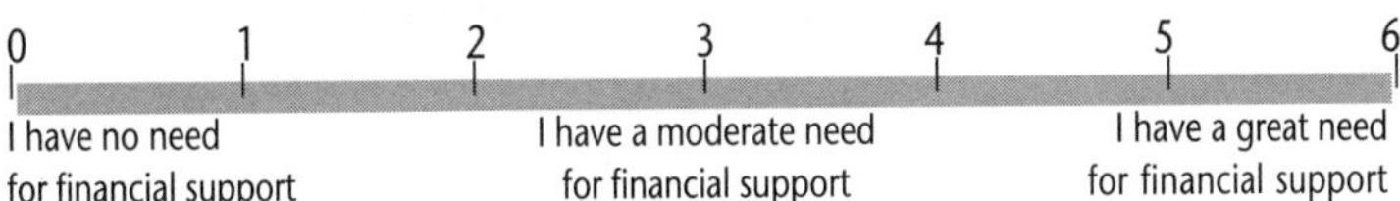

If or when your spouse *is not* willing to support you financially, how do you feel? (Circle the appropriate letter.)

a. Very unhappy
b. Somewhat unhappy
c. Neither happy nor unhappy
d. Happy not to be financially supported

If or when your spouse supports you financially, how do you feel? (Circle the appropriate letter.)

a. Very happy
b. Somewhat happy
c. Neither happy nor unhappy
d. Unhappy to be financially supported

B. **Evaluation of spouse's financial support:** Indicate your satisfaction with your spouse's financial support by circling the appropriate number.

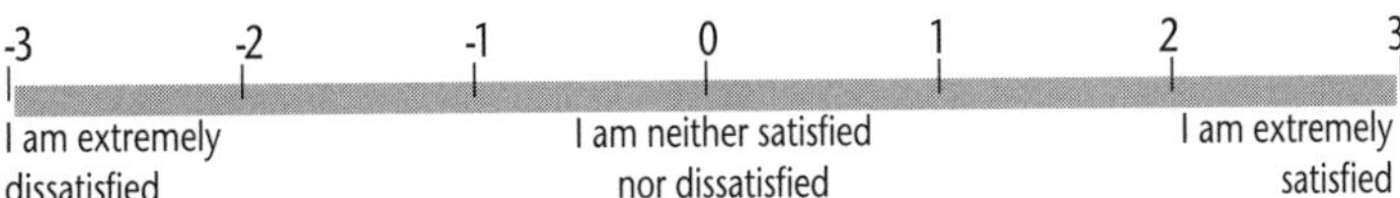

How much money would you like your spouse to earn to support you?

____

How many hours each week would you like your spouse to work? _____

If your spouse is not earning as much as you would like, is not working the hours you would like, does not budget the way you would like, or does not earn an income the way you would like, explain how your need for financial support could be better satisfied in your marriage. _____

____

____

____

____

____

____

8. **Domestic support.** Creation of a home environment for you that offers a refuge from the stresses of life; managing the home and care of the children—if any are at home—including but not limited to cooking meals, washing dishes, washing and ironing clothes, housecleaning.

   A. **Need for domestic support:** Indicate how much you need domestic support by circling the appropriate number.

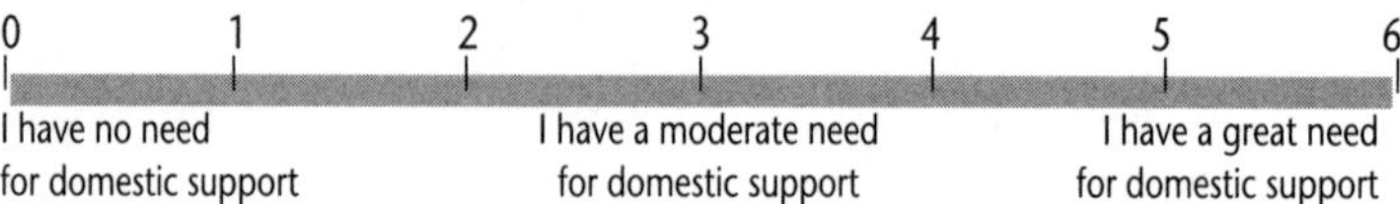

If your spouse *is not* willing to provide you with domestic support, how do you feel? (Circle the appropriate letter.)

a. Very unhappy
b. Somewhat unhappy
c. Neither happy nor unhappy
d. Happy not to have domestic support

If or when your spouse provides you with domestic support, how do you feel? (Circle the appropriate letter.)

a. Very happy
b. Somewhat happy
c. Neither happy nor unhappy
d. Unhappy to have domestic support

   B. **Evaluation of spouse's domestic support:** Indicate your satisfaction with your spouse's domestic support by circling the appropriate number.

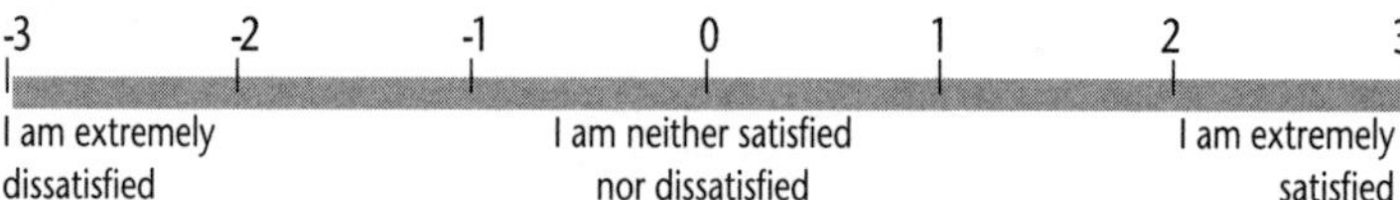

My spouse provides me with all the domestic support I need. Yes No

I like the way my spouse provides domestic support. Yes No

If your answer is no to either of the above questions, explain how your need for domestic support could be better satisfied in your marriage.________________________________

9. **Family commitment.** Scheduling sufficient time and energy for the moral and educational development of your children; reading to them, taking them on frequent outings, educating himself or herself in appropriate child-training methods and discussing those methods with you; avoiding any child-training method or disciplinary action that does not have your enthusiastic support.

   A. **Need for family commitment:** Indicate how much you need family commitment by circling the appropriate number.

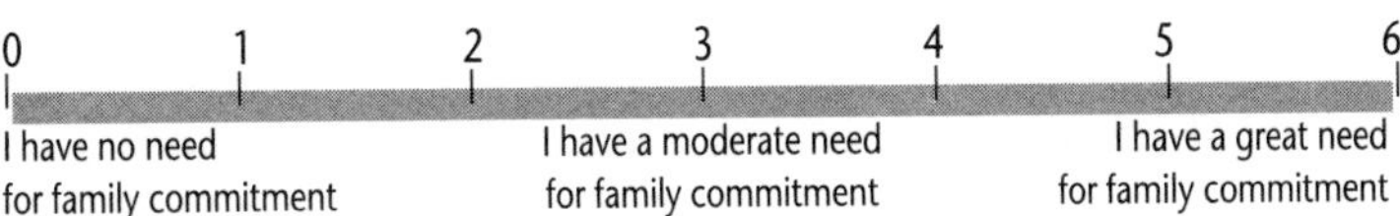

If or when your spouse *is not* willing to provide family commitment, how do you feel? (Circle the appropriate letter.)

a. Very unhappy
b. Somewhat unhappy
c. Neither happy nor unhappy
d. Happy he/she's not involved

If or when your spouse provides family commitment, how do you feel? (Circle the appropriate letter.)

a. Very happy
b. Somewhat happy
c. Neither happy nor unhappy
d. Unhappy he/she's involved in the family

   B. **Evaluation of spouse's family commitment:** Indicate your satisfaction with your spouse's family commitment by circling the appropriate number.

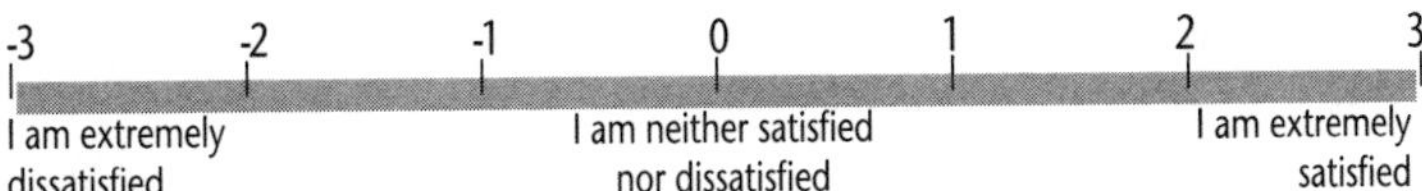

My spouse commits enough time to the family. Yes No

If your answer is no, how often would you like your spouse to join in family activities?

________ (write number) times each day/week/month (circle one).

________ (write number) hours each day/week/month (circle one).

I like the way my spouse spends time with the family. Yes No

If your answer is no, explain how your need for family commitment could be better satisfied in your marriage. ________________________

____

10. Admiration. Respecting, valuing, and appreciating you; rarely critical and expressing admiration to you clearly and often.

A. Need for admiration: Indicate how much you need admiration by circling the appropriate number.

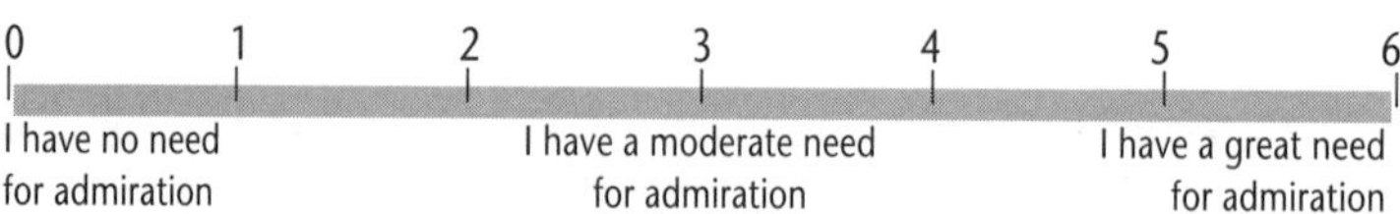

If or when your spouse *does not* admire you, how do you feel? (Circle the appropriate letter.)

a. Very unhappy
b. Somewhat unhappy
c. Neither happy nor unhappy
d. Happy not to be admired

If or when your spouse does admire you, how do you feel? (Circle the appropriate letter.)

a. Very happy
b. Somewhat happy
c. Neither happy nor unhappy
d. Unhappy to be admired

B. Evaluation of spouse's admiration: Indicate your satisfaction with your spouse's admiration of you by circling the appropriate number.

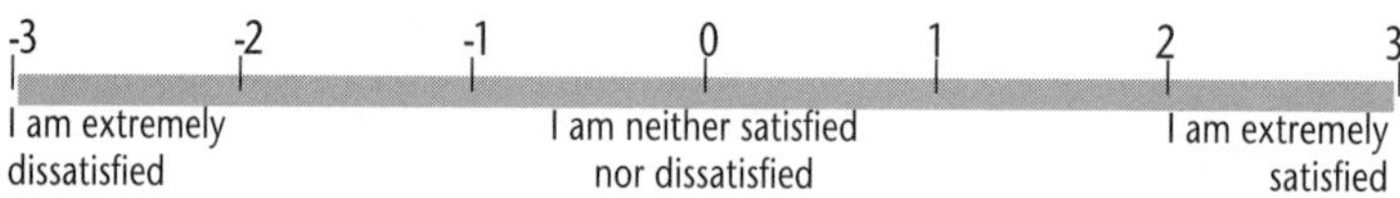

My spouse gives me all the admiration I need. Yes No

If your answer is no, how often would you like your spouse to admire you? _________ times each day/week/month (circle one).

I like the way my spouse admires me. Yes No

If your answer is no, explain how your need for admiration could be better satisfied in your marriage. ______________________________

____
____
____
____
____
____
____
____
____
____
____

Ranking of Your Emotional Needs

The ten basic emotional needs are listed below. There is also space for you to add other emotional needs that you feel are essential to your marital happiness.

In the space provided in front of each need, write a number from 1 to 5 that ranks the need's importance to your happiness. Write a 1 before the most important need, a 2 before the next most important, and so on until you have ranked your five most important needs.

To help you rank these needs, imagine that you will have only one need met in your marriage. Which would make you the happiest, knowing that all the others would go unmet? That need should be 1. If only two needs will be met, what would your second selection be? Which five needs, when met, would make you the happiest?

_________ Affection

_________ Sexual fulfillment

_________ Conversation

_________ Recreational companionship

_________ Honesty and openness

_________ Attractiveness of spouse

_________ Financial support

_________ Domestic support

_________ Family commitment

_________ Admiration

_________ ______________________________

_________ ______________________________

_________ ______________________________

_________ ______________________________

APPENDIX C

FRIENDS AND ENEMIES OF GOOD CONVERSATION INVENTORY

Name____________________________________ Date____________________

The conversations you have with your spouse can be either enjoyable or unpleasant. You will tend to have a pleasant conversation when your spouse (1) uses the conversation to inform, investigate, and understand you, (2) develops interest in your favorite topics of conversation, (3) balances the conversation, and (4) gives you undivided attention when he/she talks to you. These are some of the friends of good conversation.

You will tend to have an unpleasant conversation when your spouse (1) tries to force his or her way of thinking on you, and (2) dwells on your mistakes of the past or present, and (3) uses conversation to punish you. These are some of the enemies of good conversation.

Under the heading Friends of Good Conversation to Create, please name and describe new conversational habits that you would like your spouse to develop. For example, you may simply list one or more of the friends of good conversation listed above or you could add others that would improve conversation for you. You may even indicate that more time for conversation is needed.

If your spouse engages in conversational habits that you find annoying or inappropriate for your needs, name and describe that behavior under the heading Enemies of Good Conversation to Avoid. You may find that it isn't the behavior itself that you find inappropriate, but rather the time and place that bother you. If that's the case, explain that clearly in your description and include its appropriate form under Friends of Good Conversation to Create. If you need more space for your descriptions or would like to list more descriptions than the form allows, use another sheet of paper and attach it to this form.

Since conversation is interactive (one of you can't engage in meaningful conversation without the other participating), you and your spouse should complete separate **Friends and Enemies of Good Conversation Inventories.** After reviewing each other's tastes in conversation, try to develop habits of conversation that you both want to create, and try to avoid habits that either of you finds annoying.

Friends of Good Conversation to Create

1. ______________________________
   ____
   ____

2. ______________________________
   ____
   ____

3. ______________________________
   ____
   ____

4. ______________________________
   ____
   ____

5. ______________________________
   ____
   ____

6. ______________________________
   ____
   ____

7. ______________________________
   ____
   ____

Enemies of Good Conversation to Avoid

1. ____
____
____

2. ____
____
____

3. ____
____
____

4. ____
____
____

5. ____
____
____

6. ____
____
____

7. ____
____
____

APPENDIX D

STRATEGY TO MEET THE NEED OF CONVERSATION

Name______________________________ Date__________________

This worksheet is designed to help you create a strategy to meet your spouse's need for conversation. Complete each section to provide yourself with documentation of the process you used to select a strategy.

1. After you complete the **Friends and Enemies of Good Conversation Inventory,** describe conversational behavior that your spouse would like you to learn. ______________________________

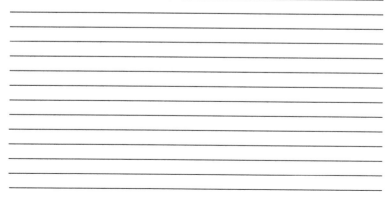

2. Describe your plan to learn the conversational behavior listed in question 1. Be certain that this plan is made with your spouse's enthusiastic support. Include a deadline to learn this conversational behavior. ______________

3. Describe your conversational behavior that your spouse would like you to avoid. ______________

4. Describe your plan to avoid the conversational behavior listed in question 3. Be certain that this plan is made with your spouse's enthusiastic support. Include a deadline to avoid this behavior. ______________

Appendix E

Friends and Enemies of Good Conversation Worksheet

Name____________________________________ Date____________________

For each conversation you have with your spouse that is over one minute in length, take a moment to evaluate its quality. As a reminder:

The friends of good conversation: (1) using the conversation to inform, investigate, and understand each other, (2) developing an interest in each other's favorite topics of conversation, (3) balancing the conversation, and (4) giving each other undivided attention. Add to this list any other conversational habits that you want your spouse to develop. ______________________________

____

____

____

____

The enemies of good conversation: (1) trying to force agreement to one's way of thinking, (2) dwelling on mistakes of the past or present, and (3) using conversation to punish. Add to this list any other conversational habits that you want your spouse to avoid. ____________________________________

____

____

____

____

Please list the instances of friends and enemies of good conversation that were made *by your spouse* during the conversation. Your spouse is to complete a similar worksheet for his or her evaluation of your conversation. After the conversation, exchange worksheets and acknowledge each other's evaluations. *Do not try to defend yourself if you do not agree with your spouse's evaluation.* Accept it and express willingness to improve the conversation at the next opportunity. Make another copy of this page if you need space for additional instances of friends and enemies of good conversation.

Friend and/or Enemy of Good Conversation

1. Day: ________ ______________________________
   Date: ________ ______________________________
   Time: ________ ______________________________
   ____
2. Day: ________ ______________________________
   Date: ________ ______________________________
   Time: ________ ______________________________
   ____
3. Day: ________ ______________________________
   Date: ________ ______________________________
   Time: ________ ______________________________
   ____
4. Day: ________ ______________________________
   Date: ________ ______________________________
   Time: ________ ______________________________
   ____
5. Day: ________ ______________________________
   Date: ________ ______________________________
   Time: ________ ______________________________
   ____

Friend and/or Enemy
of Good Conversation

6. Day: ________ ______________________________

Date: ________ ______________________________

Time: ________ ______________________________

____

7. Day: ________ ______________________________

Date: ________ ______________________________

Time: ________ ______________________________

____

8. Day: ________ ______________________________

Date: ________ ______________________________

Time: ________ ______________________________

____

9. Day: ________ ______________________________

Date: ________ ______________________________

Time: ________ ______________________________

____

10. Day: ________ ______________________________

Date: ________ ______________________________

Time: ________ ______________________________

____

11. Day: ________ ______________________________

Date: ________ ______________________________

Time: ________ ______________________________

____

Appendix F

Sexual Experience Inventory

Name________________________________ Date__________________

The sexual experience divides into five stages (1) desire, (2) arousal, (3) plateau, (4) climax, and (5) recovery. During *desire* a man feels like having sex, and a woman is willing. In the stage of *arousal* a man or woman begins to sense sexual feelings. His penis usually becomes erect, and her vagina usually begins to secrete fluid. If a man's penis and a woman's clitoris are stimulated properly, or if other sexually stimulating steps are taken, they pass into the *plateau* stage. In this stage his penis becomes very hard and her vagina contracts, providing greater resistance and a heightened sexual sensation during intercourse. The *climax,* which usually lasts only a few seconds, is the peak of the sexual experience. At this time the penis ejects semen in bursts (ejaculation), and the vagina alternately contracts and releases several times. The *recovery* stage follows, in which both partners feel peaceful and relaxed. The penis becomes soft, and the vagina, no longer secreting lubricating fluid, relaxes.

Please answer the following questions to provide information regarding your understanding of your sexual experience and your ability to create that experience.

Sexual Desire

1. How often do you experience sexual desire or willingness to have sex?
   _______ (write number) times each day/week/month/year (circle one).

2. Describe the conditions that tend to create sexual desire or willingness to have sex. ____
____
____
____

3. Are you more likely to experience sexual desire or willingness to have sex when your spouse is with you or when he or she is not with you? Why? ___
____
____
____

4. If you have difficulty experiencing sexual arousal in the presence or absence of your spouse, are you willing to create a plan with your spouse that may help you overcome that difficulty? When would you be willing to start planning? ____
____

Sexual Arousal

1. How often do you experience sexual arousal?__________(write number) times each day/week/month/year (circle one).

2. Describe the conditions that tend to create sexual arousal for you. ______
____
____

3. Are you more likely to experience sexual arousal when your spouse is with you or when he or she is not with you? Why? ____________________
____
____
____
____

4. If you have difficulty experiencing sexual arousal in the presense or absence of your spouse, are you willing to create a plan with your spouse that may help you overcome that difficulty? When would you be willing to start planning? ____
____
____
____
____

Sexual Plateau

1. How often do you experience sexual plateau?__________(write number) times each day/week/month/year (circle one).

2. Describe the conditions that tend to create sexual plateau for you. ______
____
____

3. Are you more likely to experience sexual plateau when your spouse is with you or when he or she is not with you? Why? ______________________
____
____
____
____

4. If you have difficulty experiencing sexual plateau in the presense or absence of your spouse, are you willing to create a plan with your spouse that may help you overcome that difficulty? When would you be willing to start planning?____
____
____
____
____

Sexual Climax

1. How often do you experience sexual climax?__________(write number) times each day/week/month/year (circle one).

2. Describe the conditions that tend to create sexual climax for you._______
____
____

3. Are you more likely to experience sexual climax when your spouse is with you or when he or she is not with you? Why? ______________________
____
____
____
____

4. If you have difficulty experiencing sexual climax in the presense or absence of your spouse, are you willing to create a plan with your spouse that may help you overcome that difficulty? When would you be willing to start planning? ____

Sexual Recovery

Unlike the other four stages of sexual experience, sexual recovery usually follows sexual climax natually and effortlessly. But sometimes this experience is thwarted or incomplete. Answer the following questions to help understand your sexual recovery.

1. How often do you experience sexual recovery?__________(write number) times each day/week/month/year (circle one).

2. Describe the conditions that tend to create sexual recovery for you. _____

3. Are you more likely to experience sexual recovery when your spouse is with you or when he or she is not with you? Why? _______________________

4. If you have difficulty experiencing sexual recovery in the presense or absence of your spouse, are you willing to create a plan with your spouse that may help you overcome that difficulty? When would you be willing to start planning? ____

5. Please add any information that may help in gaining an understanding of the stages of your sexual experiences. ____________________________

Appendix G

Strategy to Create a Stage of Sexual Experience

Name______________________________ Date____________________

This worksheet is designed to help you develop a strategy to create one of the five stages of sexual experience when you and your spouse make love. Complete each section to provide yourself with documentation of the process you used to select a strategy.

1. After you complete the **Sexual Experience Inventory,** describe a stage of sexual experience that you have difficulty experiencing with your spouse.

2. Describe your plan to experience the sexual stages listed in question 1. Be certain that this plan is made with your spouse's enthusiastic support. Include a deadline to overcome your difficulty.

SEXUAL EXPERIENCE WORKSHEET

Name________________________________ Date__________________

This worksheet applies to the following stage of sexual experience: ________ ________________________ Please list all instances of your effort to gain this stage of sexual experience. Indicate whether or not the stage was achieved and whether or not conditions that help you create this experience were met.

Circumstances

1. Day: ________ ____________________________________

   Date:________ ____________________________________

   Time:________ ____________________________________

   ____

2. Day: ________ ____________________________________

   Date:________ ____________________________________

   Time:________ ____________________________________

   ____

3. Day: ________ ____________________________________

   Date:________ ____________________________________

   Time:________ ____________________________________

   ____

Circumstances

4. Day: ________ ______________________________

Date:________ ______________________________

Time:________ ______________________________

____

5. Day: ________ ______________________________

Date:________ ______________________________

Time:________ ______________________________

____

6. Day: ________ ______________________________

Date:________ ______________________________

Time:________ ______________________________

____

7. Day: ________ ______________________________

Date:________ ______________________________

Time:________ ______________________________

____

8. Day: ________ ______________________________

Date:________ ______________________________

Time:________ ______________________________

____

9. Day: ________ ______________________________

Date:________ ______________________________

Time:________ ______________________________

____

Appendix I

Sexual Fulfillment Worksheet

Name________________________________ Date__________________

Please list all of your spouse's sexual behavior and your emotional reaction. If you find your spouse emotionally upset with your honest reactions, or if you are reluctant to provide honest reactions, seek professional supervision.

Type of Sexual Behavior and Your Reaction

1. Day: ________ ______________________________________
   Date:________ ______________________________________
   Time:________ ______________________________________
   ____

2. Day: ________ ______________________________________
   Date:________ ______________________________________
   Time:________ ______________________________________
   ____

Type of Sexual Behavior and Your Reaction

3. Day: ________ ____________________________________

Date:________ ____________________________________

Time:________ ____________________________________

____

4. Day: ________ ____________________________________

Date:________ ____________________________________

Time:________ ____________________________________

____

5. Day: ________ ____________________________________

Date:________ ____________________________________

Time:________ ____________________________________

____

6. Day: ________ ____________________________________

Date:________ ____________________________________

Time:________ ____________________________________

____

7. Day: ________ ____________________________________

Date:________ ____________________________________

Time:________ ____________________________________

____

8. Day: ________ ____________________________________

Date:________ ____________________________________

Time:________ ____________________________________

____

APPENDIX J

AFFECTION INVENTORY

Name________________________________ Date__________________

Under the heading Affectionate Habits to Create, please name and describe the types of affectionate behavior that you would like from your spouse. For example, if you would like your spouse to hold your hand more often, you should simply indicate how often and under which circumstance you would enjoy holding his or her hand.

If your spouse engages in affectionate behavior that you find annoying or inappropriate for your needs, name and describe that behavior under the heading Affectionate Habits to Avoid. You may find that it isn't the behavior itself that you find inappropriate, but rather the time and place that bother you. If that's the case, explain that clearly in your description and include its appropriate form under Affectionate Habits to Create. If you need more space for your descriptions or would like to list more descriptions than the form allows, use another sheet of paper and attach it to this form.

Since affection is interactive (one of you can't be affectionate without the other participating), you and your spouse should each complete a separate **Affection Inventory.** After reviewing each other's tastes in affection, try to develop habits of affection that you both want to create, and try to avoid habits that either of you finds annoying.

Name and Description of Affectionate Habits to Create

1. ____________________

2. ____________________

3. ____________________

4. ____________________

5. ____________________

6. ____________________

Name and Description of Affectionate Habits to Avoid

1. ____

2. ____

3. ____

4. ____

5. ____

6. ____

Appendix K

Strategy to Meet the Need of Affection

Name________________________________ Date________________

This worksheet is designed to help you create a strategy to meet your spouse's need for affection. Complete each section to provide yourself with documentation of the process you used to select a strategy.

1. After you complete the **Affection Inventory,** describe affectionate behavior that your spouse would like you to learn. ____________________

2. Describe your plan to learn the affectionate behavior listed in question 1. Be certain that this plan is made with your spouse's enthusiastic support. Include a deadline to learn this affectionate behavior. ________________

3. Descibe the affectionate behavior that your spouse would like you to avoid.

4. Describe your plan to avoid the affectionate behavior listed in question 3. Be certain this plan is made with your spouse's enthusiastic support. Include a deadline to avoid this behavior. ________________

Appendix L

Affection Worksheet

1992 by Willard F. Harley, Jr.

Name_________________________ Date_____________

Please list all instances of your spouse's affection. This is a very sensitive subject and not all couples can objectively handle this without professional supervision. If you find your spouse emotionally upset with your honest reactions, or if you are reluctant to provide honest reactions, seek professional help.

Type of Affection
and Your Reaction

1. Day: ________ ______________________________

   Date:________ ______________________________

   Time:________ ______________________________

   ____

2. Day: ________ ______________________________

   Date:________ ______________________________

   Time:________ ______________________________

   ____

Type of Affection
and Your Reaction

3. Day: ________ ______________________________

   Date:________ ______________________________

   Time:________ ______________________________

   ____

4. Day: ________ ______________________________

   Date:________ ______________________________

   Time:________ ______________________________

   ____

5. Day: ________ ______________________________

   Date:________ ______________________________

   Time:________ ______________________________

   ____

6. Day: ________ ______________________________

   Date:________ ______________________________

   Time:________ ______________________________

   ____

7. Day: ________ ______________________________

   Date:________ ______________________________

   Time:________ ______________________________

   ____

8. Day: ________ ______________________________

   Date:________ ______________________________

   Time:________ ______________________________

   ____

APPENDIX M

RECREATIONAL ENJOYMENT INVENTORY

1992 by Willard F. Harley, Jr.

Name________________________________ Date__________________

Please indicate how much you enjoy, or think you might enjoy, each recreational activity listed below. In the space provided by each activity, under the appropriate column (husband or wife), circle one of the following numbers to reflect your feelings: 3 = very enjoyable; 2 = enjoyable; 1 = somewhat enjoyable; 0 = no feelings one way or the other; -1 = somewhat unpleasant; -2 = unpleasant; -3 = very unpleasant. Add to the list, in the spaces provided, activities that you would enjoy that are not listed. In the third column, add the ratings of both you and your spouse *only if both ratings are positive.* The activities with the highest sum are those that you should select when planning recreational time together.

Activity	Husband's Rating	Wife's Rating	Total Rating
Acting	-3 -2 -1 0 1 2 3	-3 -2 -1 0 1 2 3	________
Aerobic exercise	-3 -2 -1 0 1 2 3	-3 -2 -1 0 1 2 3	________
Amusement parks	-3 -2 -1 0 1 2 3	-3 -2 -1 0 1 2 3	________
Antique collecting	-3 -2 -1 0 1 2 3	-3 -2 -1 0 1 2 3	________
Archery	-3 -2 -1 0 1 2 3	-3 -2 -1 0 1 2 3	________

Activity	Husband's Rating	Wife's Rating	Total Rating
Astronomy	-3 -2 -1 0 1 2 3	-3 -2 -1 0 1 2 3	________
Auto customizing	-3 -2 -1 0 1 2 3	-3 -2 -1 0 1 2 3	________
Auto racing (watching)	-3 -2 -1 0 1 2 3	-3 -2 -1 0 1 2 3	________
Badminton	-3 -2 -1 0 1 2 3	-3 -2 -1 0 1 2 3	________
Baseball (watching)	-3 -2 -1 0 1 2 3	-3 -2 -1 0 1 2 3	________
Baseball (playing)	-3 -2 -1 0 1 2 3	-3 -2 -1 0 1 2 3	________
Basketball (watching)	-3 -2 -1 0 1 2 3	-3 -2 -1 0 1 2 3	________
Basketball (playing)	-3 -2 -1 0 1 2 3	-3 -2 -1 0 1 2 3	________
Bible study	-3 -2 -1 0 1 2 3	-3 -2 -1 0 1 2 3	________
Bicycling	-3 -2 -1 0 1 2 3	-3 -2 -1 0 1 2 3	________
Boating	-3 -2 -1 0 1 2 3	-3 -2 -1 0 1 2 3	________
Bodybuilding	-3 -2 -1 0 1 2 3	-3 -2 -1 0 1 2 3	________
Bowling	-3 -2 -1 0 1 2 3	-3 -2 -1 0 1 2 3	________
Boxing (watching)	-3 -2 -1 0 1 2 3	-3 -2 -1 0 1 2 3	________
Bridge	-3 -2 -1 0 1 2 3	-3 -2 -1 0 1 2 3	________
Camping	-3 -2 -1 0 1 2 3	-3 -2 -1 0 1 2 3	________
Canasta	-3 -2 -1 0 1 2 3	-3 -2 -1 0 1 2 3	________
Canoeing	-3 -2 -1 0 1 2 3	-3 -2 -1 0 1 2 3	________
Checkers	-3 -2 -1 0 1 2 3	-3 -2 -1 0 1 2 3	________
Chess	-3 -2 -1 0 1 2 3	-3 -2 -1 0 1 2 3	________
Church services	-3 -2 -1 0 1 2 3	-3 -2 -1 0 1 2 3	________
Coin collecting	-3 -2 -1 0 1 2 3	-3 -2 -1 0 1 2 3	________
Computer programming	-3 -2 -1 0 1 2 3	-3 -2 -1 0 1 2 3	________
Computer games	-3 -2 -1 0 1 2 3	-3 -2 -1 0 1 2 3	________
Computer ______	-3 -2 -1 0 1 2 3	-3 -2 -1 0 1 2 3	________
Concerts (rock music)	-3 -2 -1 0 1 2 3	-3 -2 -1 0 1 2 3	________
Concerts (classical music)	-3 -2 -1 0 1 2 3	-3 -2 -1 0 1 2 3	________

Activity	Husband's Rating	Wife's Rating	Total Rating
Concerts (country music)	-3 -2 -1 0 1 2 3	-3 -2 -1 0 1 2 3	________
Cribbage	-3 -2 -1 0 1 2 3	-3 -2 -1 0 1 2 3	________
Croquet	-3 -2 -1 0 1 2 3	-3 -2 -1 0 1 2 3	________
Dancing (ballroom)	-3 -2 -1 0 1 2 3	-3 -2 -1 0 1 2 3	________
Dancing (square)	-3 -2 -1 0 1 2 3	-3 -2 -1 0 1 2 3	________
Dancing (rock)	-3 -2 -1 0 1 2 3	-3 -2 -1 0 1 2 3	________
Dancing (________)	-3 -2 -1 0 1 2 3	-3 -2 -1 0 1 2 3	________
Dining out	-3 -2 -1 0 1 2 3	-3 -2 -1 0 1 2 3	________
Fishing	-3 -2 -1 0 1 2 3	-3 -2 -1 0 1 2 3	________
Flying (as pilot)	-3 -2 -1 0 1 2 3	-3 -2 -1 0 1 2 3	________
Flying (as passenger)	-3 -2 -1 0 1 2 3	-3 -2 -1 0 1 2 3	________
Football (watching)	-3 -2 -1 0 1 2 3	-3 -2 -1 0 1 2 3	________
Football (playing)	-3 -2 -1 0 1 2 3	-3 -2 -1 0 1 2 3	________
Gardening	-3 -2 -1 0 1 2 3	-3 -2 -1 0 1 2 3	________
Genealogical research	-3 -2 -1 0 1 2 3	-3 -2 -1 0 1 2 3	________
Golf	-3 -2 -1 0 1 2 3	-3 -2 -1 0 1 2 3	________
Ham radio	-3 -2 -1 0 1 2 3	-3 -2 -1 0 1 2 3	________
Handball	-3 -2 -1 0 1 2 3	-3 -2 -1 0 1 2 3	________
Hiking	-3 -2 -1 0 1 2 3	-3 -2 -1 0 1 2 3	________
Hockey (watching)	-3 -2 -1 0 1 2 3	-3 -2 -1 0 1 2 3	________
Hockey (playing)	-3 -2 -1 0 1 2 3	-3 -2 -1 0 1 2 3	________
Horseback riding	-3 -2 -1 0 1 2 3	-3 -2 -1 0 1 2 3	________
Horse shows (watching)	-3 -2 -1 0 1 2 3	-3 -2 -1 0 1 2 3	________
Horse racing	-3 -2 -1 0 1 2 3	-3 -2 -1 0 1 2 3	________
Horseshoe pitching	-3 -2 -1 0 1 2 3	-3 -2 -1 0 1 2 3	________
Hot air ballooning	-3 -2 -1 0 1 2 3	-3 -2 -1 0 1 2 3	________
Hunting	-3 -2 -1 0 1 2 3	-3 -2 -1 0 1 2 3	________

Activity	Husband's Rating	Wife's Rating	Total Rating
Ice fishing	-3 -2 -1 0 1 2 3	-3 -2 -1 0 1 2 3	________
Ice skating	-3 -2 -1 0 1 2 3	-3 -2 -1 0 1 2 3	________
Jogging	-3 -2 -1 0 1 2 3	-3 -2 -1 0 1 2 3	________
Judo	-3 -2 -1 0 1 2 3	-3 -2 -1 0 1 2 3	________
Karate	-3 -2 -1 0 1 2 3	-3 -2 -1 0 1 2 3	________
Knitting	-3 -2 -1 0 1 2 3	-3 -2 -1 0 1 2 3	________
Metalwork	-3 -2 -1 0 1 2 3	-3 -2 -1 0 1 2 3	________
Model building	-3 -2 -1 0 1 2 3	-3 -2 -1 0 1 2 3	________
Monopoly	-3 -2 -1 0 1 2 3	-3 -2 -1 0 1 2 3	________
Mountain climbing	-3 -2 -1 0 1 2 3	-3 -2 -1 0 1 2 3	________
Movies	-3 -2 -1 0 1 2 3	-3 -2 -1 0 1 2 3	________
Museums	-3 -2 -1 0 1 2 3	-3 -2 -1 0 1 2 3	________
Opera	-3 -2 -1 0 1 2 3	-3 -2 -1 0 1 2 3	________
Painting	-3 -2 -1 0 1 2 3	-3 -2 -1 0 1 2 3	________
Photography	-3 -2 -1 0 1 2 3	-3 -2 -1 0 1 2 3	________
Pinochle	-3 -2 -1 0 1 2 3	-3 -2 -1 0 1 2 3	________
Plays	-3 -2 -1 0 1 2 3	-3 -2 -1 0 1 2 3	________
Poetry (writing)	-3 -2 -1 0 1 2 3	-3 -2 -1 0 1 2 3	________
Polo (watching)	-3 -2 -1 0 1 2 3	-3 -2 -1 0 1 2 3	________
Pool (or billiards)	-3 -2 -1 0 1 2 3	-3 -2 -1 0 1 2 3	________
Quilting	-3 -2 -1 0 1 2 3	-3 -2 -1 0 1 2 3	________
Racquetball	-3 -2 -1 0 1 2 3	-3 -2 -1 0 1 2 3	________
Remodeling (home)	-3 -2 -1 0 1 2 3	-3 -2 -1 0 1 2 3	________
Rock collecting	-3 -2 -1 0 1 2 3	-3 -2 -1 0 1 2 3	________
Roller-skating	-3 -2 -1 0 1 2 3	-3 -2 -1 0 1 2 3	________
Rowing	-3 -2 -1 0 1 2 3	-3 -2 -1 0 1 2 3	________
Rummy	-3 -2 -1 0 1 2 3	-3 -2 -1 0 1 2 3	________

Activity	Husband's Rating	Wife's Rating	Total Rating
Sailing	-3 -2 -1 0 1 2 3	-3 -2 -1 0 1 2 3	________
Sculpting	-3 -2 -1 0 1 2 3	-3 -2 -1 0 1 2 3	________
Shooting (skeet, trap)	-3 -2 -1 0 1 2 3	-3 -2 -1 0 1 2 3	________
Shooting (pistol)	-3 -2 -1 0 1 2 3	-3 -2 -1 0 1 2 3	________
Shopping (clothes)	-3 -2 -1 0 1 2 3	-3 -2 -1 0 1 2 3	________
Shopping (groceries)	-3 -2 -1 0 1 2 3	-3 -2 -1 0 1 2 3	________
Shopping (vehicles)	-3 -2 -1 0 1 2 3	-3 -2 -1 0 1 2 3	________
Shopping (________)	-3 -2 -1 0 1 2 3	-3 -2 -1 0 1 2 3	________
Shuffleboard	-3 -2 -1 0 1 2 3	-3 -2 -1 0 1 2 3	________
Sightseeing	-3 -2 -1 0 1 2 3	-3 -2 -1 0 1 2 3	________
Singing	-3 -2 -1 0 1 2 3	-3 -2 -1 0 1 2 3	________
Skiing (water)	-3 -2 -1 0 1 2 3	-3 -2 -1 0 1 2 3	________
Skiing (downhill)	-3 -2 -1 0 1 2 3	-3 -2 -1 0 1 2 3	________
Skiing (cross-country)	-3 -2 -1 0 1 2 3	-3 -2 -1 0 1 2 3	________
Skin diving (snorkeling)	-3 -2 -1 0 1 2 3	-3 -2 -1 0 1 2 3	________
Skydiving	-3 -2 -1 0 1 2 3	-3 -2 -1 0 1 2 3	________
Snowmobiling	-3 -2 -1 0 1 2 3	-3 -2 -1 0 1 2 3	________
Softball (watching)	-3 -2 -1 0 1 2 3	-3 -2 -1 0 1 2 3	________
Softball (playing)	-3 -2 -1 0 1 2 3	-3 -2 -1 0 1 2 3	________
Spearfishing	-3 -2 -1 0 1 2 3	-3 -2 -1 0 1 2 3	________
Stamp collecting	-3 -2 -1 0 1 2 3	-3 -2 -1 0 1 2 3	________
Surfing	-3 -2 -1 0 1 2 3	-3 -2 -1 0 1 2 3	________
Swimming	-3 -2 -1 0 1 2 3	-3 -2 -1 0 1 2 3	________
Table tennis	-3 -2 -1 0 1 2 3	-3 -2 -1 0 1 2 3	________
Taxidermy	-3 -2 -1 0 1 2 3	-3 -2 -1 0 1 2 3	________
Television	-3 -2 -1 0 1 2 3	-3 -2 -1 0 1 2 3	________
Tennis	-3 -2 -1 0 1 2 3	-3 -2 -1 0 1 2 3	________

Activity	Husband's Rating	Wife's Rating	Total Rating
Tobogganing	-3 -2 -1 0 1 2 3	-3 -2 -1 0 1 2 3	________
Video games	-3 -2 -1 0 1 2 3	-3 -2 -1 0 1 2 3	________
Video production	-3 -2 -1 0 1 2 3	-3 -2 -1 0 1 2 3	________
Video movies (watching)	-3 -2 -1 0 1 2 3	-3 -2 -1 0 1 2 3	________
Volleyball	-3 -2 -1 0 1 2 3	-3 -2 -1 0 1 2 3	________
Weaving	-3 -2 -1 0 1 2 3	-3 -2 -1 0 1 2 3	________
Woodworking	-3 -2 -1 0 1 2 3	-3 -2 -1 0 1 2 3	________
Wrestling (watching)	-3 -2 -1 0 1 2 3	-3 -2 -1 0 1 2 3	________
Yachting	-3 -2 -1 0 1 2 3	-3 -2 -1 0 1 2 3	________
____________	-3 -2 -1 0 1 2 3	-3 -2 -1 0 1 2 3	________
____________	-3 -2 -1 0 1 2 3	-3 -2 -1 0 1 2 3	________
____________	-3 -2 -1 0 1 2 3	-3 -2 -1 0 1 2 3	________
____________	-3 -2 -1 0 1 2 3	-3 -2 -1 0 1 2 3	________
____________	-3 -2 -1 0 1 2 3	-3 -2 -1 0 1 2 3	________
____________	-3 -2 -1 0 1 2 3	-3 -2 -1 0 1 2 3	________
____________	-3 -2 -1 0 1 2 3	-3 -2 -1 0 1 2 3	________
____________	-3 -2 -1 0 1 2 3	-3 -2 -1 0 1 2 3	________
____________	-3 -2 -1 0 1 2 3	-3 -2 -1 0 1 2 3	________
____________	-3 -2 -1 0 1 2 3	-3 -2 -1 0 1 2 3	________
____________	-3 -2 -1 0 1 2 3	-3 -2 -1 0 1 2 3	________
____________	-3 -2 -1 0 1 2 3	-3 -2 -1 0 1 2 3	________
____________	-3 -2 -1 0 1 2 3	-3 -2 -1 0 1 2 3	________
____________	-3 -2 -1 0 1 2 3	-3 -2 -1 0 1 2 3	________
____________	-3 -2 -1 0 1 2 3	-3 -2 -1 0 1 2 3	________
____________	-3 -2 -1 0 1 2 3	-3 -2 -1 0 1 2 3	________
____________	-3 -2 -1 0 1 2 3	-3 -2 -1 0 1 2 3	________
____________	-3 -2 -1 0 1 2 3	-3 -2 -1 0 1 2 3	________
____________	-3 -2 -1 0 1 2 3	-3 -2 -1 0 1 2 3	________

Appendix N

Strategy to Meet the Need of Recreational Companionship

Name_______________________________ Date__________________

This worksheet is designed to help you create a strategy to meet your spouse's need for recreational companionship. Complete each section to provide yourself with documentation of the process you used to select a strategy.

1. After you complete the **Recreational Enjoyment Inventory,** list the recreational activities that both you and your spouse enjoy. ________________

2. Describe your plan to engage in these recreational activities together. Be certain that this plan is made with your spouse's enthusiastic support. Include a deadline to be spending your recreational time together. _____

Appendix O

Recreational Companionship Worksheet

Name______________________________ Date________________

Please list all recreational activities shared by you and your spouse, and describe your emotional reaction to the time you spent together. If you enjoyed the time together, explain what made it enjoyable. If you disliked the time together, explain what made it unpleasant. Try to avoid unpleasant aspects of your time together when you next engage in that activity. This is sometimes a sensitive subject, and not all couples can objectively handle this without professional supervision. If you find your spouse emotionally upset with your honest reactions, or if you are reluctant to provide honest reactions, seek professional help.

Recreational Activity and Your Reaction

1. Day: ________ ____________________________________

   Date:________ ____________________________________

   Time:________ ____________________________________

   ____

2. Day: ________ ____________________________________

   Date:________ ____________________________________

   Time:________ ____________________________________

   ____

Recreational Activity and Your Reaction

3. Day: ________ ______________________________

Date:________ ______________________________

Time:________ ______________________________

____

4. Day: ________ ______________________________

Date:________ ______________________________

Time:________ ______________________________

____

5. Day: ________ ______________________________

Date:________ ______________________________

Time:________ ______________________________

____

6. Day: ________ ______________________________

Date:________ ______________________________

Time:________ ______________________________

____

7. Day: ________ ______________________________

Date:________ ______________________________

Time:________ ______________________________

____

8. Day: ________ ______________________________

Date:________ ______________________________

Time:________ ______________________________

____

About the Author

Willard F. Harley, Jr., Ph.D., is a clinical psychologist and marriage counselor. Over the past twenty-five years he has helped thousands of couples overcome marital conflict and restore their love for each other. His innovative counseling methods are described in the books and articles he writes. One of his books, *His Needs, Her Needs,* has been a best-seller since it was published in 1986 and has been translated into German, French, Dutch, and Chinese. Dr. Harley also leads training workshops for couples and marriage counselors and has appeared on hundreds of radio and television programs.

Willard Harley and Joyce, his wife of over thirty years, live in White Bear Lake, Minnesota. They are parents of two married children who are also marriage counselors.

Dr. Harley would be delighted to hear from you. His web site is: http://www.marriagebuilders.com